WHAT RESEARCH *REALLY* SAYS ABOUT TEACHING AND LEARNING TO READ

What Research Really Says about Teaching and Learning to Read

Edited by

STEPHEN B. KUCER
Washington State University–Vancouver

National Council of Teachers of English
1111 W. Kenyon Road, Urbana, Illinois 61801-1096

Manuscript Editor: JAS Group
Staff Editor: Bonny Graham
Interior Design: Jenny Jensen Greenleaf
Cover Design: Pat Mayer

NCTE Stock Number: 56759

It is the policy of NCTE in its journals and other publications to provide a forum for the open discussion of ideas concerning the content and the teaching of English and the language arts. Publicity accorded to any particular point of view does not imply endorsement by the Executive Committee, the Board of Directors, or the membership at large, except in announcements of policy, where such endorsement is clearly specified.

Every effort has been made to provide current URLs and email addresses, but because of the rapidly changing nature of the Web, some sites and addresses may no longer be accessible.

Library of Congress Cataloging-in-Publication Data

What research really says about teaching and learning to read / edited by Stephen B. Kucer.
    p. cm.
  Includes bibliographical references and index.
  ISBN 978-0-8141-5675-9 ((pbk.))
  1. Reading. 2. Language arts. 3. Language experience approach in education. 4. Curriculum planning. 5. Reading teachers—In-service training. I. Kucer, Stephen B., 1950–
  LB1050.6.W48 2008
  428.4071—dc22
                                                              2008031907

CONTENTS

INTRODUCTION

From the Beginning: Power for the Teacher

YETTA M. GOODMAN
University of Arizona

What Research Really *Says about Teaching and Learning to Read* reflects the focus among language and literacy scholars concerned with informing classroom teachers with knowledge and research about the teaching of reading. The English language arts curriculum in school settings is now at a time in American education where the power of the teacher is being eroded by forces that place great trust in tests and statistical manipulation rather than in the power of a caring and thoughtful professional. Lack of respect for classroom teachers is not historically unusual in the United States, however; yet recent research makes it abundantly clear that the teacher in the classroom is most responsible for the academic achievement of the students (Darling-Hammond & Bransford, 2005). More than ever before, support for teachers is necessary to help them continue their development of professional knowledge, and to expand on their classroom experiences to understand their role in the teaching and learning of language.

The concern to inform English language arts professionals lies in the origins of the National Council of Teachers of English (NCTE). Hook (1979) makes the case that NCTE began as a gathering of "protesters against curricular rigidity imposed by colleges on the American high school" (p. 3). Hook also makes the case that the founders were organizers and builders. The founders, teachers, and teacher educators were responding to the imposition of mandates and tests on the English curriculum of

American high schools. Elementary school teachers also joined the protest that same year.

The content of this volume expands on the mission of NCTE members to respond to uninformed impositions by those outside of the classroom, and to build an organization of teachers and teacher educators who would inform their profession by providing background knowledge, theory, and research that can be adapted to their own settings. Through the authors in this book, members of the Commission on Reading, NCTE sustains its mission to support classroom teachers in continuing to develop the expertise they need to be successful in developing curricula in their classrooms that provide language-learning opportunities for all their students. The authors also provide guidelines and specific aids for classroom teachers to use as resources and references to develop a safe learning environment in which students have opportunities to use language, including reading and writing, as a tool for exploring the world.

Since my own entry into teaching, I have been imbued with the notion that curriculum is most effective for learners when the teacher is centrally involved in negotiating the curriculum with students. John Dewey (1938) makes clear that a curriculum embodies all the experiences of the teacher and students as they come together to learn.

In the 1950s, as I was learning to become a teacher, we discussed ideas and explored opportunities for teachers to develop their own curricula in negotiation with their students. I valued the language-experience approach to the teaching of reading, which stressed building on children's relevant and personally meaningful experiences in and out of the classroom to write their own reading materials and to expand on their learning. I used adaptations of language experience with my self-contained eighth graders, to engage them in writing a cantata based on the history of our new intermediate school in the city of Redondo Beach, California; and we published a literacy magazine based on their writings. We adapted Taba's (1962) concepts about curriculum inquiry, and built habitats to compare the students' immigrant communities to the communities in which their parents had grown up in Mexico, Japan, China, and European countries. There was so much the students had to read and write in order to answer their many, and often changing, questions about their world.

When I went into teaching, I knew I would integrate speaking, listening, reading, and writing with my science and social studies programs. I knew that children enjoyed learning best when the experiences were interesting and relevant to their lives, and when they had choice in the materials they read and wrote. I knew that classrooms could be organized in ways similar to social-group work settings, in which children could collaborate, solve problems, discuss, argue, and take leadership roles in organizing their classrooms with my expertise and help. My interactions with students were based on trust that kids are always learning, and on an understanding that the classroom community in which we were learning together was of utmost importance to our development as a community of teachers and learners. My students were capable of working in small groups and on their own, as I worked with them to provide safe spaces and opportunities in which they were learning to read and write while they were learning about their world. When I started teaching in 1952, the term *progressive education* was rarely used. It was the McCarthy period in American education, but the experiences that many of my colleagues and I were putting into practice in the classrooms were rooted in the theories, philosophies, and concepts of progressive education, with the focus of using oral and written language as a tool to learn across the curriculum.

My professional involvement in language arts education in the 1980s included my NCTE presidency (1979–1980) at the same time that Dorothy Strickland was president of the International Reading Association (IRA). Charlotte Huck, who had been president of NCTE four years earlier (1975–1976), proposed a series of conferences for teachers and teacher educators to showcase the research being done worldwide in reading, writing, and oral language that was especially relevant to elementary language arts. Dr. Huck believed that if the knowledge were easily accessible to teachers and teacher educators, it would have significant impact on language arts curricula. Although Dr. Huck was not able to obtain funds to support the project, when Dorothy Strickland and I became presidents, we enthusiastically picked up on the idea and worked together to develop a series of conferences. Huck, Strickland, and I wrote a proposal accepted by both the IRA and NCTE executive boards, and for more than five years, eighteen national and regional conferences were held in cities across the United States, as well as one in Dublin, Ireland, at the World Reading Congress. The conferences were called *Oral and Written Language Development Research: Impact on the Schools* (Goodman, Haussler, & Strickland, 1980; Jaggar & Smith-Burke, 1985). In their presidential years, Sheila Fitzgerald and Bea Cullinan extended the conferences to focus on classroom application and strategies for improving language and literacy instruction. The conferences were organized so that "a new theoretical and integrated base for the teaching of the language arts including reading would be the result and that its impact on the elementary school would be great" (Goodman, Haussler, & Strickland, 1980, p. 2).

The names of the people who spoke at these impact conferences include prominent researchers and language theorists who continue to influence the English language arts to this day. Language arts teachers, teacher educators, and researchers were introduced to and worked together with Vera John Steiner, Joan Tough, Don Graves, Charles Read, Frank Smith, Emilia Ferriero, Gordon Wells, and many more. Michael Halliday introduced his idea about children learning language, learning through language, and learning about language. Marie Clay fascinated us with the description of a teacher education program that had teachers observing a reader with a teacher behind a two-way mirror, followed by intensive discussion about their observations.

The conferences included scholars from many nations and involved elementary classroom teachers as presenters, planners, and leaders. The walls of the conference rooms showcased children's work. Presenters read children's books to the adult audiences. Garth Boomer, a prominent Australian English educator, got down from the traditional speaker's platform and moved chairs into circles to establish an environment for the purpose of serious talk among professionals.

Winners of the NCTE David H. Russell Research Award also influenced the knowledge base on language arts education. Louise Rosenblatt received her award in 1980 for her concept of transaction in reading. As elementary teachers expanded their use of trade books in classrooms, Rosenblatt's concepts of efferent and aesthetic stances during reading helped them think about ways to engage their students in responding thoughtfully and personally to literature. Nanci Atwell received the research award for her work on writing, helping teachers think about ways to engage middle school students in their own writing; and Vivian Paley received the award for using talk and dramatic play with very young children.

Through the support of Rosemary Winklejohann, NCTE developed opportunities for individual and groups of teachers to bring their teacher-developed language arts programs to a panel of experts for suggestions and evaluation.

The Commission on Reading added support for teachers' knowledge as they developed many projects, and advised NCTE in ways that supported the belief that teachers continuously develop their teaching of reading as they build their knowledge and experience to invigorate rich language environments and opportunities in their classrooms. Much of the focus of the work of the Commission is to assure that teacher-developed language arts programs are at the heart of teachers' work. Pamphlets, checklists, and commercial reading and language arts programs are helpful to teachers, but only if teachers use such materials as tools to inform their own decisions about curriculum development. The teacher is the decision maker in the classroom.

What Research Really *Says about Teaching and Learning to Read* emerged from deliberations by recent members of the Commission on Reading, who believe that teachers are decision makers about their curricula. The matrixes and documents developed by the Commission were written to highlight the knowledge about the teaching and learning of reading that would support teachers in organizing their classroom environment. The documents were developed over a period of time so they could be presented to teachers, teacher educators, and reading researchers for reflection and response. In this way, the documents were put into practice based on the experience and knowledge of a range of professionals in the field. The importance of the documents is that they are meant to guide and engage teachers to consider their own knowledge about their students and their own beliefs about the teaching and learning of reading. The documents are meant to engage teachers in exploring the usefulness of the documents, and to encourage teachers to adapt the information gathered to their own settings. The documents reflect the idea that teachers are searching for multiple ways to be reflective about their literacy teaching.

Reading First and No Child Left Behind (NCLB) have been written as mandates for the teaching of reading in the classroom. The research used to support the reading provisions ignores a wide range of reading theories and diversity of research, and establishes a one-size-fits-all procedure for the teaching of reading. The *Decision-Making Matrix*, the accompanying documents, and the articles in this volume are written to provide a more complete view of the theories, knowledge, and practices available in the English language arts community about reading teaching and learning. The authors represent in their work a diversity of research results, using individual readers and readers in classroom settings to provide profiles of readers engaged in language arts learning and teaching.

What Research Really *Says about Teaching and Learning to Read* is organized into four sections to highlight the documents and the discussions that have taken place in their development. In Part I, Patrick Shannon provides a critique of the Commission's focus over the years on "resisting the collective consciousness of the corporate scientific and state forces within the English language arts," and Ruth Rigby provides a history of the Commission documents. Both chapters establish the Commission's belief that knowledgeable and experienced teachers are central to the teaching and learning of language arts in the classroom.

Part II provides chapters that highlight the reading research that led to the development of the guidelines in the matrix and the documents. Here, the nature of reading is embedded in relation to curriculum building on what is known about the linguistic, cognitive, and sociocultural diversity of readers in our schools. Various authors explore the nature of learning that results in language inventions and the development of reading proficiency in children of many ages and different language and cultural communities, as well as learners with a wide range of reading proficiencies, including English as a Second Language (ESL) readers and readers with various school-imposed labels. The authors discuss readers' inventions about language and concepts as the children learn the relationships between context, subject matter, content of the classroom, and literacy engagements.

Part III is organized to focus specifically on the documents themselves: to share possibilities for their uses in professional development, to expand on teachers' adaptations to their own settings, and to provide support in language across the curriculum development. The documents expand beyond the narrow view of research that drives much of governmental mandates on teachers and developing readers.

The final section presents the documents themselves, which are embedded in the rich context of knowledge and research in the previous chapters. Teachers, curriculum developers in schools, reading coaches, and a range of literacy professionals can use the documents to inform their decision-making process, to support the development of classrooms rich in opportunities for students of all ages to use reading and writing to learn about their world.

References

Darling-Hammond, L., & Bransford, J. (Eds.). (2005). *Preparing teachers for a changing world: What teachers should learn and be able to do*. San Francisco: Jossey Bass.

Dewey, J. (1938). *Experience and education*. New York: Macmillan.

Goodman, Y., Haussler, M., & Strickland, D. (Eds.). (1980). *Oral and written language development research: Impact on schools*. Newark, DE: International Reading Association.

Hook, J. N. (1979). *A long way together: A personal view of NCTE's first sixty-seven years*. Urbana, IL: National Council of Teachers of English.

Jaggar, A., & Smith-Burke, M. (Eds.). (1985). *Observing the language learner*. Newark, DE: International Reading Association; Urbana, IL: National Council of Teachers of English.

Taba, H. (1962). *Curriculum development: Theory and practice*. New York: Harcourt, Brace & World.

I

HISTORICAL FRAMEWORK

CHAPTER ONE

Resistance Is Futile?

PATRICK SHANNON
Penn State University

In "The Best of Both Worlds" episode of *Star Trek: The Next Generation,* Locutus, a member of the alien race known as the Borg, informs the crew of *Starship Enterprise D* that they cannot resist his power to connect their minds and bodies to a collective consciousness that will bridge the gap between the artificial and organic worlds. With a simple biochip implanted behind their ears, the crew will join a technological collective that promises to make their work more efficient, their actions more effective, and their thoughts more rational. At the same time, they will enjoy the creature habits of their own world—its beauty, desires, and comforts. Locutus thinks the crew will jump at this opportunity to go with the flow. When it becomes clear to the crew that the connection is not symbiotic, and that they will lack a voice in the collective, Locutus proves willing to use his power against their reluctance. Any resistance is futile, or so he thinks.

The field of English language arts has faced its own Borg since the publication of the *A Nation at Risk* report in 1983. Since that time, corporate, scientific, and government forces have invited, inveigled, and pushed teachers toward a collective consciousness of high standards, standardized curricula, and testing in order to improve the American workforce. The promise has been that these technologies will remove bias from the system and ensure that all students become proficient, self-motivated learners ready to retool themselves continuously in order to keep their place in the new global economy. If teachers and other school personnel will accept these technologies as a collective consciousness of American schooling, then their work will become more efficient, effective, and rational. Resistance to this technological implant is futile—or so experts, business, and the government thought.

Throughout this period, the members of the Commission on Reading of the National Council of Teachers of English (NCTE) have assumed the identities of the crew of *Starship Enterprise D* in order to question the claims and consequences of the technological-over-human movement in American schools. Like its fictional counterpart, the Commission is composed of diverse members who hold various views of English language arts. As a group, however, the Commission appears to continue the work of the Dartmouth Conference of 1967 using its philosophy as the Commission's base principles. Then, the Commission promotes discovery/process models over mastery/competency or surrender/heritage models of curriculum (Mandel, 1980), arguing that English curricula should center "on the personal and inner life, helping the child to order, extend, and enrich his experience, instead of imparting a body of knowledge or mere techniques" (Muller, 1967, p. 40). Moreover, advocates claim the same rights for teachers.

> Our first concern, therefore is that teachers of English at all levels should have more opportunities to enjoy and refresh themselves in their subject, using language in operation for all its central purposes—in imaginary drama, writing and speech as well as in response to literature. Teachers without this experience—who would never think of writing a poem, flinch at the idea of acting, and rarely enter into a discussion of the profound human issues in everyday experience—are themselves deprived and are likely in turn to limit the experience of their pupils. (Dixon, 1967, p. 107)

In what follows, I review four acts of resistance from the Commission on Reading. Although different members planned and completed each of the acts, the four acts demonstrate a continued critique of power within the field of English language arts and a commitment to teacher agency in the classroom over basal (core) reading materials, standardized tests and testing, national standards, and federal attempts to mandate teaching practices.

The First Act: Resistance to Basal Readers

NCTE appointed the Commission on Reading to inform the executive board members on issues of concern and promise in the field of reading education. In 1986, under the direction of Dorothy Watson, the Commission convened to discuss the recently published *Becoming a Nation of Readers* report from the National Academy of Education (Anderson, Hiebert, Scott, & Wilkinson, 1985). That report was represented as a state-of-the-art document concerning reading instruction and was meant to re-create reading instruction in its own image. Although authors of the report were mildly critical of basals for failing to translate the most recent research into their materials, they concluded that improvements in reading instruction would have to pass through basal publishers because of the historical importance of basals in the twentieth century. In effect, researchers, commercial publishers, and state governments considered basals to be the one best, although currently imperfect, system for teaching reading. Improving basals, they argued, would bring about a collective consciousness among teachers in order to provide efficient and effective instruction. The Commission on Reading took exception to *Becoming a Nation of Readers* and charged Ken Goodman to produce a different perspective on the state of reading education.

In November 1987, new Commission director Connie Weaver convened an invitational conference during the NCTE Annual Convention in Los Angeles. Panels of publishers, teachers, administrators, researchers, and basal authors responded to early drafts of what was called "the Goodman report" and made suggestions for revision. The Goodman report was far more critical of basals than was *Becoming a Nation of Readers*. From the Goodman report's perspective, basals (1) underestimated what children know about language and text; (2) misrepresented how children learn language; (3) limited the text available to readers; (4) supplanted the teacher's authority during reading instruction; and (5) placed commercial concerns before students' and teachers' best interests.

Goodman submitted the final report to the Commission on Reading at the 1988 NCTE Spring Conference. Weaver and the Commission members accepted the document and submitted it for expedited publication through NCTE. Although the Commission had initiated the study and the NCTE Research Foundation had funded it, the NCTE Executive Committee balked at publication, suggesting that it would require a year or more of careful review before a decision on publication could be made. Sensing efforts to keep the report from the public, the Commission released the report to Goodman, who published it privately as *Report Card on Basal Readers* (Goodman, Shannon, Freeman, & Murphy, 1988).

The Second Act: Resistance to Standardized Tests

In 1992, the Commission on Reading met during the NCTE Annual Convention to discuss the potential impact of President George H. W. Bush's *America 2000: An Educational Agenda* (United States Department of Education, 1991) on reading education. Congress established the National Council of Education Standards and Testing (NCEST) to "advise on the desirability and feasibility of national standards and tests, and to recommend long-term policies, structures, and mechanisms for setting voluntary education standards and planning an appropriate system of tests" (1992, p. 1). With two governors (Carroll Campbell and Roy Romer); noted conservatives (Lynne Cheney and Chester Finn Jr.); corporate executives (David Kearns and Kay Whitmore); and with Lauren Resnick from the University of Pittsburgh and Mark Tucker of the National Center of Education and the Economy as members, NCEST concluded that national standards and tests were not only feasible, but necessary if American schools were to once again produce human capital to meet the demands of a global economy. Again, members of the Commission questioned the assumption that a competence model would best serve future plans for English language arts education. With even voluntary academic standards a remote possibility at the time, the Commission proposed a series of papers to report on the current state of standardized reading tests.

At the 1993 NCTE Annual Convention in Pittsburgh, four members of the Commission on Reading presented its report. Sharon Murphy asked, "What counts as evidence?" and used the metaphor of the legal system to distinguish between artifact and testimony. She characterized reading tests as an attempt to produce an artifact that would trump the testimony of students, parents, and teachers. Although reading test scores are assumed to be objective, Murphy used the test items and expected answers to demonstrate that the tests simply hid the subjectivity of the test designers and the officials who made decisions about the content of the test and the forms the test could take before the artifacts were produced.

I spoke directly to those decisions, treating reading tests as historical artifacts that had enjoyed a ninety-year social life at the time of the convention. My thesis was that tests were meant to sort people by criteria that the test designers and reviewers thought to be appropriate or true at the time of their construction and that were simply accepted when the tests were used subsequently. Those subjectivities and criteria have not always been honorable, enabling reading tests to confirm cultural biases about the inferiority of certain ethnic groups and races in the name of science.

> The illusions of scientific objectivity—standardization, universality, and mathematical precision—obscured cultural, racial, and social class biases encoded in the formats, procedures, and topics of reading tests. The results from these tests became the self-fulfilling prophecies that produced biased treatments of different social groups under the guise of scientific truth. In this way, reading tests not only define reading and measure school and programmatic success, but they verify White middle and upper class superiority. (Shannon, 1998, p. 85)

Peter Johnston (1998) described the shifting criteria within the evaluation of reading tests. Although the validity of tests continued to be considered most important, the consequences of the interpretations and uses of tests were now connected directly to thoughts about test validity. Johnston detailed the ways in which tests scores were and could be used: to position teachers and students, to alter curricula, to label schools, and to skew considerations of equity. He ended with a statement that foretold the current role of reading tests in schools:

> But the tests are not without blame: they represent the reification of the belief system. A test that offers 10 decoding subtests and one comprehension subtest reflects as well as projects a particular view of literacy, a view of a significant group of people, and once the view is sanctioned by science in the form of a test, the view has the authority to dominate a conversation. (p. 100)

Jane Hansen (1998) spoke about alternatives to reading tests. Her talk was based on her study of the ways in which students, parents, administrators, and teachers characterize students as readers during conversations with her. She was pleasantly surprised to find that few mentioned test scores in their descriptions, and noted that many of the factors these informants considered salient were often neglected in test-driven evaluation schemes. First, her respondents thought that reading was a social accomplishment in which readers developed as a natural extension of literate environments. Home, community, and school environments matter deeply. Second, they defined literacy in broad terms, acknowledging many types of literacies that flourish outside of school but often are outlawed in school. Third, they reported that passions are involved in reading. Hansen concluded that if we cared about developing a nation of readers, then we should attend to these factors rather than ones that are easily measured.

These four authors submitted their papers to the Commission for consideration and commentary, and then forwarded them to the NCTE publications office as a proposal for a book. The Commission hoped that the book would reach a greater public than the NCTE resolutions on testing had reached, providing NCTE members and others with more developed arguments concerning the federal calls for national testing in reading. Again, the NCTE publication officials responded that the Commission on Reading did not have the authority to sanction a position on testing, and that the manuscript would only be reviewed as any other independent proposal. With that response, Sharon Murphy accepted responsibility for the texts, applied and received a grant from the NCTE Research Foundation, expanded the arguments by analyzing the items of all existing reading achievement tests, and published the work as *Fragile Evidence: A Critique of Reading Assessment* (Murphy, 1998).

The Third Act: Resistance to National Standards

Miles Myers was hired as executive director of NCTE in 1990 with the charge to bring the organization into the national conversation about school reform. To gain potential recognition, Myers believed that NCTE had to deliver the national standards sought in *America 2000,* and then *Goals 2000: The Educate America Act* (United States, 1994). He approached the Center for the Study of Reading (CSR) about submitting a proposal to the National Board of Professional Teaching Standards regarding creation of standards for English certification, and he became a co-director (with P. David Pearson of CSR) of the Literacy Unit of the New Standards Project. In 1991, Myers encouraged the presidents of NCTE and the International Reading Association (IRA) to indicate their willingness to become involved in the creation of national standards for English language arts. At the NCTE Annual Convention that fall, the officers of NCTE sought a "clear mandate" (Myers as quoted in McCollum-Clark, 1995, p. 137) for national standards from its constituent organization. Only the Commission on Reading was on record as reporting concern over NCTE's involvement in the standards movement. Despite those concerns, NCTE joined with CSR and IRA to accept a $3 million federal grant to produce national standards within two years.

In 1992, Director Diane Stephens and the members of the Commission published a letter to that Joint Committee of NCTE, CSR, and IRA expressing their concerns about national content standards. The letter asked the Joint Committee to recognize the threat that standardization brings to marginalized groups, the antidemocratic practice of a centralized group setting standards for a decentralized school system, and the reality that standards would lead to national testing. In that year's "Trends and Issues Report" to the NCTE Executive Committee, the Commission called for "an open discussion in print (*The Council Chronicle*) in which writers from multiple points of view are allowed to explore the committee structure for the production of standards, plans and drafts for writers and editors, and the proposed use of the standards document once produced" (as quoted in McCollum-Clark, 1995, p. 138). According to the only study of NCTE involvement in the standards project (McCollum-Clark, 1995), the *Council Chronicle* was used only for press releases from the Joint Committee, describing the work of the standards committees. No open debate took place in print for consideration by the NCTE membership.

After a year of work, the federal government cancelled the remainder of the grant, withheld almost half of the initial allotment, and kept the second installment of more than $1 million because the Joint Committee was writing generative and delivery standards rather than prescriptive standards. The federal government sought standards that declared what students should know about English; what they should be able to do with English; how that knowledge and those skills should be taught; and how it would be determined that students possessed that knowledge and those skills. After the rebuke, CSR dropped out of the Joint Committee, Janet Emig and P. David Pearson withdrew from leadership roles, and NCTE and IRA decided to switch the project from writing national standards to producing professional standards. In 1995, Myers explained that the project continued in order to increase the federal funding for public schools, to provide a measure for adequate curricula within schools, and to elevate the content and skills included in English language arts curricula. By attempting to produce national reading standards and being labeled a failure when that did not happen, however, NCTE had gambled and lost its authority to comment on the government's subsequent use and measurement of standards. When IRA and NCTE delivered their joint statement of standards in 1996, the *New York Times* editors wrote:

> A curriculum guide for teaching English has just been released in a tongue barely recognizable as English. . . . Nowhere in their twelve rules will you find the prescriptive verbs "should" or

"ought." Simple declarative sentences are equally hard to find.
... The only plausible reason one can think of for such circumlo-
cutions is that the writers were paralyzed by caution. (1996, p.
A22)

The Fourth Act: Resistance to Federal Mandates for Teaching

Under the direction of Jane Braunger in 2004, the Commission
on Reading convened to discuss the impact of the 2001 No Child
Left Behind (NCLB) legislation on reading education in American classrooms. That legislation promoted the findings of the
National Reading Panel (NRP) report and its definition of evi-
denced-based decision making. The NRP limited itself to considering only experimental research on five topics that could be folded
easily into a statistical meta-analysis to determine which elements
of alphabetics, phonics, fluency, vocabulary, and comprehension
should be pursued during reading instruction. Agreeing with many
concerned educators, the Commission on Reading considered the
NRP's report and its subsequent use in NCLB to be shortsighted
on at least two fronts. First, the decisions concerning topics seemed
to be idiosyncratic to the panel members. Second, the limitation
of evidence to experimental results eliminated much of the recent
research on reading and the teaching of reading. Stephen B. Kucer
and Jane Braunger accepted the challenge to produce short, accessible reports on elementary and secondary school students'
reading that would address both these concerns. Margaret Phinney
and Penny Silvers led the development of a decision-making ru-
bric to provide an alternative to the federal government's biased
model for choosing basals.

While discussion of these three documents (*On Reading,
Learning to Read, and Effective Reading Instruction: An Over-
view of What We Know and How We Know It; A Call to Action:
What We Know about Adolescent Literacy and Ways to Support
Teachers in Meeting Students' Needs*; and *Features of Literacy
Programs: A Decision-Making Matrix*) compose the body of this
volume, it is important to note that they are responses, perhaps
even refutations of, the federal government's attempts to direct

reading education in American classrooms. And the Department of Education inspector general's report (United States Department of Education, 2006) on the design and implementation of NCLB's Reading First initiative demonstrates that the government's efforts are anything but fair and objective.

Is Resistance Futile?

Captain Picard dealt the Borg a fatal blow, and the threat of collective consciousness was vanquished completely on *Star Trek*. The Commission on Reading has not ended the discourses of science, business, and government in reading education. Despite the *Report Card on Basal Readers* (Goodman et al., 1988), core-reading programs (new name for basals) are mandated in many classrooms and are used in nearly all. According to the inspector general's 2006 report, the federal government had a list of five basals that it deemed to be essential to progress in closing the achievement gaps. The publishers of those materials and standardized tests are considered to be "Bush stocks" after the passage of the NCLB legislation. Depending on whether state or national test scores are considered, those gaps are closing or widening.

Despite *Fragile Evidence* (Johnston, 1998), there are more standardized reading tests in American schools than at any other time in our history. The basal publishers supply tests of their basals' content. Some districts require annual standardized norm-referenced achievement tests. In order to comply with NCLB, state departments of education require annual tests of reading in grades 3 through 8, and then once in high school. Every other year, a subset of school districts in each state administers the National Assessment of Educational Progress (NAEP), enabling the federal government to compare test results among the fifty states. With the rise of continuous testing and the establishment of high-stakes tests for students, teachers, and schools, entrepreneurs have moved into this market to sell schools materials and services to help their students prepare to take the tests.

Despite the Commission's protests, NCTE wrote professional standards that played some part in the development of English language arts standards in all states. Rather than increase the influence of the organization, the joint project left NCTE without an effective presence within the national debate about policy for reading education. NCTE now passes resolutions about its concerns for reading education, but its proven failure in the production of standards diminishes its impact on state policymakers. As the Commission on Reading predicted, standards are tied directly to testing, reading curricula have been essentially nationalized through core materials, and instruction for minority (but not for majority) students has been standardized.

So the Borg were correct. Resistance is futile. If basals, tests, and standards are still in play, and the federal government is increasing its influence in classrooms across the country, then a collective consciousness about reading education has been realized. What good has come from the four acts of resistance by the Commission on Reading? Keep in mind that "The Best of Both Worlds" was a two-part episode, and two hours is an eternity in TV time. Picard and his crew needed both hours to defeat the Borg. Let me suggest that we are just starting our metaphorical second episode. Here's why I'm optimistic.

First, the Commission has made progress within NCTE. This book is evidence of that, and of the able leadership of Ruth Rigby and Jane Braunger. *Report Card on Basal Readers* (Goodman et al., 1988) and *Fragile Evidence* (Johnston, 1998) had to be published outside the organization. NCTE never devoted space for an open debate among its membership about standards while they were being negotiated. But the three recent Commission on Reading documents included in this book were offered on the NCTE website nearly a year before the book was even conceived. One outcome of the acts of resistance is that the NCTE leadership seems to have caught up with the Commission.

Second, the Commission continues to provide alternatives for teachers to use and strategies to subvert mandates with empirical evidence. Instead of basal readers, the Commission argues for children's books, films, songs, and games. It champions social practices that children bring with them to school, emphasizing the strengths of languages, cultures, and individuals as the foundation for reading education. It argues to reduce the role of standardized testing in reading education, promoting ethical uses of those tests, and argues to increase attention to the social practices of reading beyond the classroom. Moreover, the Commission supports teachers' professional judgment as the best authority for assessments.

Finally, the Commission on Reading refuses to stand by silently while science, business, and government discourses work to disempower teachers and students by offering standardized practices that lead to domesticated literacies. If these discourses were not powerfully active in the field, the Commission would not need to be resistant. However, when experts limit social science research to experimentation based on physical science principles, this requires the Commission to stand in opposition. When business makes reading instruction into a series of markets, this compels the Commission to reemphasize the human essence of reading and teaching. The federal bribing and bullying of schools to employ a narrow vision of reading's potential invites the Commission to defend the principles expressed in the NCTE declaration.

Resistance does not ensure victory—even during the second episode. Rather, resistance can be thought of as friction, impeding easy movement. If the Commission on Reading's work over the last twenty-five years has impeded dominance of science, business, and government discourses on reading education, then resistance is not futile. Offering resistance in the face of power reflects, but also advances, the democratic best of our field.

References

Anderson, R., Hiebert, E., Scott, J., & Wilkinson, I. (1985). *Becoming a nation of readers: The report of the Commission on Reading.* Washington, DC: National Academy of Education.

Dixon, J. (1967). *Growth through English.* Reading, UK: National Association for the Teaching of English.

Goodman, K., Shannon, P., Freeman, Y., and Murphy, S. (1988). *Report card on basal readers.* Katonah, NY: Richard C. Owens.

Hansen, J. (1998). Evaluation is all day, noticing what is happening: Multifaceted evaluations of readers. In S. Murphy (Ed.), *Fragile evidence: A critique of reading assessment* (pp. 105-24). Mahwah, NJ: Erlbaum.

Johnston, P. (1998). The consequences of the use of standardized tests. In S. Murphy (Ed.), *Fragile evidence: A critique of reading assessment* (pp. 89–102). Mahwah, NJ: Erlbaum.

Mandel, B. (Ed.). (1980). *Three language-arts curriculum models: Prekindergarten through college.* Urbana, IL: National Council of Teachers of English.

McCollum-Clark, K. (1995). *NCTE, corporate philanthropy, and national education standards.* Unpublished dissertation, Penn State University.

Muller, H. (1967). *The uses of English: Guidelines for the teaching of English from the Anglo-American Conference at Dartmouth College.* New York: Holt Rinehart & Winston.

Murphy, S. (Ed.). (1998). *Fragile evidence: A critique of reading assessment.* Mahwah, NJ: Erlbaum.

Myers, M. (1995). Why participate? *College Composition and Communication, 46*(3), 438–40.

National Commission on Excellence in Education. (1983). *A nation at risk: The imperative for education reform.* Washington, DC: Government Printing Office.

National Council on Education Standards and Testing (NCEST). (1992). *Raising standards for American education.* Washington, DC: Government Printing Office.

National Institutes of Health. National Institute of Child Health and Human Development (NICHD). (2000). *Report of the National Reading Panel. Teaching children to read* (NIH Publication No. 00-4769). Washington, DC: Government Printing Office.

New York Times, The. (1996, March 14). How not to write English. Editorial. p. A22. Retrieved June 13, 2008, from http://query.nytimes.com/gst/fullpage.html?res=9C07E1DF1639F937A25750C0A960958260

Shannon, P. (1998). A selective social history of the use of reading tests. In Murphy, S. (Ed.), *Fragile evidence: A critique of reading assessment* (pp. 75–88). Mahwah, NJ: Erlbaum.

United States Congress, House of Representatives. (1994). *Goals 2000: Educate America Act.* 103rd Congress, second session. H.R. 1804; P.L. 103-227. Washington, DC: Government Printing Office. Retrieved July 1, 2008, from http://www.ed.gov/legislation/GOALS2000/TheAct/index.html

United States Congress, House of Representatives. (2001). *No Child Left Behind Act of 2001*. 107th Congress, first session. H.R. 1. Washington, DC: Government Printing Office.

United States Department of Education. (1991). *AMERICA 2000: An education strategy: Sourcebook*. Washington, DC: Government Printing Office.

United States Department of Education. (2006). *The Reading First program's grant application process: Final inspection report (EDE-OIG/113-F0017)*. Washington, DC: Author. Retrieved July 1, 2007, from http://www.ed.gov/about/offices/list/oig/aireports/i13f0017.pdf

A History of the NCTE Commission on Reading Documents: Three Documents That Challenge the Limited Scientific Research Base Given Authority by the National Reading Panel Report

RUTH E. RIGBY

School District of Lee County, Florida

I n November 2001 the National Council of Teachers of English (NCTE) Commission on Reading met in Baltimore, Maryland, following the NCTE Annual Convention. The Commission is "a deliberative and advisory body which each year identifies and reports . . . on key issues in the teaching of reading . . . and suggests topics for future publications on reading" (Commission on Reading, 2008). At this meeting, dialogue among representative reading researchers, curriculum specialists, university professors, teachers, and teacher educators began shaping itself into a serious and passionate plea to create documents showcasing valid and reliable research in reading that had been dismissed by the National Reading Panel (NRP) report, issued just months before in April 2000 (National Institutes of Health, 2000a, 2000b). Those reading commissioners, poised around a table that day, provided an honest appraisal of what reading practices had been left behind in the federal government's authoritative NRP report, and determined a path of advocacy for these orphaned teaching practices.

National Reading Panel Deliberately Chooses a Narrow View of Reading

What emerged in discussion included the undisputed fact that NRP, by its own acknowledgment of the sheer volume of research in the area of reading, limited its research to five components of reading (National Institutes of Health, 2000a, 2000b); this same panel further limited its research in these five components of reading to include only scientifically based research. These two narrowings left important scholarly research in reading by the wayside.

Two types of educational research could have been examined by the fourteen-member NRP. Simply put, scientific, or *quantitative*, research determines impact by comparison of results for a control group and a treatment group. These controlled experiments exemplify scientific research, and this experimental or quasi-experimental research served as the criterion for selection by NRP. The other type of research, no less valid or reliable, is *qualitative* research. Typically, qualitative researchers collect thick, ethnographic data written in the form of case studies or correlational studies. The National Reading Panel rejected qualitative research. It opted for a narrow view of reading.

The deliberate choice by NRP to examine only scientifically based reading research aligned with a theoretical stance that defines reading as a technical skill to be mastered through the hierarchical acquisition of discrete skills, one skill at a time, especially the skill of phonics. "With no powerful voices from other philosophical camps on the panel, it was easy for this majority to believe that theirs was the only legitimate view. Without debate, the panel accepted as the basis for its investigations a model composed of a three-part hierarchy: decoding, fluency, and comprehension" (Yatvin, 2002, p. 366). If qualitative research had been studied by NRP, a theoretical stance that "reading is a complex, purposeful, social, and cognitive process" (Commission on Reading, 2004b, para. 2) of constructing meaning from varied text would have been evident, including the importance of comprehension, contextualized skill instruction, prior knowledge, and social collaboration to construct meaning with the text.

What was, in the year 2000, a newly emerging language of reading has now become an authoritative language of reading on the lips not only of educators, but also of policymakers, testing companies, and textbook publishers. The five components of scientific reading research—phonemic awareness, phonics, fluency, vocabulary, and comprehension—now resonate in the federal government's 2001 No Child Left Behind (NCLB) legislation and through Reading First mandates. Reading First initiatives, which focus on kindergarten through third-grade beginning reading programs, mandate compliance by attaching federal funding only to programs implementing NRP's *scientifically based reading instruction*. "The phrase appears thirty-one times in the House version of the bill and almost as many times in the Senate version of the bill" (Coles, 2001, p. 206).

National Reading Panel's Narrow View Is Misrepresented

Adding to the Commission on Reading's concern about a narrow research base was the egregious *Summary* of the *Reports of the Subgroups of the National Reading Panel*. The *Summary* misinformed its educator audience with inaccuracies of the actual number of studies, as well as misrepresentations of NRP's own reading research conclusions. This *Summary* "reduces a six-hundred-page Subgroup Report to a thirty-two page document, and condenses the eighty-six pages of the Phonics Subgroup Report to less than four pages" (Garan, 2001, p. 67). The *Summary*, as well as a fifteen-minute video (*Teaching Children to Read*) and press releases, were prepared and presented to the public by Widmeyer Communications, the same public relations firm that had marketed McGraw-Hill's *Open Court* reading program during George W. Bush's Texas literacy drive (Metcalf, 2002, para. 21). Much has been written to unveil inaccuracies and caution educators about the use of flawed research that makes generalizations to diverse student groups (Altwerger, 2005; Coles, 2000). In fact, a *Minority Report*, written by NRP panelist Joann Yatvin, explains these concerns as well as other inaccuracies, yet it appears buried behind the Appendix of the NRP report, her revelations unrevealed to the public (Garan, 2001).

Inaccuracies between NRP Report and NRP Summary Document

Although it is not the primary purpose of this chapter to elaborate on opposition to the NRP findings, details from a significant critique drill down to the essence of the disparity between the NRP report and the widespread *Summary*. In the article "What Does the *Report of the National Reading Panel* Really Tell Us about Teaching Phonics?" (2001), Garan uses the exact words of NRP members rather than relying on the *Summary*, video, or press releases. The following is a snapshot of discrepancies Garan uncovered between the data in the *Reports of the Subgroups of the National Reading Panel* and the *Summary* marketed to educators and the general public.

Garan stated, "The methodology is flawed, and the results as reported in the *Summary* are not supported by the [P]anel's own data or by their own statements. For example, my reference to the small number of studies used in the NRP report and the unreliability of the research base are not simply my opinion, but are limitations that are identified by the Panel itself" (2001, p. 71).

"Thirty-eight phonics studies, eight of which the Panel determined were of questionable reliability," (Garan, 2001, p. 63) were used to draw conclusions about the impact of systematic phonics instruction on six different isolated skills. Garan charted this subgroup report data from information in the full NRP report (Garan, 2001). Analysis of the effects of phonics instruction on these fourteen data points revealed the effects as high, moderate, small, or none. The effect of phonics instruction on decoding words with regular spelling patterns only, for at-risk kindergarten and first-grade students, was high: .98. The remaining thirteen data points indicated that five were moderate; one was small to moderate; three were small; and three demonstrated no effect size (Garan, 2001). The actual NRP report stated, "There were insufficient data to draw any conclusions about the effects of phonics instruction with normally developing readers above first grade" (Metcalf, 2002, para. 20), but the *Summary* stated there were "significant benefits for students in kindergarten through sixth grade and for children having difficulty learning to read" (National Institutes of Health, 2000b, p. 9). In fact, the impact of phonics diminishes with older readers (grades 2 through 6), "confirming that children do not appear to transfer isolated phonics expertise to authentic text" (Garan, 2001, p. 68).

The phonics studies conducted with problem readers were generalized in the *Summary* to apply also to normally progressing readers, Limited English Proficient (LEP), and English as a Second Language (ESL) populations. Yet the studies used to make this generalization did not include any representative samples of these types of readers (Garan, 2001), which violates sound research methods.

Impact of Misrepresentations

The grave impact of these misrepresentations is that our country's children are subjected to practices of reading instruction that are known to have been misinterpreted—or rather, interpreted—to convey a preconceived message. For teachers, these misrepresentations authoritatively push out successful teaching practices, including the use of authentic stories by real authors; thematic studies that integrate language functions; contextualized skill instruction based on responsive teaching; self-selected independent reading; author studies; and even writing.

Even more appalling is the morphing of the generalization about systematic phonics instruction to be applied also to adolescent readers! In Florida, for example, a three-hundred-hour reading endorsement training program, strictly defined and monitored by the state, credentials a teacher as highly qualified to teach reading above grade 6. The reading endorsement instruction for these teachers is limited to the five components of reading identified by NRP, and emphasizes phonics. Unless teachers educate themselves on the broad base of reading research omitted from their state training, they will be uninformed and seemingly brainwashed to implement practices developed from a narrow, scientific research base that is admittedly insufficient. Again, the exact words of the NRP report stated "there were insufficient data to draw any conclusions about the effects of phonics instruction with normally developing readers above first grade" (Metcalf, 2002, para. 20).

Some of the most prominent criticisms of the use of the NRP report uncover what is perhaps a hidden agenda. By limiting reading instruction to low-level tasks in the guise of sound, scientifically based reading research, the accountability for proficiency in these tasks can in turn be easily measured by accountability testing. Improvement in reading as measured by mastery of hierarchical, discreet, and isolated skills can be marked off on the nation's reading report card.

Testing companies and textbook publishers profit from the national reading policy. They provide scripted teacher books, basal student books, isolated skill workbooks, decodable booklets, and test preparation supplements that appear in approved lists meeting the criteria for scientifically based research.

When education leaders joined President George W. Bush on his first day in the White House, guest Harold McGraw III, publisher, stated, "It's a great day for education, because we now have substantial alignment among all the key constituents—the public, the education community, business and political leaders—that results matter" (Metcalf, 2002, para. 5). Nine months later, President Bush's read-aloud exercise with a second-grade class stopped abruptly, as his chief of staff Andrew Card whispered to him. The day was September 11, 2001. Even though the hoped-for excitement of the upcoming new education reform being celebrated that morning dissolved, the education reform legislation was enacted as the No Child Left Behind Act on January 8, 2002. Years later, the impact of NCLB is being questioned by educators and by the public. In a survey of 2,000 teachers charged with implementing NCLB, 76 percent believed that the Act has had at least a somewhat negative influence on teaching and learning in English/reading classrooms. "If we want schools that are equitable and accountable, where teachers have more freedom to use proven educational methods to educate their children, and schools where all children have the opportunity to learn to their highest abilities and parents have more choices, we need less emphasis on prepping for a single test, more emphasis on significant teaching and formative local assessment, and much more emphasis on all students learning and teachers teaching" (Commission on Reading, 2004b, para. 2).

Reading Research Not Examined by NRP

In keeping with the mission of the Commission on Reading to identify and report on key issues in the teaching of reading, over time, three documents emerged as tools for advocating valid and reliable research in reading that had been hidden by the bravado of the NRP report. These three NCTE documents are *On Reading, Learning to Read, and Effective Reading Instruction: An Overview of What We Know and How We Know It*; *A Call to Action: What We Know about Adolescent Literacy and Ways to Support Teachers in Meeting Students' Needs*; and *Features of Literacy Programs: A Decision-Making Matrix*. These three reading documents are included in the Appendixes of this book, and subsequent chapters of this book elaborate on the enactment of teaching practices aligned to the research base of the documents.

Chapters in this book that are focused on learning to read define reading as a "complex and purposeful socio-cultural, cognitive, and linguistic process in which readers simultaneously use their knowledge of spoken and written language, their knowledge of the topic of the text, and their knowledge of their culture to construct meaning with text" (Commission on Reading, 2004b, para. 2). "Characteristics of effective reading instruction focus on authentic experiences with texts, multiple daily reading experiences, explicit demonstrations of reading strategies, ongoing assessment to inform instruction, creative and critical student response to texts, inquiry into language study, student collaborations, and partnerships with families to extend school learning" (Shaw, 2005).

The adolescent literacy research base presented in the chapters of this book reflects the multiple ways in which adolescents "use literacy as a social and political endeavor in which they engage to make meaning and to act upon their worlds" (Commission on Reading, 2004a, para. 4). Teachers must "recognize and value the multiple literacy resources students bring to the acquisition of school literacy" by showing, demonstrating, and making visible "how literacy operates within the academic disciplines"; by providing adolescents "with sustained experiences in diverse texts; by offering opportunities to examine print, electronic, and visual media through student-led discussions; by offering ongoing opportunities for students to reflect about how they engage with texts" (Shaw, 2005, p. 2).

The third document provides a broad-based matrix of features for teachers and curriculum developers to consider when identifying standards-aligned criteria to make decisions about the selection of instructional materials and programs. Features include content of text materials; instructional methodologies of comprehension and word study; opportunities for student engagement; assessment; and professional resources and development. Each feature provides the opportunity for conversation centered on the research base of each feature (Commission on Reading, 2005).

The most prominent use of these three documents has been at NCTE Annual Convention sessions, with invitation for participants to access them at the NCTE website for further use among colleagues. Over time, the audience has expanded to include participants of the International Reading Association (IRA), through cosponsored convention sessions. Publication in professional journals has also given some exposure to these documents. Each presentation of these NCTE reading documents has resulted in overwhelming enthusiasm for their clearly stated research base, usefulness as tools for dialogue about reading instruction, and affirmation that "reading is not a technical skill acquired once and for all in the primary grades, but rather a developmental process" (Commission on Reading, 2004b, para. 2).

Classroom teachers especially have been empowered by these documents to teach with authority what is just and good for students. Teacher educators have taught future teachers with these documents in ways intended to open conversation, and to construct beliefs about reading that are founded on fact.

Because the value of these reading documents has been affirmed multiple times, the Commission on Reading now offers them to a wider audience through this book. It is also the goal of this book to elaborate on powerful reading research that has been purposefully left out of our country's national reading mandates—left out by the NRP decision to narrow the reading research base, and left out by the marketing strategists' selective summarizing and selective overgeneralizations of the unabridged text of the

NRP report. The authors hope that not only educators, but also policymakers—those who make decisions about our children's reading education—will assimilate an additional research-based perspective when making authoritative decisions about reading instruction. The results do matter. Powerful research can be enacted and supported in the classrooms of America when teachers, education leaders, and policymakers are provided with whole truth, not half-truth.

References

Altwerger, B. (Ed). (2005). *Reading for profit: How the bottom line leaves kids behind.* Portsmouth, NH: Heinemann.

Coles, G. (2000). *Misreading reading: The bad science that hurts children.* Portsmouth, NH: Heinemann.

Coles, G. (2001). Reading taught to the tune of the "scientific" hickory stick. *Phi Delta Kappan, 83*(3), 204–12.

Commission on Reading of the National Council of Teachers of English. (2004a). *A call to action: What we know about adolescent literacy and ways to support teachers in meeting students' needs.* Retrieved May 29, 2008, from http://www.ncte.org/about/policy/guidelines/118622.htm

Commission on Reading of the National Council of Teachers of English. (2004b). *On reading, learning to read, and effective reading instruction: An overview of what we know and how we know it.* Retrieved May 28, 2008, from http://www.ncte.org/about/policy/guidelines/118620.htm

Commission on Reading of the National Council of Teachers of English. (2005). *Features of literacy programs: A decision-making matrix.* Retrieved May 29, 2008, from http://www.ncte.org/library/files/About_NCTE/Overview/ReadingMatrixFinal.pdf

Commission on Reading of the National Council of Teachers of English. (2008). *Charge.* Retrieved July 6, 2008, from http://www.ncte.org/about/gov/commissions/106919.htm

Council Chronicle Online. (2006, September 6). Literacy educators and the public deeply concerned about NCLB. National Council of Teachers of English. Retrieved May 29, 2008, from http://www.ncte.org/pubs/chron/highlights/125383.htm

Garan, E. M. (2001). What does the *Report of the National Reading Panel* really tell us about teaching phonics? *Language Arts, 79*(1), 61–71.

Metcalf, S. (2002, January 28). Reading between the lines. *Nation.* Retrieved May 29, 2008, from http://thenation.com

National Institutes of Health. National Institute of Child Health and Human Development. (2000a). *Report of the National Reading Panel: Teaching children to read. Reports of the subgroups* (NIH Publication #00-4754).Washington, DC: Government Printing Office.

National Institutes of Health. National Institute of Child Health and Human Development. (2000b). *Report of the National Reading Panel: Teaching children to read. Summary report* (NIH Publication #00-4769). Washington, DC: Government Printing Office.

Shaw, M. L. (2005). NCTE Commission on Reading takes proactive positions on reading and reading instruction. *Council-Grams.* National Council of Teachers of English. Retrieved May 29, 2008, from http://www.ncte.org/about/gov/cgrams/res/120008.htm?source =gs

Vasquez, V. (2004). *Negotiating critical literacies with young children.* Mahwah, NJ: Erlbaum.

Yatvin, J. (2002). Babes in the woods: The wanderings of the National Reading Panel. *Phi Delta Kappan, 83*(5), 364–69.

II

WHAT DOES THE RESEARCH SAY?

CHAPTER THREE

What We Know about the Nature of Reading

STEPHEN B. KUCER

Washington State University–Vancouver

The very nature of literacy has long been contested. Historically, the debates—largely cognitive or psycholinguistic in nature—have centered on the degree to which readers utilize the print available, the role of context in word identification, and whether aspects of the reading process are automated (e.g., Adams & Bruck, 1995; Goodman, K., 1996; National Institutes of Health, 2000; Smith, 2004; Stanovich, 2000). Currently, the debate has expanded to include not only the role of the linguistic and cognitive dimensions in reading, but the sociocultural as well (e.g., Gee, 1996; Gonzalez, Moll, & Amanti, 2005; New London Group, 1996; Luke, 1995).

The Commission on Reading was cognizant of these ongoing and expanding debates as it crafted the guideline *On Reading, Learning to Read, and Effective Reading Instruction* (2004; see Appendix A for the document.) The stance of the Commission was that its members would take a multifaceted view of reading, relying on research that was conducted within contextualized situations. In so doing, we hoped to avoid narrow and reductionistic understandings of the reading process. For as Ed Young (1992) reminds us in *Seven Blind Mice*, "Knowing in part may make a fine tale, but wisdom comes from seeing the whole" (n.p.). Not only did this stance help us move beyond simply telling a fine tale, it also provided rich possibilities for classroom connections.

The dimensions of literacy represented in Figure 3.1 (Kucer, 1991; Kucer, 2005; Kucer & Silva, 2006) provide a visual overview of this chapter, which expands on the work of the Commission. In this rendering, every literacy event—in this case

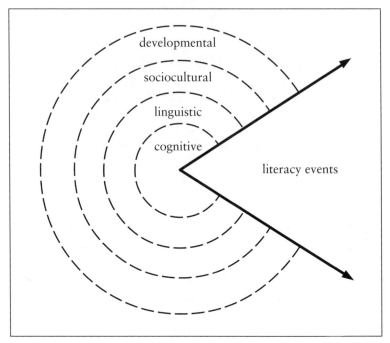

FIGURE 3.1. *Dimensions of literacy.*

reading—is envisioned as dynamic and multidimensional in nature. Being literate means having the ability to effectively and efficiently negotiate the dimensions of written language within particular situations. Reflecting and extending the work of Luke (1995, 1998) and Freebody and Luke (1990), the linguistic dimension conceives of the reader as a "code breaker," the cognitive as a "meaning maker," the sociocultural as a "text user and text critic," and the developmental dimension as a "scientist and construction worker." Readers draw upon all four of these knowledge resources when engaged with any written language event.

To facilitate understanding, each of the four dimensions is addressed somewhat separately. In actuality, however, they are embedded or embodied in one another, as represented in Figure 3.1. Each dimension impacts and is impacted by all the others. Additionally, the dimensions are used in tandem; that is, real-world literacy always involves all four of the dimensions operating together. We need, therefore, to resist the notion that particular dimensions, such as the linguistic, are learned or used before other dimensions, such as the sociocultural, when the individual reads.

Finally, readers are typically unable to consciously and explicitly talk about much of their dimensional knowledge. They are, however, able to employ these resources when transacting with print. This implicit knowledge is in contrast to school knowledge, which typically learners must be able to explicitly "talk about" in very direct ways in order for it to be recognized or "counted" as knowledge. Such a distinction between implicit and explicit knowledge is important to recognize as we examine the nature of reading and consider ways to help our students develop the implicit knowledge that undergirds all literacy use.

The Linguistic Dimension: The Reader as Code Breaker

The linguistic dimension represents all the reader understands about how written language operates as a vehicle for communication. Smith (2004) has termed this visible aspect of language the *surface structure*. The surface structure consists of various systems or cues (Goodman, K., 1996), such as text structure, genre, semantics, syntax, orthographics, and graphophonemics. As the word *system* implies, there are rules for how the cues are organized internally. The syntactic cue system, for example, represents the rules that govern the grammatical arrangements of words within the sentence. Similarly, the orthographic system specifies the spelling patterns within words, and the graphophonemic system reflects the relationship between letters and sounds. Based on literacy experiences—or lack thereof—in various communicative contexts, the individual may have more or less knowledge of, or control over, particular systems than others.

Readers, however, do not typically encounter individual systems of language or isolated cues—except perhaps in school contexts. Rather, they encounter *texts*, units of meaning of any size that form a unified whole and that are intended to communicate to some community of people (de Beaugrande, 1980; Gee, 1996; Halliday, 1973, 1974). These texts may be nonlinguistic as well as linguistic. Paintings, photographs, dances, and musical scores are all texts or "configurations of signs [cues] that provide a potential for meaning" (Smagorinsky, 2001, p. 137). More important for our purposes is the fact that many texts are multimodal; they contain linguistic as well as nonlinguistic systems. Pictures, tables, figures, colors, and various font sizes and shapes are frequently part of what makes a text a text (Waller, 1996). The advent of computer technology has expanded the multimodality of texts as well. The use of sound and video, along with the embedding of hypertexts, expands our notion of what texts are traditionally thought to be (Kinzer & Leander, 2003; Lankshear & Knobel, 2002; Leu, 2000; Wysocki, 2004). And, in addition to their multimodality, electronic texts can disrupt the linearity of written texts because of the nonlinear nature of hypertext (RAND Reading Study Group, 2002). Regardless of the nature of the text, readers use their linguistic resources, their knowledge of other communication systems, and the cues provided by the author as a blueprint or guide to work their way through the written code.

The various systems of language that make up a text are interrelated and operate together. Letters and their corresponding sounds are embedded within spelling patterns; letters, sounds, and spelling patterns are embedded within words; letters, sounds, spelling patterns, and words are embedded within syntax; and so on. This interrelationship among systems results in redundancy, which "exits whenever the same information is available from more than one source" (Smith, 2004, p. 63). For example, in English the letters that can immediately follow a word beginning with the letter *t* are restricted to *h, r, a, e, i, o, u,* and *y.* Or, the grammatical category of the word following the adjective *big* is most likely to be a noun. And this noun is most likely to be a particular kind of person, place, or thing given the topic of the sentence and our knowledge of the world (Rumelhart, 2004; Smith, 2004; Weaver, 2002). As we will see in the next section on the cognitive dimension of literacy, the redundancy of the linguistic system allows readers to be selective in the amount of print that they ultimately select for processing. Readers need not rely on all the linguistic sources available because redundancy is built into the system.

It is beyond the scope of this chapter to delineate all of the various linguistic cues available to the reader. However, the graphophonemic system will be briefly addressed because of the privilege it has received in many reading programs within our schools. It is on this system of language that much of the debate over the nature of the reading process and beginning and "remedial" reading instruction is centered. The graphophonemic system expresses the rules for relating letters and sounds within the language. In English, this relationship involves twenty-six letters and approximately forty-four sounds. The challenge is that there are far more individual sounds in the spoken language than forty-four, and they must be systematically linked to a much more limited number of letters. A rule system for the linking of letters and sounds must account for this discrepancy.

Two attempts at generating a rule system that accounts for letter-sound relationships in English are particularly noteworthy as well as revealing. Berdiansky, Cronnel, and Kroehler (1969) examined the letter-sound relationships in 6,092 one- and two-syllable words in the comprehension vocabularies of six- to nine-year-old children. For this corpus of words, 211 letter-sound relationships were found (83 for the consonants, 128 for the vowels). And 166 rules existed (60 for the consonants, 106 for the vowels), each representing at least ten instances of the given letter-sound correspondence. Accompanying these rules were forty-five exceptions (23 consonants, 22 vowels).

In a second study, Clymer (1996) identified forty-five phonic rules or generalizations that were taught to children in four basal readers. After identifying the generalizations, Clymer developed a word list that included all of the words introduced in the four basals as well as the words from Gates's *A Reading Vocabulary for the Primary Grades*. The list contained 2,600 words. Each generalization was then applied to all words in the list that were relevant to the generalization. The degree to which the generalization generated the correct pronunciation was computed as a percentage and labeled the *percent of utility*. Clymer found that a significant number of the phonic generalizations taught to children fail to apply. He concluded by noting that if the criteria of 75 percent application were set to determine the usefulness of any generalization, only eighteen out of forty-five rules would be helpful. This research largely corroborates work by Emans (1967) and Bailey (1967).

As is readily apparent, any attempt to teach and/or learn all of the rules and exceptions as the sole basis for reading and spelling development would be difficult at best. What is also interesting is that the rule-governed nature of the letters in the English alphabet varies across consonants and vowels. Letter consonants are much more consistent in the sounds they represent, whereas letter vowels are far more variable. This accounts for the much greater number of letter-sound correspondences found among vowels, as well as the greater number of rules necessary to account for these correspondences.

The variability between letters and sounds in English has led many educators to lament the English spelling system. However, the "irregularity" of English spelling may not be as erratic as it first appears if we move beyond a strictly alphabetic analysis of the language. This is because the relationship between letters and sounds in English orthography is not based solely on the alphabetic principle. Meaning also plays a critical role. Such written words as <feet> and <feat>; <sea> and <see>; and <rowed>, <rode>, and <road> are spelled differently even though they have identical pronunciations because of the influence of meaning. Consequently, their spelling represents not so much a link with spoken language as it does a link to meaning. Spelling in English marks meaning as much as it marks sound. The general rule in English is that when words sound alike but have different meanings, the words are spelled differently. English orthography, when possible, accommodates meaning rather than sound (Chomsky, 1970; Strauss, 2005; Templeton, 1992; Templeton & Morris, 2000).

On the other hand, when elements of meaning are shared by various words, the tendency of the English language is to maintain a shared spelling. The <s> is pronounced differently in <dogs>, <cats>, and <horses> yet spelled the same way because <s> at the end of nouns typically signifies plurality. Similarly, the <g> in <sign> may not be heard yet is included because of the semantic relationship between <sign> and <signature> in which the <g> is pronounced. A second general rule in English is that when parts of words are related semantically, the spelling is the same for these parts even when the sound varies.

Given the spelling-meaning-sound relationships represented in English, readers need not necessarily go through sound to access word meaning. In fact, an overreliance on sound may actually inhibit the reader's ability to understand. In the two phrases <the cross-eyed bear> and <the cross I'd bare> spelling, not sound, indicates the meaning being represented. The use of a spelling system that is not exclusively based on sound has another advantage. It assures that regardless of what dialect(s) one speaks, the spelling will be the same. Some dialects distinguish between /pin/ and /pen/; others do not. Some dialects pronounce /oil/ and /all/ in the same way; others do not. However, the pairs of morphemes are spelled differently, even though in some speech communities one would need to use context to distinguish which word is being used. English speakers use the same written language system although they speak different dialects (Smith, 2004).

The Cognitive Dimension: The Reader as Meaning Maker

An examination of the cognitive dimension of literacy moves us from a focus on the language itself to an examination of the individual who is transacting with the print. A cognitive discussion of literacy concerns those mental processes, strategies, or procedures that the individual engages so as to construct meaning. Because in the construction of meaning there is a meeting of a mind (cognition) and a text (linguistic), this part of the chapter can best be conceived as a psycholinguistic extension of the previous linguistic discussion. The cognitive dimension is divided into four sections. The first addresses the role of perception in the reading processes, the second the strategies used in reading. This is followed by a look at reading in two languages and a discussion of how readers comprehend.

Readers Perceiving

Although contested by some (e.g., National Institutes of Health, 2000; Stanovich, 2000), many researchers argue that the perception of any particular system of language—for example, letters, words, syntax—is impacted by the linguistic context in which the system is embedded (e.g., Cattell, 1885; Paulson & Freeman, 2003; Rumelhart, 2004). K. Goodman (1993, 1996) and Smith (2004), among others, have argued that readers selectively "pick" from the graphic display. Not all available print is processed; rather, the brain selects just what is necessary to construct meaning. In fact, the brain actually utilizes "strategies to limit the amount of perceptual information it uses to just enough for making sense of the print and confirming its predictions. Perception is what you *think* you see" (Goodman, K., 1996, p. 40). This perceptual information is not limited to the graphics of a particular word. Readers also utilize the syntactic and semantic environment within which any word is embedded to build their expectations. Readers are able to effectively and efficiently predict upcoming words based on the previous meanings and language structures they have encountered as well as their selective sampling of the print. Word identification is therefore impacted and facilitated by multiple sources of information, that is, the various systems of language and the background knowledge of the reader.

The very nature of words themselves, according to Weaver (2002) and Wilde (2000), contributes to the reader's ability to engage in selective sampling. Consonants are far more important to identify than vowels because they provide the reader with more information about a word's identity. There are more consonants than vowels in the English language, and they occur more frequently within words than do vowels. Additionally, as we saw in the discussion of the linguistic dimension, the rules for linking letters to sounds are fewer, and are far more systematic and regular for constants than for vowels. Similarly, the beginnings and endings of words are more useful than the middles in cueing word recognition. Readers can better predict a word from its beginning and ending than from its middle. As is evident, when it comes to perception and reading, all letters are not created equal.

Readers Reading

The reading process is based on a relationship between a reader and writer. The process unfolds within a context of situation, the environment that brings the reader to the text in the first place. The situational context gives rise to the literacy event or activity, influences the individual's purpose for reading, and has a direct impact on how the print on the page is sampled. If the reader is looking for specific information, for example, scanning may be initiated. The reader ignores much of the print, focusing attention only on the specific information being sought. Skimming might be employed when the reader is seeking general knowledge of the text, whereas a much closer reading is initiated when a fuller, more detailed understanding of a text is desired. If the purpose is to recall the information in a text—rather than simply to fully understand it—the reader may need to process the text several times. Finally, the need to memorize will repeatedly focus the reader's attention on the surface level of the discourse. In general, proficient readers are flexible in the way they process a text, guided by their purpose.

Based on the reader's language and background experiences, as well as the purpose for reading, reading is initiated. The reader transacts with the written text using various strategies to construct meaning. These strategies might be understood as being similar to the tools a carpenter uses to build a house. The carpenter employs hammers, saws, and rulers to nail, cut, and measure the wood that will form the house. Similarly, the reader samples visual information, predicts meaning, and integrates meanings into a coherent whole (Goodman, K., 1996; Goodman, Y., & Goodman, K., 2004).

Throughout the entire process of constructing an understanding of the text, the reader monitors and evaluates the meanings being generated. The reader asks such questions as "Does what I am reading make sense?" "Does it sound like language?" "Does it meet my purpose for reading?" "Does it make sense in the situation?" Continuing the carpenter analogy, this would be similar to the carpenter looking at what is being built and evaluating whether it reflects what is intended. When the answer to such questions is "no"—that is, the use of the reading strategies has not been completely successful—the reader has a number of options available (Kucer, 1995, p. 23). The reader can

stop reading and rethink what was read,

reread previous portions of the text,

read ahead to gather more information,

read on to see if there is need to revise,

form a tentative prediction and read on to see if it makes sense,

substitute a different meaning,

sound it out,

ignore the problem,

seek assistance from an outside source (dictionary, encyclopedia, another reader),

use text aids (illustrations, charts, graphs, headings, subheadings),

stop reading altogether.

Readers Reading in Two Languages

Reading in two languages is an increasingly common phenomenon in the United States. This fact was recognized by the federal government in the formation of the National Literacy Panel on Language-Minority Children and Youth, which was charged with investigating what was known about the teaching and learning of non-English-speaking students (McCardle, 2006). The result of this panel's work was the report *Developing Literacy in Second-Language Learners* (August & Shanahan, 2006), which synthesized much of the current research in this area.

By its very nature, the bilingual population is extremely varied, and the degree of biliteracy can vary among bilingual students (Brisk & Harrington, 2000). Bernhardt (2000) noted that second-language reading is "a diverse, complicated, and frustrating landscape to traverse, let alone explain or predict" (p. 791). This variation manifests itself in such things as whether students develop biliteracy simultaneously or sequentially. If sequential, is the home or school language developed first? There is also the issue of whether the home language is maintained at school as the English language is introduced, or if the school language becomes a substitute for the home language (Sen & Blatchford, 2001). Additionally, the degree of oral proficiency in both the first and second language impacts the literacy processes. Finally, according to Bernhardt, biliteracy is influenced by the extent to which the first language has been developed in written form, and by the linguistic similarity between the two languages.

To address all these possible variations is beyond the scope of this chapter. The focus here is on comparing and contrasting the cognitive processes used when individuals are proficient readers—efficient and effective—in their home (first) language and in the English (second) language. However, because of the varied circumstances and experiences encountered by bilingual students, care needs to be taken not to overgeneralize the findings from the biliteracy research.

Biliterate students are not engaged in altogether different processes when reading in two languages. In general, there is a positive and supportive relationship between the processes and strategies used in the first and second languages (Allen, 1991; Carrasquillo, Kucer, & Abrams, 2004; Cummins, 1991; Fitzgerald, 1995; Jimenez, Garcia, & Pearson, 1995, 1996; Weber, 1996). Individuals who are proficient in two written language systems are frequently able to employ strategies used successfully in the first language in the second language as well (Freeman, Y., & Freeman, D., 2006). In both languages, readers monitor their processing through such metacognitive procedures as evaluating, revising (for example, rereading, reading on, and substituting), and predicting upcoming meanings and structures. Biliterates make inferences, draw conclusions, and ask questions. In English as well as in the home language, readers draw on their background knowledge of content and the systems of language to make sense of the ideas being encountered. Vocabulary items that are similar in both languages—cognates—such as the Spanish word <producto> for the English word <product> are also relied on in the making of meaning.

Differences in biliterate readers are also evident. Biliterates may translate—code switch—from one language to the other, and this translation occurs in both directions. Occasionally, miscues made in English can be attributed to the use of syntactic knowledge of the first language. This is especially the case when the reader has a strong spoken command of the first language and less command of the second. The ability to use first-language strategies in both second-language reading and writing is strongly associated with well-developed English oral language as well as developed literacy in the home language (Genesee, Geva, Dressler, & Kamil, 2006; Geva, 2006; Lesaux & Geva, 2006). However, as readers develop oral proficiency in the second language, they typically develop increased reading fluency in the second language as well (Bernhardt, 2000).

Although readers successfully employ a wealth of available strategies when reading in both languages, the extent to which monitoring and revision strategies are necessary may vary. It is not uncommon for biliterates to encounter unknown vocabulary more frequently than do monolinguals. This problem may be compounded when encountering academic text in the second language. In addition to lexical items, biliterates engaged in academic text can encounter unknown grammatical structures or unfamiliar text structures (Scarcella, 2002). Like proficient monolinguals, proficient biliterate readers are able to apply various strategies to determine the meanings of these words and thus allow them to attend to grammatical and text structures. However, the repeated need to engage these revision strategies may impact the degree to which the reader is able to comprehend the text. Compared to native English speakers, biliterates tend to monitor comprehension and engage reading strategies more slowly (Fitzgerald, 1995). The cognitive energy required to make such repairs may limit the attention the reader is able to apply to understanding the overall meanings of the text. This is in contrast to monolingual readers, who typically encounter fewer unknown words and therefore may find it less necessary to engage in revision.

The need for additional monitoring and revision is not language specific, however. The content and structure of the text, as well as opportunities to read in the language under consideration, determine the need to monitor and repair—not whether the text is in the reader's first or second language. It is not uncommon that the biliterate reader's first oral and written language is not English. However, if the school setting does not honor and maintain the reader's home language, and if academic subjects are encountered largely in English, monitoring and repair may be more frequent in the child's home language than in English.

Interestingly, in her review of the research on biliterates, Fitzgerald (1995) found that regardless of the language being read, unfamiliar content had a more significant impact on the biliterate reader than unfamiliar text structure. Weber (1996), Allen (1991), and K. Goodman and Y. Goodman (1978) reported similar findings concerning the relationship between background and linguistic knowledge more generally. Background knowledge tends to "trump" or have a dominating influence on the reading process.

Similar patterns are found when proficient bilingual students reading in English are compared and contrasted with proficient monolingual students reading in English. Both groups engage metacognitive strategies and monitor for meaning. They generate inferences, recall superordinate ideas, and focus more on content than on function words. At times, however, the bilingual readers do not use context as effectively as monolingual readers and monitor their comprehension more slowly. These differences, however, may be developmental; that is, with time and experience, the bilingual readers will come to use context as effectively as the monolingual readers. More important, they will be proficient in reading two languages rather than one.

Readers Comprehending

The goal of any reader is to understand the text being encountered within a particular situation for a particular reason or purpose. The prior experiences of the reader exert a powerful influence on how the reader transacts with the text and how the text is ultimately understood, whether in traditional print form (Alexander & Jetton, 2000; Kintsch, 1998; Tierney & Pearson, 1994; Weaver, 2002) or in hypertext form (Lawless, K., Brown, S., Mills, R., & Mayall, H., 2003). In general, the better the match between the reader's and the writer's background, the better able the reader will be to comprehend the author's message.

Experiences or background knowledge represent not only an understanding of objects, things, or content. More important, the background of the reader represents an awareness of how what is known is to be used in transactions with the world. Just as any text embodies the situation in which it was written, so too does background knowledge embody the situation in which it was generated (Gee, 2004; McVee, Dunsmore, & Gavelek, 2005; Smagorinsky, 2001). Knowledge the reader brings to the page is always constrained, supported, and framed by the situations from which the knowledge was created and used.

Given this action- and situation-oriented nature of background knowledge, it should not be surprising that the comprehension of what a "word" means is always based on the linguistic and situational context in which it is embedded. Words have multiple meanings or at least shades of meaning (Anderson & Nagy, 1996). Word meanings shift and slide depending on the linguistic and situational context in which they are embedded, as do the ideas to which they refer (Labov, 1973). Further complicating the issue is the fact that the situational "context is not really something that can be seen and heard, it is actually something people make assumptions about" (Gee, 1996, p. 75). Therefore, it might be more accurate to talk of readers *interpreting* rather than comprehending words and texts within particular situations, so as to capture the dynamic nature of the process.

A critical factor in understanding a text is the building of coherence (Halliday, 1974; Kintsch, 1998; van Dijk, 1980; van Dijk & Kintsch, 1983). Readers attempt to conceptually link each idea to those ideas immediately around it, and in a general sense to the other meanings in the text. Van den Broek and Kremer (2000) suggest that one way in which readers build coherence is by being particularly sensitive to referential and causal relations throughout a text. Referential relations refer to objects, people, and events that are repeated throughout the text. Readers must remember that these entities have been referenced earlier in their reading. Causal relations indicate how different events or facts impact one another. As events unfold, their meanings are better understood if they can be linked to the previous events that caused or impacted them.

As meaning is constructed within any particular situation, it is not uncommon for the reader to be cognitively changed. That is, what the reader knows when the transaction with print terminates may be qualitatively and/or quantitatively different than when the transaction was initiated. In some instances, the meanings constructed through print fit within the experiences of the reader; a congruency exists between the individual, the situation, and the information. The addition of information to the individual's background results in an elaboration or extension of existing knowledge. The new knowledge is simply added, or assimilated, to what is already known.

There are also instances when the information to be generated through print does not easily match the reader's experiences. The reader may lack the knowledge to make sense of the information presented within a particular situation. In order for the information to be understood by the reader, a restructuring or accommodation of what is known is required. Accommodation typically requires more attention and cognitive resources on the part of the reader. In general and to varying degrees, both assimilation and accommodation occur as the reader attempts to make sense of what is being read.

The Sociocultural Dimension: The Reader as Text User and Text Critic

The sociocultural dimension of literacy shifts our attention from the text (linguistic) and the mind (cognitive) to that of the group (social). It represents the reader's knowledge of how to use texts in socially appropriate ways and the ability to read critically. Not simply an individual act of language and cognition, literacy use also represents patterned social acts of a group. Texts and minds are always embedded within literacy practices, are socially situated and ideologically formed (Gee, 1996, 2004). Literacy practices are recurring or patterned literacy events within a particular community or social group (Heath, 1983; Reder, 1994; Scribner & Cole, 1978). Literacy occurs, therefore, not simply because an individual possesses and applies the necessary linguistic and cognitive strategies and processes, but because group membership requires it (Devine, 1994). Luke (1995, 1998), in fact, argues that there are no private acts of literacy, only social ones.

Two aspects of the sociocultural dimension of literacy are examined: (1) the nature of literacy events and practices used by various social groups to mediate their interactions with the world, and (2) the nature of texts and reading critically.

The Nature of Literacy Events and Literacy Practices

By our very nature, we are social beings and belong to various social groups. Smith (1988) refers to such membership as *belonging to clubs*. We all belong, for example, to cultural, socio-economic, linguistic, gender, and family groups. We may be part of religious organizations and possibly hold membership in such psychological groups as being a jock, brain, or yuppie. According to Ferdman (1990), our social identity consists of the totality of the various groups in which we hold membership.

Each social group or community has its own set of guidelines for what is required to be a member in good standing. That is, there are ways of thinking and behaving that are appropriate to the group. These guidelines impact the individual's beliefs and behaviors, and frame his or her interpretations of, and interactions with, others. Because the individual belongs to a number of social groups, he or she typically has multiple frameworks for behaving and for constructing and understanding experiences.

Literacy practices are one expression of the knowledge, values, and behaviors of any group. Each group "has rules for socially interacting and sharing knowledge in literacy events" (Heath, 1982, p. 50). Each group sponsors the use of particular texts and their reading in particular ways (Brandt, 1998, 2001). Therefore, the literacy behaviors of the individual express the literacy practices of the various social groups of which the individual is a member. Table 3.1 (Kucer, 2005; Kucer & Silva, 2006) contains a list of typical reoccurring literacy practices that have been found in a number of studies (e.g., Anderson & Stokes, 1984; Heath, 1983; Taylor & Dorsey-Gaines, 1988).

Recently, the literacy practices of a number of social groups have been explored. For illustrative purposes, two groups are examined, schools and religious. Most readers probably will have had experiences with both from which they can draw.

Schools are a primary site for literacy sponsorship in American society. Both adults and children expect that literacy will be formally taught and sustained throughout the students' academic

TABLE **3.1.** Some Common Literacy Practices

Type of Practice	Definition	Genre Examples
Daily Living	Literacy activities that relate to ordinary family life, including obtaining food, maintaining shelter and health, managing finances, shopping, paying bills, caring for children.	Shopping lists, bills and checks, budgets
Entertainment or Recreational	Literacy activities that relate to passing the time in an enjoyable or interesting manner.	Television guides, theater listings and reviews, magazines, newspapers, books
Spiritual	Literacy activities related to worship or metaphysical endeavors.	Hymnals, bulletins and newsletters, scripture reading, order of the service guidelines
Work-related	Literacy activities related to one's place of employment.	Office memorandums, order forms, applications, policies and procedures, guidelines
Social-interactional	Literacy activities related to written communication with friends or relatives; literacy used to build and maintain social relationships.	Friendly letters, email, greeting cards
Educational	Literacy activities related to increasing one's knowledge.	Textbooks, reports and papers, "how to" materials, school forms, academic journals
News-related	Literacy activities to gain information about local, state, regional, national, or world events or third parties.	Newspapers and news magazines, flyers, bulletins
Archival-related	Literacy activities related to materials that are saved and referenced when necessary.	Report cards, birth certificates, paid bills, insurance policies, telephone numbers, leases

careers. Like any institution, schools have specific rules or norms for how language is to be used and how texts are to be formed. These rules and forms may affirm, build on, and extend the way in which language is used in the learner's home; may require adaptation in language rules and forms; or may directly contradict home language patterns (Heath, 1983; Scollon & Scollon, 1981).

A central feature in many classroom lessons is the initiation-reply-evaluation (IRE) sequence. As documented by Cazden (2001) and Heath (1983), the teacher initiates the IRE sequence by asking a question. In contrast to authentic questions, it is clear to all involved that the teacher knows the answers to the questions being asked. A student is then identified to respond or reply to the question, and the teacher explicitly evaluates the adequacy of the response. In contexts other than the classroom, it would be considered inappropriate for a questioner to openly evaluate the acceptability of a provided answer (Gee, 1996).

In addition to norms for school texts and lessons, there are also rules for what text meanings are to be the focus of attention within the IRE lesson sequence. In the early grades, much attention is given to the asking and answering of "what" questions, for example, "What did the boy do after he planted the seed?" Selective attention is given to the segmentation of items and meanings in the text as they are discussed and analyzed. Students are expected to listen as an audience to the questions and answers, and then to respond and display what they know when called on. This display of knowledge, however, may be limited to the factual meanings in the text that the teacher has solicited; the incorporation of nonschool experiences into the answers is often discouraged.

Not only does such school-based literacy sponsorship contradict the ways in which many families frame literacy use in their homes (e.g., Heath 1982, 1983; Michaels, 1981; Purcell-Gates, 1996; Purcell-Gates, L'Allier, & Smith, 1995; Scollon, R., & Scollon, S., 1981), it also fails to correspond to literacy use in other social contexts. For example, a great deal of research has examined the use of literacy within religious contexts (e.g., Elster, 2003; McMillon & Edwards, 2000; Moss, 1994, 2001). Moss examined the form and function of sermons within African American churches. In contrast to school-based texts, the discourse of the sermons did not represent or function as independent entities. Rather, sermons had a dialogic quality and were created and sustained through a collaboration between the minister and the congregation. There was not a fixed boundary between the minister and the worshipers. In fact, the active participation and contributions of the believing community were needed to complete the text. Sermons were also heavily contextualized. References were made to both current and historical events of relevance to the African American fellowship. These references served to lessen the distance between the pastor and the congregants. It was through the sermon itself that the pastor attempted to demonstrate that he was not above or beyond the worshipers, but rather one with them.

Within an Israeli Orthodox Jewish context, Elster (2003) documented similarly different understandings of, and interactions with, sacred texts from those commonly found in secular schools. For the most part, the texts under study are restricted to the *Torah* and *Talmud*, are continually and orally reread and studied, and are regulatory in their function. That is, the texts seek to impact moral behavior and spiritual aspirations. The ritual oral reading of the *Torah* scroll is to be accomplished without "deviation from the words of the written text" (p. 674). Secular schools, in contrast, involve the reading of a continually evolving variety of texts reflecting a variety of functions. Oral reading, although a strategy used in early reading instruction, seldom continues as a regular instructional event in the upper grades.

Although literacy is intimately woven into the very fabric of daily life in most communities within the United States, the relationship between school and community literacy use may vary. The previous religious literacy examples serve as a much-needed reminder that there are many paths to becoming and being literate in our society. Middle-class norms for reading and writing may reflect the literacy norms found in many schools; however, they are not the only route to becoming a reader and writer. McMillon and Edwards (2000) have documented, for instance, how a young child, Joshua, was a developing and engaged literacy user in Sunday school. In contrast, he struggled as a reader in preschool literacy programs because he was unfamiliar with the acceptable standards for participation in school-based literacy practices.

The Nature of Texts and Reading Critically

Knowing how to appropriately engage in the literacy practices of the various communities in which one holds membership is one aspect of the sociocultural dimension of reading. The second is the ability to read the word and the world through a critical lens (Freire, 1998). Texts represent and are sponsored by particular groups representing particular ideologies or beliefs (Bigelow & Peterson, 1998; Brandt, 1998, 2001; Buckingham & Sefton-Green, 1994; Pennycook, 2001). As such, texts, whether encountered inside or outside of the classroom, have the potential to significantly impact both literacy and concept development. Because meanings are seldom if ever neutral—they always assert a particular perspective related to a particular individual as a member of a particular group—text meanings reflect particular worldviews of particular groups. Just as important, meanings have the ability to cover up other meanings, to suppress other stories, other voices. Meanings reveal as well as conceal.

The Eurocentric knowledge that many Americans have about colonial explorations of the Western Hemisphere, for example, covers or hides meanings that represent an indigenous perspective (Bigelow, 1989; Bigelow, Miner, & Peterson, 1991). Use of the words and phrases *discover, New World, savage Indians,* and *America* positions both Europeans and native peoples. Alternate positions and perspectives are reflected in such words as *steal, homeland, one with nature,* and *civilized.* However, these words and the views they represent are often not encountered in school and other institutional discourse. When the origin and nature of knowledge are viewed from this perspective, the "socialness" of knowing is made visible. Knowledge is understood to be socially constructed and promoted by like-minded individuals. Knowledge reflects a particular view, a particular position of writer and reader, at a particular point in time, and within a particular context.

In our previous cognitive discussion on comprehension, we found that readers construct meanings from their transactions with written discourse. This transaction is conceived as being among reader, text, and author. As part of this transaction, the reader's own particular background knowledge impacts in a very direct way how any text is comprehended. However, we have also seen that readers and writers have multiple social identities. These identities reflect and are formed by the particular experiences that members of the group have had with one another and with other groups in the wider society. Therefore, the background a reader brings to the page represents not only his or her own unique experiences, but also the experiences of the various groups in which the individual holds membership. These group identities impact how the individual interprets any piece of written discourse. The cognitive transaction is widened beyond the individual, and conceives of reader, writer, and text as reflections and products of relevant interpretive communities.

Given the positions that authors endeavor to make readers assume, proficient readers engage in critical analysis as they work their way through text. They reflect on such issues as (1) Who made, constructed, or originated the perspective and ideas in this text? (2) Who might benefit from this perspective and these ideas? (3) Who might need to learn this perspective and these ideas? (4) Why might someone choose to learn this perspective and these ideas? (5) Who might be harmed from this perspective and these ideas? (6) What alternate perspectives and ideas might be constructed? In essence, readers attempt to make explicit that which is often implicit in nature (Edelsky, 1999, 2006; Heffernan & Lewison, 2005; Leland, Harste, & Huber, 2005; Lewison, Flint, & Van Sluys, 2002; Lewison, Leland, & Harste, 2008).

The Developmental Dimension: The Reader as Scientist and Construction Worker

The developmental dimension addresses what we know concerning how the learner becomes a code breaker, meaning maker, text user, and critic. It concerns both the processes and the participants involved in learning the linguistic, cognitive, and sociocultural dimensions of literacy. This relationship between the developmental dimension and the linguistic, cognitive, and sociocultural is why in Figure 3.1 the developmental engulfs or is wrapped around the other dimensions. Each reading event reflects those dimensions of literacy that the individual does and does not control in any given situation. Potentially, development never ends, as individuals may encounter reading experiences that involve using reading in new and novel ways. These experiences offer the opportunity for additional learning that results in developmental advances. Therefore, *becoming* literate rather than *being* literate more accurately describes our ongoing relationship with written language (Leu, 2000).

The following chapters in this book address in very specific ways what we know about promoting reading development in our students. The last section of this chapter briefly frames the processes by which this learning occurs. Learners are actively involved in the developmental process, building for themselves an understanding of the way written language operates linguistically, cognitively, and socioculturally. Adults and more capable literacy users play a mediational role in this process, supporting and scaffolding the learners' development.

The individual goes about learning language knowledge much as a scientist goes about developing scientific knowledge: through data collection, rule generation, rule testing, and rule modification. The dimensions of language are actually constructed or built by the learner. The learner discovers the linguistic, cognitive, and sociocultural regularities or patterns of the language based on the language data available, the situation in which the language is embedded, and the mediation provided. Actively involved in the developmental process, the learner is anything but a passive recipient of the language. Rather, the learner experiences or encounters language data expressed by others. In an attempt to make sense of this data, the learner generates hypotheses or rules for how a particular aspect of the language might operate. Using these hypotheses as a guide, the learner engages in language use and receives feedback from others. Based on the feedback provided, the hypotheses are modified as warranted.

Until recently, the notion of the learner generating rules for understanding written language was largely ignored. Written language development was thought to come about through direct, segmented, and skill-by-skill instruction. However, we now know that learners also attempt to make sense of the print that surrounds them (Dyson, 2003; Teale & Sulzby, 1991). There is little evidence to suggest that written language is to any great extent learned through imitation. The individual's stance is not to replicate or copy the language that he or she encounters. Rather, the learner attempts to understand the social and cognitive meanings being expressed and the systems of language that serve as the avenue for their expression. Through such attempts at understanding, the language is constructed.

Teachers' behaviors and the materials they use are the primary mediational vehicles within most classrooms. Mediations represent the support structures, or scaffolds, that are built around a learner (Bruner 1986; Gee, 2004; Vygotsky, 1978). These configurations, similar to those surrounding a building under construction, provide the social assistance necessary for the learner to meaningfully engage in the particular undertaking at hand, such as reading a book to locate specific information. The power of such scaffolds is that the learner encounters the entire activity within a meaningful, purposeful context. And, although the learner may be capable of engaging in only portions of the activity, he or she is aware of the entire scope of the unfolding literacy event.

With time, experience, and growing competency on the part of the learner, the teacher begins to lessen the support provided— deconstructs the scaffold. The learner is encouraged to take on responsibility for certain aspects of the activity that were once performed solely by the teacher, or by the teacher and learner working collaboratively. As the scaffold is dismantled, what the teacher once did is now the responsibility of the learner. More specifically, potential abilities represent those aspects of literacy that the learner has the capability or capacity to develop. As described by Vygotsky (1978), potential abilities are like buds on a tree that with time and nourishment will bloom into flowers and ultimately bear fruit. The nourishment provided by the teacher is the social and collaborative support structure built around the learner—the scaffold. Independent abilities, in contrast, are those reading behaviors that the individual is able to employ without the support or assistance of others. These strategies and processes, once social and external in nature, are now internal, autonomous, and self-governing. The distance between potential and independent abilities is what Vygotsky termed the *zone of proximal development (ZPD)*. It is within this zone that the teacher and student collaboratively operate.

As teachers encourage—and students move toward—independence, it is important to keep in mind the inherent variability of literacy development. Traditionally, "mastery" has been the goal of much classroom instruction. Through mastery, the child was supposed to be capable of consistently and effectively applying the learned skill across space, time, and contexts. When the child experienced problems with this application, "reinforcement" or "remediation" of the skills was the typical instructional response. Previously introduced skills were revisited and practiced so as to ensure or maintain their mastery.

Development, however, is not the same as mastery. Rather, development represents the learner's growth in the ability to effectively and efficiently apply the literacy strategies across an ever-widening range of situations. However, texts and situations with which the learner encounters difficulty will still exist. Of course, this developmental process can be applied to most of us. Development typically continues throughout the course of one's life as long as literacy is encountered and used in new or novel ways. Additionally, literacy contexts always exist in which we are less than proficient, if only because we lack experience or interest in these situations.

Conclusion and Summary

What we know about the nature of reading is that it is a multidimensional, transactional, and complex process. Readers draw upon their linguistic, cognitive, and sociocultural resources as they crack the code, generate meaning, and use and critique written language. These ongoing engagements with texts offer individuals the possibilities of continually *becoming* literate, increasing the range of texts and situations in which they can successfully operate as readers.

References

Adams, M., & Bruck, M. (1995). Resolving the "great debate." *American Educator, 19*(2), 10–20.

Alexander, P., & Jetton, T. (2000). Learning from text: A multidimensional and developmental perspective. In M. Kamil, P. Mosenthal, P. D. Pearson, & R. Barr (Eds.), *Handbook of reading research: Vol. 3* (pp. 285–310). Mahwah, NJ: Erlbaum.

Allen, V. (1991). Teaching bilingual and ESL children. In J. Flood, J. Jensen, D. Lapp, & J. Squire (Eds.), *Handbook of research on teaching the English language arts* (pp. 356–64). New York: Macmillan.

Anderson, A., & Stokes, S. (1984). Social and institutional influences on the development and practice of literacy. In H. Goelman, A. Oberg, & F. Smith (Eds.), *Awakening to literacy* (pp. 24–37). Exeter, NH: Heinemann.

Anderson, R., & Nagy, W. (1996). Word meanings. In R. Barr, M. Kamil, P. Mosenthal, & P. D. Pearson (Eds.), *Handbook of reading research: Vol. 2* (pp. 690–724). Mahwah, NJ: Erlbaum.

August, D., & Shanahan, T. (Eds.). (2006). *Developing literacy in second-language learners: Report of the National Literacy Panel on Language-Minority Children and Youth.* Mahwah, NJ: Erlbaum.

Bailey, M. H. (1967). The utility of phonic generalizations in grades one through six. *Reading Teacher, 20,* 413–18.

Berdiansky, B., Cronnel, B., & Kroehler, J. (1969). *Spelling–sound relations and primary form–class descriptions for speech-comprehension vocabularies of 6–9 year-olds* (Tech. Rep. No. 15). Inglewood, CA: Southwest Regional Laboratory for Educational Research and Development.

Bernhardt, E. (2000). Second-language reading as a case study of reading scholarship in the 20th century. In M. Kamil, P. Mosenthal, P. D. Pearson, & R. Barr (Eds.), *Handbook of reading research: Vol. 3* (pp. 791–811). Mahwah, NJ: Erlbaum.

Bigelow, W. (1989). Discovering Columbus: Rereading the past. *Language Arts, 66*(6), 635–43.

Bigelow, W., Miner, B., & Peterson, R. (1991). Rethinking Columbus. In W. Bigelow, B. Miner, & R. Peterson (Eds.), *Rethinking schools.* Milwaukee, WI: Rethinking Schools.

Bigelow, W., & Peterson, B. (Eds.). (1998). *Rethinking Columbus: The next 500 years* (2nd ed.). Milwaukee, WI: Rethinking Schools.

Brandt, D. (1998). Sponsors of literacy. *College Composition and Communication, 49*(2), 165–85.

Brandt, D. (2001). Literacy learning and economic change. In S. Beck & L. Olah (Eds.). *Perspectives on language and literacy: Beyond the here and now* (pp. 201–20). Cambridge, MA: Harvard Educational Review.

Brisk, M. E., & Harrington, M. M. (2000). *Literacy and bilingualism.* Mahwah, NJ: Erlbaum.

Bruner, J. (1986). *Actual minds, possible worlds.* Cambridge, MA: Harvard University Press.

Buckingham, D., & Sefton-Green, J. (1994). *Cultural studies goes to school: Reading and teaching popular media.* Bristol, PA: Taylor & Francis.

Carrasquillo, A., Kucer, S. B., & Abrams, R. (2004). *Beyond the beginnings: Literacy interventions for upper elementary English language learners.* Clevedon, UK: Multilingual Matters.

Cattell, J. M. (1885). The inertia of the eye and brain. *Brain, 8,* 295–312.

Cazden, C. (2001). *Classroom discourse: The language of teaching and learning* (2nd ed.). Portsmouth, NH : Heinemann.

Chomsky, C. (1970). Reading, writing, and phonology. *Harvard Educational Review, 40*(2), 287–309.

Clymer, T. (1996). The utility of phonic generalizations in the primary grades. *Reading Teacher, 50*(3), 182–87.

Commission on Reading of the National Council of Teachers of English. (2004). *On reading, learning to read, and effective reading instruction: An overview of what we know and how we know it.* Retrieved February 5, 2005, from http://www.ncte.org/about/over/positions/category/read/118620.htm

Cummins, J. (1991). Interdependence of first- and second-language proficiency in bilingual children. In E. Bialystok (Ed.), *Language processing in bilingual children* (pp. 70–89). Cambridge, UK: Cambridge University Press.

de Beaugrande, R. (1980). *Text, discourse, and process.* Norwood, NJ: Ablex.

Devine, J. (1994). Literacy and social power. In B. Ferdman, R. M. Weber, & A. Ramirez (Eds.), *Literacy across languages and cultures* (pp. 221–37). Albany: State University of New York Press.

Dyson, A. H. (2003). *The brothers and sisters learn to write: Popular literacies in childhood and school cultures.* New York: Teachers College Press.

Edelsky, C. (Ed.). (1999). *Making justice our project.* Urbana, IL: National Council of Teachers of English.

Edelsky, C. (2006). *With literacy and justice for all: Rethinking the social in language and education* (3rd ed.). Mahwah, NJ: Erlbaum.

Elster, C. (2003). Authority, performance, and interpretation in religious reading: Critical issues of intercultural communication and multiple literacies. *Journal of Literacy Research, 35*(1), 663–92.

Emans, R. (1967). The usefulness of phonic generalizations above the primary grades. *Reading Teacher, 20,* 419–25.

Ferdman, B. (1990). Literacy and cultural identity. *Harvard Educational Review, 60*(2), 181–204.

Fitzgerald, J. (1995). English-as-a-second-language learners' cognitive reading processes: A review of research in the United States. *Review of Educational Research, 65*(2), 145–90.

Freebody, P., & Luke, A. (1990). Literacies' programs: Debates and demands in cultural context. *Prospect: The Australian Journal of TESOL, 5*(3), 7–16.

Freeman, Y., & Freeman, D. (2006). *Teaching reading and writing in Spanish and English* (2nd ed.). Portsmouth, NH: Heinemann.

Freire, P. (1998). *Teachers as cultural workers: Letters to those who dare teach.* Boulder, CO: Westview Press.

Gee, J. (1996). *Social linguistics and literacies: Ideology in discourses* (2nd ed.). Bristol, PA: Taylor & Francis.

Gee, J. (2004). *Situated language and learning: A critique of traditional schooling.* New York: Routledge.

Genesee, F., Geva, E., Dressler, C., & Kamil, M. (2006). Synthesis: Cross-linguistic relationships. In D. August & T. Shanahan (Eds.), *Developing literacy in second-language learners: Report of the National Literacy Panel on Language-Minority Children and Youth* (pp. 153–83). Mahwah, NJ: Erlbaum.

Geva, E. (2006). Second-language oral proficiency and second-language literacy. In D. August & T. Shanahan (Eds.), *Developing literacy in second-language learners: Report of the National Literacy Panel* on *Language-Minority Children and Youth* (pp. 123–39). Mahwah NJ: Erlbaum.

Gonzalez, N., Moll, L., & Amanti, C. (2005). *Funds of knowledge: Theorizing practices in households, communities, and classrooms.* Mahwah, NJ: Erlbaum.

Goodman, K. (1993). *Phonics phacts.* Portsmouth, NH: Heinemann.

Goodman, K. (1996). *On reading.* Portsmouth, NH: Heinemann.

Goodman, K., & Goodman, Y. (1978). *Reading of American children whose language is a stable rural dialect of English or a language other than English* (NIE-C-00-3-0087). Washington, DC: National Institute of Education, U.S. Department of Health, Education and Welfare.

Goodman, Y., & Goodman, K. (2004). To err is human: Learning about language processes by analyzing miscues. In R. Ruddell & N. Unrau (Eds.), *Theoretical models and processes of reading* (5th ed., pp. 620–39). Newark, DE: International Reading Association.

Halliday, M. A. K. (1973). *Explorations in the functions of language.* London: Arnold.

Halliday, M. A. K. (1974). *Language and social man.* London: Longman.

Heath, S. (1982). What no bedtime story means: Narrative skills at home and school. *Language in Society, 11*(1), 49–76.

Heath, S. (1983). *Ways with words: Language, life, and work in communities and classrooms.* Cambridge: Cambridge University Press.

Heffernan, L., & Lewison, M. (2005). What's lunch got to do with it? Critical literacy and the discourse of the lunchroom. *Language Arts, 83*(2), 107–17.

Jimenez, R., Garcia, G., & Pearson, P. D. (1995). Three children, two languages, and strategic reading: Case studies in bilingual/monolingual reading. *American Educational Research Journal, 32*(1), 67–97.

Jimenez, R., Garcia, G., & Pearson, P. D. (1996). The reading strategies of bilingual Latina/o students who are successful English readers: Opportunities and obstacles. *Reading Research Quarterly, 31*(1), 90–112.

Kintsch, W. (1998). *Comprehension: A paradigm for cognition.* Cambridge: Cambridge University Press.

Kinzer, C., & Leander, K. (2003). Technology and the language arts: Implications of an expanded definition of literacy. In J. Flood, D. Lapp, J. Squire, & J. Jensen (Eds.), *Handbook of research on teaching the English language arts* (2nd ed., pp. 546–65). Mahwah, NJ: Erlbaum.

Kucer, S. B. (1991). Authenticity as the basis for instruction. *Language Arts, 68*(7), 532–40.

Kucer, S. B. (1995). Guiding bilingual students "through" the literacy processes. *Language Arts, 72*(1), 20–29.

Kucer, S. B. (2005). *Dimensions of literacy: A conceptual base for teaching reading and writing in school settings* (2nd ed.). Mahwah, NJ: Erlbaum.

Kucer, S. B., & Silva, C. (2006). *Teaching the dimensions of literacy.* Mahwah, NJ: Erlbaum.

Labov, W. (1973). The boundaries of words and their meanings. In C. J. Bailey & R. Shuy (Eds.), *New ways of analyzing variation in English* (pp. 340–73). Washington, DC: Georgetown University.

Lankshear, C., & Knobel, M. (2002). Do we have your attention? New literacies, digital technologies, and the education of adolescents. In D. Alvermann (Ed.), *Adolescents and literacies in a digital world* (pp. 19–39). New York: Peter Lang.

Lawless, K., Brown, S., Mills, R., & Mayall, H. (2003). Knowledge, interest, recall, and navigation: A look at hypertext processing. *Journal of Literacy Research, 35*(3), 911–34.

Leland, C., Harste, J., & Huber, K. (2005). Out of the box: Critical literacy in a first-grade classroom. *Language Arts, 82*(4), 257–68.

Lesaux, N., & Geva, E. (2006). Synthesis: Development of literacy in language-minority students. In D. August & T. Shanahan (Eds.), *Developing literacy in second-language learners: Report of the National Literacy Panel on Language-Minority Children and Youth* (pp. 53–74). Mahwah, NJ: Erlbaum.

Leu, D. (2000). Literacy and technology: Deictic consequences for literacy education in an information age. In M. Kamil, P. Mosenthal, D. Pearson, & R. Barr (Eds.), *Handbook of reading research: Vol. 3* (pp. 743–70). Mahwah, NJ: Erlbaum.

Lewison, M., Flint, A. S., & Van Sluys, K. (2002). Taking on critical literacy: The journey of newcomers and novices. *Language Arts, 79*(5), 382–92.

Lewison, M., Leland, C., & Harste, J. (2008). *Creating critical classrooms: K–8 reading and writing with an edge.* New York: Erlbaum.

Luke, A. (1995). When basic skills and information processing just aren't enough: Rethinking reading in new times. *Teachers College Record,* 97(1), 95–115.

Luke, A. (1998). Getting over method: Literacy teaching as work in "new times." *Language Arts,* 75(4), 305–13.

McCardle, P. (2006). Foreword. In D. August & T. Shanahan (Eds.), *Developing literacy in second-language learners: Report of the National Literacy Panel on Language-Minority Children and Youth* (pp. ix–xi). Mahwah, NJ: Erlbaum.

McMillon, G. T., & Edwards, P. (2000). Why does Joshua "hate" school . . . but love Sunday school? *Language Arts,* 78(2), 111–20.

McVee, M., Dunsmore, K., & Gavelek, J. (2005). Schema theory revisited. *Review of Educational Research,* 75(4), 531–66.

Michaels, S. (1981). Sharing time: Children's narrative styles and differential access to literacy. *Language and Society,* 10, 423–42.

Moss, B. (1994). Creating a community: Literacy events in African-American churches. In B. Moss (Ed.), *Literacy across communities* (pp. 147–78). Cresskill, NJ: Hampton.

Moss, B. (2001). From the pews to the classrooms: Influences of the African American church on academic literacy. In J. Harris, A. Kamhi, & K. Pollock (Eds.), *Literacy in African American communities* (pp. 195–211). Mahwah, NJ: Erlbaum.

National Institutes of Health. National Institute of Child Health and Human Development (NICHD). (2000). *Report of the National Reading Panel: Teaching children to read* (NIH Publication No. 00-4769). Washington, DC: Government Printing Office.

New London Group. (1996). A pedagogy of multiliteracies: Designing social futures. *Harvard Educational Review,* 66(1), 60–92.

Paulson, E., & Freeman, A. (2003) *Insight from the eyes: The science of effective reading instruction.* Portsmouth, NH: Heinemann.

Pennycook, A. (2001). *Critical applied linguistics: A critical introduction.* Mahwah, NJ: Erlbaum.

Purcell-Gates, V. (1996). Stories, coupons, and the TV Guide: Relationships between home literacy experiences and emergent literacy knowledge. *Reading Research Quarterly, 31*(4), 406–28.

Purcell-Gates, V., L'Allier, S., & Smith, D. (1995). Literacy at the Harts' and the Larsons': Diversity among poor, innercity families. *Reading Teacher, 48*(7), 572–78.

RAND Reading Study Group. (2002). *Reading for understanding: Toward an r&d program in reading comprehension.* Santa Monica, CA: RAND.

Reder, S. (1994). Practice-engagement theory: A sociocultural approach to literacy across languages and cultures. In B. Ferdman, R. M. Weber, & A. Ramirez (Eds.), *Literacy across languages and cultures* (pp. 33–74). Albany: State University of New York Press.

Rumelhart, D. (2004). Toward an interactive model of reading. In R. Ruddell & N. Unrau (Eds.), *Theoretical models and processes of reading* (5th ed., pp. 1149–79). Newark, DE: International Reading Association.

Scarcella, R. (2002). Some key factors affecting English learners' development of advanced literacy. In M. Schleppegrell and M. C. Colombi (Eds.), *Developing advanced literacy in first and second languages* (pp. 209-26). Mahwah, NJ: Lawrence Erlbaum.

Scollon, R., & Scollon, S. (1981). *Narrative, literacy, and face in interethnic communication.* Norwood, NJ: Ablex.

Scribner, S., & Cole, M. (1978). Literacy without schooling: Testing for intellectual effects. *Harvard Educational Review, 48*(4), 448–61.

Sen, R., & Blatchford, P. (2001). Reading in a second language: Factors associated with progress in young children. *Educational Psychology, 21*(2), 189–202.

Smagorinsky, P. (2001). If meaning is constructed, what is it made from? Toward a cultural theory of reading. *Review of Educational Research, 71*(1), 133–69.

Smith, F. (1983). *Essays into literacy.* Exeter, NH: Heinemann.

Smith, F. (2004). *Understanding reading* (6th ed.). Mahwah, NJ: Erlbaum.

Stanovich, K. (2000). *Progress in understanding reading: Scientific foundations and new frontiers.* New York: Guilford Press.

Strauss, S. (2005). *The linguistics, neurology, and politics of phonics: Silent "e" speaks out.* Mahwah, NJ: Erlbaum.

Taylor, D., & Dorsey-Gaines, C. (1988). *Growing up literate: Learning from inner-city families.* Portsmouth, NH: Heinemann.

Teale, W., & Sulzby, E. (1991). Emergent literacy. In R. Barr, M. L. Kamil, P. B. Mosenthal, & P. D. Pearson (Eds.), *Handbook of reading research: Vol. 2* (pp. 418–52). New York: Longman.

Templeton, S. (1992). New trends in an historical perspective: Old story, new resolution— Sound and meaning in spelling. *Language Arts, 69*(6), 43–52.

Templeton, S., & Morris, D. (2000). Spelling. In M. Kamil, P. Mosenthal, D. Pearson, & R. Barr (Eds.), *Handbook of reading research: Vol. 3* (pp. 525–543). Mahwah, NJ: Erlbaum.

Tierney, R., & Pearson, P. D. (1994). Learning from text: A framework for improving classroom practice. In R. Ruddell, M. Ruddell, & H. Singer (Eds.), *Theoretical models and processes of reading* (4th ed., pp. 496–513). Newark, DE: International Reading Association.

van den Broek, P., & Kremer, K. (2000). The mind in action: What it means to comprehend during reading. In B. Taylor, M. Graves, and P. van den Broek (Eds.), *Reading for meaning: Fostering comprehension in the middle grades* (pp. 1–31). New York: Teachers College Press.

van Dijk, T. A. (1980). *Macrostructures.* Hillsdale, NJ: Erlbaum.

van Dijk, T. A., & Kintsch, W. (1983). *Strategies of discourse comprehension.* New York: Academic Press.

Vygotsky, L. S. (1978). *Mind in society: The development of higher psychological processes.* Cambridge, MA: Harvard University Press.

Waller, R. (1996). Typography and discourse. In R. Barr, M. Kamil, P. Mosenthal, & P. D. Pearson (Eds.), *Handbook of reading research: Vol. 2* (pp. 341–80). Mahwah, NJ: Erlbaum.

Weaver, C. (2002). *Reading process and practice* (3rd ed.). Portsmouth, NH: Heinemann.

Weber, R. (1996). Linguistic diversity and reading in American society. In R. Barr, M. Kamil, P. Mosenthal, & P. D. Pearson (Eds.), *Handbook of reading research: Vol. 2* (pp. 97–119). Mahwah, NJ: Erlbaum.

Wilde, S. (2000). *Miscue analysis made easy: Building on student strengths*. Portsmouth, NH: Heinemann.

Wysocki, A. F. (2004). The multimedia of texts: How onscreen and paper texts incorporate words, images, and other media. In C. Bazerman & P. Prior (Eds.), *What writing does and how it does it: An introduction to analyzing texts and textual practices* (pp. 123–63). Mahwah, NJ: Erlbaum.

Young, E. (1992). *Seven blind mice*. New York: Philomel.

CHAPTER FOUR

What We Know about the Learning and Development of Reading K–12: Thirteen Core Understandings about Reading and Learning to Read

JANE BRAUNGER
Strategic Literacy Initiative
WestEd

JAN PATRICIA LEWIS
Pacific Lutheran University

This chapter discusses thirteen core understandings that knowledgeable teachers have about reading: understandings informed by various research traditions and demonstrated by the classroom environments that such teachers design (cf. Braunger & Lewis, 2006). The book that explains these core understandings in detail, *Building a Knowledge Base in Reading*, significantly informed the Commission on Reading documents found in Appendixes A, B, and C in this book. As teachers, parents, and policymakers act in their respective roles on these understandings, they support all students to develop the sophisticated literacy skills required for personal, social, civic, and economic fulfillment.

The core understandings reflect the nature of reading as language, which is always about meaning and communication. However, they also illustrate that reading is a learned rather than an acquired language behavior. Reading is dependent on mastering a written code based on the alphabetic principle. Allington and Cunningham (1996) sum up the essential tension: "reading and writing are meaning constructing activities, but they are dependent on words" (p. 49). The core understandings that follow summarize current research on best practice in literacy instruction that keeps the focus on reading as a construction of meaning, while developing a wide range of print-based skills and strategies necessary for the effective use of literacy. Following the initial publication of these core understandings (Braunger & Lewis, 1997), we heard repeatedly from teachers, teacher educators, and policymakers about how useful they found this collection and explanation of research on literacy instruction, with its compilation of research-based instructional recommendations. Over the past few years, however, the research climate has been narrowed by an increasingly simplistic model of what works in the teaching of reading—scientifically based reading instruction as described in this book. This focus on establishing a single line of cause and effect has led to a problem with research in reading: the preferred topics for funded research are increasingly the smallest components of reading that can be controlled or studied in experimental settings. Instructional recommendations based on such studies tend to focus on direct instruction of discrete skills, for example, phonemic awareness and phonics.

In contrast to the narrow criterion of scientifically based instruction, the International Reading Association (IRA) has proposed *evidence-based* instruction as the hallmark of literacy instruction, recognizing the many types of research that provide insights into teaching and learning. The IRA's position paper on evidence-based reading instruction (2002) asserts that reading research makes it clear that "there is no single instructional program or method that is effective in teaching all children to read" (par. 2).

Thirteen Core Understandings about Reading and Learning to Read

The challenge to public schools to bring all students to high levels of literacy is unprecedented and complex. The task is made even more daunting by a lack of public consensus on (1) literacy goals and (2) the relevant knowledge base to inform initial and continuing reading instruction.

The thirteen core understandings contribute to an important professional dialogue, and help build a consensus on literacy and its knowledge base by detailing what is known about how children learn to read and grow as readers, and about the environments that support the process. This chapter outlines and briefly describes salient research in support of the thirteen core understandings discussed in more detail in *Building a Knowledge Base in Reading* (Braunger & Lewis, 2006).

1. Reading is a construction of meaning from written text. It is an active, cognitive, and affective process.
From the earliest stages, reading is for comprehension. Lest this goal be lost in current debates on how best to teach beginning reading, the RAND Reading Study Group (2002) identified comprehension research as a priority from primary grades through secondary school.

Readers do not take in print and receive words off the page. They actively engage with the text and build their own understanding. With comprehension as the goal, readers purposefully sample print, constructing meaning efficiently and effectively (Duke & Pearson, 2002; Goodman, K., 1996; Kucer & Tuten, 2003; Smith, 2004).

Reading is a sociocultural process. That is, it occurs within a situation whose participants, time, place, and expectations will affect the reader and the meaning he or she constructs with the text (Gee, 1996; Halliday, 1973, 1975). A learner taught to read in ways that emphasize construction of meaning with texts that are semantically and syntactically authentic will develop a useful model of reading (Cambourne, 2002).

2. Background knowledge and prior experience are critical to the reading process.
The work of Anderson and Pearson (1984) and Rumelhart (1980) has demonstrated the importance of prior knowledge in reading. According to this view, called *schema theory*, readers understand what they read only as it relates to what they already know.

It is important for teachers to understand and build on the range of background knowledge, both overall and specific, that students bring to school. The more students read and write, the more their prior knowledge grows, which in turn strengthens their ability to construct meaning as they read (Allington & Cunningham, 1996; Sweet, 1993).

Numerous studies have confirmed the importance of extensive reading to build vocabulary and background knowledge (Anderson & Nagy, 1992; Stahl, 1998). Because words, and the concepts and knowledge they represent, are learned incrementally, extensive reading provides the repeated encounters with a new word necessary for a reader to develop a good working knowledge of that word, and by extension, to build new schema, or background knowledge associated with it (McKeown, Beck, Omanson, & Pople, 1985; Nagy, Anderson, & Herman, 1987).

For middle and high school students, the need to acquire and apply new schema suited to various academic discourses is critical. In addition, these students need to learn discipline-based ways of reading to access valued concepts and information (Kucer, 2005; Schoenbach, Greenleaf, Cziko, & Hurwitz, 1999). For adolescents, even a little background knowledge in a domain related to the content of a subject area text can improve comprehension of that text (Snow & Biancarosa, 2003).

It is important for teachers to be aware of the schema students bring to a text, as well as the ones they may need to develop. Especially in settings with students from culturally and linguistically diverse backgrounds, teachers need to be alert for mismatches between students' schema and the structure, content, and language of texts they are expected to read.

3. Social interaction is essential in learning to read.

Learning and literacy are acquired through social interactions. They are cultural and historical activities, representing how a cultural group or discourse community interprets the world and communicates this information from one generation to another (RAND Reading Study Group, 2002).

It is important to talk about *how* and *why* one reads as well as *what* one reads. Vygotsky (1978) emphasizes the importance of social interactions to drive any learning process. Bruner (1975) and Applebee and Langer (1983) elaborate on this notion with their descriptions of scaffolding—the interaction between the learner and the more sophisticated others that provides guidance, support, and models as new learning takes place. In this process, metacognition develops: that is, the ability to be aware of what one does as a reader; to talk about what is read; and to consciously realize problems and reach solutions (Pressley, 2002; cf. Sweet, 1993).

Critical knowledge of both the reading processes and what one does as a strategic reader is built through discussion (Eeds & Wells, 1989; Langer, 1993). Research on dialogic instruction in middle and high schools found that classrooms with high academic demands, and a great emphasis on discussion-based approaches to learning, show higher end-of-year achievement across all ability levels (Applebee, Langer, Nystrand, & Gamoran, 2003).

As Vygotsky (1978) first proposed and myriad studies have since proved, learners gradually internalize and effectively control ways of thinking, learning, and doing that they originally acquire and practice in supportive social interactions.

4. Reading and writing develop together.

Research shows that writing leads to improved reading achievement, reading leads to better writing performance, and combined instruction leads to improvements in both areas (DeFord, 1981; Smith, 1994; Tierney & Shanahan, 1991). Extensive opportunities for students to write in the variety of genres that teachers want them to comprehend as readers actually builds capacity in both areas; students learn to read like writers and write like readers (Duke & Pearson, 2002). Current research clearly reaffirms that engaging learners in many combined reading and writing experiences leads to a higher level of thinking than when either process is taught alone.

5. Reading involves complex thinking.

Research across disciplines, but particularly in cognitive and developmental psychology and education, has shown that reading (like all language modes) is the result of particular cognitive processes (Caine & Caine, 1991, 1997; Scherer, 1997). Readers consciously orchestrate a variety of thinking skills to make meaning of the texts they read. For example, the most basic mental operations—decoding, lexical access, and syntactic parsing—become automatic for proficient readers. But more sophisticated operations, such as constructing a mental model and generating inferences from text (RAND Reading Study Group, 2002), continue to demand readers' cognitive attention.

Written language relies on four cueing systems, representing types of knowledge that readers use as they interact with text: (1) pragmatic (social context), (2) semantic (meaning), (3) syntactic (structural), and (4) graphophonic (the alphabetic, orthographic, sound-symbol aspects). All of these systems must be operating in tandem for optimal meaning.

Readers' active thinking while reading text is a transaction (Rosenblatt 1978, 1995) that results in the construction of personal meaning. Readers ultimately grapple with ideas and information; print is only the entry point for this interaction (Alfassi, 1998; Duke & Pearson, 2002; Greenleaf, Schoenbach, Cziko, & Mueller, 2001; Guthrie, Wigfield, & VonSecker, 2000). A model of reading as thinking is the basis of U.S. national standards (National Council of Teachers of English & International Reading Association, 1996), and of various state standards developed in successive years.

6. Environments rich in literacy experiences, resources, and models facilitate reading development.

Learners need many opportunities to interact with print in meaningful ways. Both social and physical factors are important for creating supportive environments for successful literacy acquisition and development. Although physical context is important, it is the social interactions of these activities that make them so significant in literacy learning (Teale, 1982).

Learners in purposefully arranged rooms demonstrate more creative productivity, greater use of language-related activities, more engaged and exploratory behavior, and more social interaction and cooperation than do learners in randomly or poorly defined settings (Moore, G., 1986; Neuman & Celano, 2001).

Supportive classroom environments are often held together by the presence of a metalanguage: that is, an intentional use of vocabulary to describe the structural and language processes expected by the teacher. Allington and Johnston (2002a, 2002b) found that the single most striking feature of effective fourth-grade classrooms was the nature of the conversations that flowed within them. Teachers and students authentically talked about books, the use of language and literacy processes, and metacognitive processes of reading. Langer (2002) and Applebee et al. (2003) found similar patterns in effective high school English teachers: that is, *shared cognition.*

Rich and supportive literacy environments include opportunities to hear the reading aloud of skilled readers, observe adults who read often themselves, receive adult support for children's literacy activities, and experience routine use of materials for reading and writing at home and at school (Durkin, 1974–1975; Richardson, 2000; Taylor, 1983; Teale, 1984).

The classroom can be viewed as a community, similar to the everyday communities where students live. Effective classrooms for teaching and learning language and literacy in grades K through 12 build and respect community (Allington & Johnston, 2002a, 2002b; Langer, 2002; Pearson, 1996; Pressley, Allington, Wharton-McDonald, Block, & Morrow, 2001; Schoenbach, Branger, Greenleaf, & Litman, 2003; Taylor, Pearson, Clark, & Walpole, 1999). Clearly, vibrant and interactive classroom communities support literacy learning at all levels of development.

7. Engagement in the reading task is key in successfully learning to read.

Learners must be motivated to read for authentic purposes that are connected to their own lives in meaningful ways. In fact, students who are not motivated to read will simply not benefit from reading instruction (Guthrie & Wigfield, 2000; Kamil, 2003).

Motivation and engagement are intricately related in reading. Guthrie, Van Meter, Hancock, Alao, Anderson, and McCann (1998) describe engagement as "the motivated use of strategies to gain conceptual knowledge during reading" (p. 261). A motivated individual initiates and continues a particular activity, returning to a task with sustained engagement even as it becomes more difficult (Maehr, 1976).

The National Reading Research Center (NRRC) found that increasing competence builds motivation, and increasing motivation leads to more reading. In fact, motivation and subsequent engagement can even compensate for factors such as low family income and limited educational background, allowing learners to become agents of their own reading growth (Guthrie & Wigfield, 2000).

Instructional models that focus on motivation and engagement are particularly important to improve outcomes for middle and high school students seen as struggling readers. The link between engagement and achievement is strong (Guthrie & Wigfield, 2000; Guthrie & Davis, 2003). An engagement model of instruction can help students develop not only skills and strategies but also a reader identity, which is essential to functioning in the literate community.

8. Children's understandings of print are not the same as adults' understandings.

There are two crucial questions: (1) What understandings are vital (for example, that print carries a message and it should make sense) at the earliest stages of reading? (2) What more sophisticated conventional understandings do children grow into as they learn to read independently? The aspects of linguistic and metalinguistic awareness—children's knowledge of *wordness* (cf. Clay, 1979; Yaden & Templeton, 1986)—must be included in this discussion. Children must become aware of language as written, and then gain more sophisticated concepts about print, including being able to talk about and describe its aspects and processes as they understand them.

Goswami (2000) summarizes the current status of understanding of phonological processing at three levels: syllable, onset and rhyme, and phoneme. How do children begin to perceive the individual sounds of language? Substantive research shows that young children do not analyze speech into phonemes before they begin to read in the way literate adults have traditionally thought they do (Bruce, 1964; Ehri & Wilce, 1980; Treiman & Baron, 1981; Tumner & Nesdale, 1985). It appears that it is much easier for young children to first identify spoken syllables than to abstract either words or sounds from the stream of speech (cf. Adams, 1990; Goswami, 2000; Moustafa, 1997).

The ability to segment phonemes appears to be a consequence of literacy development, or at least grows in tandem with it (Goswami, 2000; Lie, 1991; Mann, 1986; Morais, Bertelson, Cary, & Algeria, 1986; Perfetti, Beck, Bell, & Hughes, 1987; Read, Zhang, Nie, & Ding, 1986; Winner, Landerl, Linortner, & Hummer, 1991). Scholes (1998) found that literate adults use their knowledge of spelling to help them do phonemic awareness tasks. This again supports the notion that young children perceive phonemic knowledge in developmentally appropriate, albeit different, ways.

When designing instructional experiences, teachers must consider the factors that support children's learning about print and that are appropriate to children's current understandings.

9. Children develop phonemic awareness and knowledge of phonics through a variety of literacy opportunities, models, and demonstrations.

Much time and effort has been devoted to investigations and consequent discussions about how children learn to apply the alphabetic principle—those understandings of print that are the critical difference between oral and written language—in order to read and write. The importance of developing early word identification skill is evident (Carnine & Grossen, 1993; Juel, 1991; National Institutes of Health, 2000; Pearson, 1993; Snow, Burns, & Griffin, 1998; Stanovich, 1991). Unfortunately, these discussions have become as much political as educational, with policy and instructional decisions often based more on rhetoric than on research (Cunningham, 1992; Yatvin, Weaver, & Garan, 2003).

Currently, the debate has come to focus primarily on two factors: (1) the place of phonemic awareness (discerning that spoken language is composed of separate speech sounds; the ability to segment the speech stream of a spoken word), and (2) the place of phonics (the teaching of particular parts of language, specifically rules for phoneme-grapheme relationships) in early reading instruction.

The work of Snow et al. (1998), in *Preventing Reading Difficulties in Young Children*, provided a substantive synthesis of research that

- found that phonological awareness is an important predictor of success in beginning reading tasks, and is a critical instructional component in preventing reading difficulties in young children.

- recommends that beginning reading instruction be designed to provide explicit instruction and practice with sound structures that lead to phonemic awareness; familiarity with spelling-sound correspondences, and common spelling conventions and their use in identifying printed words; sight recognition of frequent words; and independent reading, including read-alouds. Explicit instruction of comprehension strategies should be included (pp. 322–23).

Subsequently, the National Reading Panel (NRP) (National Institutes of Health, 2000) assumed the preeminent role as a synthesis of research to inform instruction particularly around phonemic awareness and phonics. This report

- found that teaching children to manipulate the sounds of language helps them learn to read, and suggested that no more than a total of eighteen hours of focused training, based early on the instructional curriculum, is the most beneficial.

- while supporting systematic instructions in phonics, emphasizes the goal of phonics instruction as a means to an end, and notes that the role of the teacher needs to be better understood and defined beyond the boundaries of a particular curriculum design (pp. 2–96).

Several studies suggest contrasting views of the importance and role of phonological and phonemic awareness (Bus & van Ijzendoorn, 1999; Swanson, Trainin, Necoechea, & Hammill, 2003; Troia, 1999). Swanson et al. suggest that the importance of phonological awareness may have been overstated in the literature (p. 432). So the question is *how much, how, when,* and *under what circumstances* are phonemic awareness and phonic knowledge included in instruction? It is important for all stakeholders to stand back and consider: are we asking the right questions in regard to what children need to know, based upon what we now know?

The term *systematic* phonics instruction has been particularly controversial. Those advocating a phonics-centered approach emphasize that explicit systematic phonics lessons are necessary for learning to read and write (Adams & Bruck, 1995; Beck & Juel, 1995; Chall, 1983; Ehri, 1991; Foorman, Francis, Fletcher, Mehta, & Schatschneider, 1998). Strickland (1998) offers an alternative definition: "Instruction is systematic when it is planned, deliberate in application, and proceeds in an orderly manner. This does not mean a rigid profession of 'one size fits all' instruction. Rather, it means a thoughtfully planned program that takes into account learner variability" (p. 51).

Phonemic awareness, in its simplest definition, is the ability to segment, delete, and combine speech sounds into abstract units. The research of the last two decades emphasizes that phonemic awareness plays a critical role in the development of the ability to decode and to read for meaning (Adams, 1990; Juel, 1988, 1991; cf. National Institutes of Health, 2000; Snow, et al., 1998; see also Core Understanding 8). The weight of evidence, irrespective of the mode of instruction, suggests that phonemic awareness is a necessary but not sufficient condition for the development of decoding and reading. Some students may need more explicit instruction in phonemic awareness; but in general, phonemic awareness develops through instruction that includes such features as language play, reading aloud, and rich experiences with language, environmental print, patterned stories, and big books.

Wharton-McDonald, Pressley, and Hampston (1998) found that the most effective first-grade teachers taught decoding skills explicitly and provided their students with many opportunities to engage in authentic reading. Their data suggest that what teachers do to promote application of phonics knowledge during the reading of connected text is what matters most; for example, teachers as coaches (cf. Cantrell, 1999; Dahl, Scharer, Lawson, & Grogan, 1999; Juel & Minden-Cupp, 2000; Xue & Meisels, 2004).

With reference to older readers, research shows that by fourth grade, the relationship between phonic knowledge and successful reading no longer shows a strong correlation (Chall, 1983). When considering older readers, Ivey and Baker (2004) propose two critical questions: (1) Does the chosen instruction help students read better? (2) Does it make students want to read more? Ivey and Baker find no evidence to suggest that focusing on sound-, letter-, or word-level instruction will benefit older readers in any way. The literature clearly supports a combination of a wide variety of teaching strategies, focused on all aspects of the reading process, as critical to the support of struggling readers. While they may need more explicit and differently designed instruction to support their learning needs, these readers do not need a focused reliance on instruction in phonic knowledge and phonemic awareness activities.

10. Children learn successful reading strategies in the context of real reading.
Much research and scholarship on the process of reading comprehension has been grounded in studies of good readers (Duke & Pearson, 2002). In general, expert readers are active, purposeful, strategic, and metacognitive. Sweet (1993) describes such readers as using strategies to construct meaning before, during, and after reading. Readers' strategies include plans for solving problems they encounter in their reading experiences. A strategic reader (Paris, Lipson, & Wixson, 1983; Paris, Wasik, & Turner, 1991) is a problem solver who draws from his or her toolbox of metacognitive strategies to repair any comprehension failure that might arise (Pearson, 1993). Critical strategies to develop for learning from text include inferencing, predicting, reading selectively, identifying important information, monitoring comprehension, summarizing, and questioning (Cooper, 1993; Duke & Pearson, 2002; Pressley, 2002; Sweet, 1993). These are best learned in the context of authentic reading.

When readers learn strategies in the context of in-depth content learning, they are more likely to understand them as purposeful tools that they can and will use to support their understanding of new texts (Greenleaf et al., 2001; Guthrie et al., 1998; Langer, 2001; RAND Reading Study Group, 2002).

11. Children learn best when teachers employ a variety of strategies to model and demonstrate reading knowledge, strategy, and skills.

Research on effective reading teachers has highlighted the need for teachers to be flexible, well trained, and knowledgeable about their students. Teachers must be able to design instruction to meet their students' individual needs; employ scaffolding strategies to promote higher-level thinking before, during, and after the reading process; and model, demonstrate, and explicitly teach a wide range of strategies in a variety of contexts (Allington & Johnston, 2002a, 2002b; Langer, 2002; Pressley et al., 2001; Taylor et al., 1999).

Following are examples of appropriate instruction models to support effective reading instruction.

ENGAGEMENT

Guthrie and Davis (2003) emphasize that cognitive strategy instruction is ineffective if isolated from rich content designed to engage learners, particularly adolescent readers, in using the strategy.

"BALANCED" APPROACHES

Pressley, Rankin, and Yokoi (1996) describe a balanced approach as extremely complicated. Many studies support the use of a balance of instructional focus and application in authentic literacy events (Anderson, Wilkinson, & Mason, 1991; Fisher & Adler, 1999; Milligan & Berg, 1992; Sacks & Mergendoller, 1997). Rankin-Erickson and Pressley (2000) found whole-language and skills instruction were complementary (cf. Morrow, Gambrell, & Pressley, 2003; Pressley, 1998).

APPRENTICESHIP

Teachers can help students become skilled readers of academic texts by making the invisible processes involved in comprehending such texts visible and accessible as students engage in meaningful literacy activities (Schoenbach et al., 2003). Teachers act as mentors to student apprentices, modeling and scaffolding critical processes, with a goal of student independence in reading challenging texts.

A number of research studies have found direct instruction via scripted lessons to be less effective for reading achievement. Taylor et al. (1999) found that a negative relationship existed between a highly teacher-directed stance toward instruction and student reading growth in grades 2 through 6. Ryder, Burton, and Silberg (2003) found that highly scripted, teacher-directed methods of teaching reading in grades 1 through 3 were not as effective as methods that allowed a more flexible approach. Moustafa and Land (2002) found scripted reading instruction to be less effective than reading instruction where teachers are allowed to exercise their professional knowledge and match instruction to instructional needs. Pressley et al. (2001) found that the instruction many effective reading teachers report delivering to struggling readers differs only in length and intensity, not in format, design, or philosophical stance.

The International Reading Association (2000) suggested that effective reading teachers scaffold, or coach, learners as they grow and develop as readers. Important studies have highlighted scaffolding in effective reading instruction (Pressley et al., 2001; Snow et al., 1998; Allington & Johnston, 2002a, 2002b; Applebee et al., 2003).

Research supports the idea that effectively organizing for instruction is critical to the successful teaching of reading. Using flexible patterns of grouping can also support this view (Flood, J., Lapp, Flood, S., & Nagel, 1992; Opitz, 1998; Wilkinson & Townsend, 2000). Taylor et al. (1999) found that schools "beating the odds" focused on small-group instruction in reading interventions. Schumm, Moody, and Vaughn (2000) and Taylor et al. (1999) found that whole-class instruction, when used exclusively, clearly fails to meet the needs of individual children, particularly those with special needs.

Understanding the role of texts in teaching and learning to read is important. Beginning readers must be given a wide range of text structure when learning to read. Teachers must be explicit in the purposes for, and uses of, texts (Heibert, 1998; Hoffman, Roser, Salas, Patterson, & Pennington, 2000). The use of decodable texts has been debated. Heibert suggests the difference of opinion is not so much about whether decodable texts are *ever* useful, but about how much, and for whom, to use such texts. Heibert also suggests that simplifying the text to the lowest denominator of high-frequency words does not facilitate the task of learning to read in the manner that the generation of educational psychologists advocating this type of text believed. Literature models the natural and expected language structures of English, and of often-used texts (Fisher, Flood, & Lapp, 2003). Predictable texts provide scaffolds for beginning readers to predict both meaning and word identification of familiar stories. For adolescents, knowledge of text structures is essential to fluent reading (Snow & Biancarosa, 2003). Wide reading, across genres, is also critical for adolescents.

Following are examples of learning goals essential to effective reading instruction.

COMPREHENSION

Research indicates that a wide range of comprehension strategies should be taught to support readers across all developmental levels (Keene & Zimmerman, 1997; Pressley, 2000; Wilhelm, 2001).

QUESTIONING

Models include QARs (Raphael, 1986), Reciprocal Teaching (Palinscar & Brown, 1984), and QtA (Beck, McKeown, Hamilton, & Kucan, 1997).

DISCUSSION AND RESPONSE TO TEXT

Those who participate in discussions are active learners who engage in the construction of knowledge (Gambrell, 1996). When students are encouraged to verbalize their ideas and questions, cognitive development is supported. They learn how to identify uncertainties in their understandings, explain and justify their positions, seek information to help them resolve uncertainties, and learn to see alternative points of view (Almasi, 1995; Brown & Palinscar, 1989; Doise & Mugny, 1984; Johnson & Johnson, 1979; Mugny & Doise, 1978).

USE OF METACOGNITIVE STRATEGY TO MONITOR MEANING

Readers must be capable of awareness of ways to improve their reading, monitor their own comprehension, and gain conscious control of their strategies as they read (Clay, 1991a; Snow & Biancarosa, 2003).

VOCABULARY

Nagy and Scott (2000) describe vocabulary development as the way in which students add words to their reading and writing vocabulary for daily use and how they learn the meanings of new words. They suggest that an important aspect of vocabulary acquisition is the ability to consider a wide variety of sources of information that can help readers become more aware of the subtle differences in word meanings.

FLUENCY

Fluent reading is a critical component of reading development. Dowhower (1991) suggests that the ultimate goal of reading is the construction of meaning; thus it is important to determine the role of fluency in a reader's comprehension. She offers two roles for fluency: the contribution of automatic word recognition to comprehension and prosody, and the ability to read with appropriate expression. Rasinksi (2004) is concerned with the current emphasis on speed and accuracy over meaning.

WORD IDENTIFICATION

Readers use a variety of cues to gain access to texts (Clay, 1991a). These include visual (symbolic) cues, structural (syntactic) cues, and semantic (meaning) cues. Word identification occurs through decoding strategies, which often employ knowledge of patterns and structures of language; through recognition of familiar sight vocabulary; and through the use of context clues to validate word recognition.

Teaching strategies for effective reading instruction are also critical. Cambourne (2001) found that effective activities meet three criteria: (1) they engage learners in the activity; (2) they allow students to internalize and transfer knowledge, skill, and strategy; and (3) they promote collaborative, independent, and interdependent learning.

Students must have opportunities to employ strategies that are appropriate before, during, and after reading. Following are examples of effective teaching strategies.

INDIVIDUAL (INDEPENDENT) READING

Formal and informal opportunities for independent reading can provide opportunities to apply reading strategies independently; provide time for sustained reading behavior; challenge readers to work on their own, using strategies on a variety of texts; challenge readers to solve words independently while reading texts well within their own control; promote fluency through rereading; build confidence through sustained, successful reading; and offer opportunities for students to support one another while reading (Clay, 1991a; Holdaway, 1979; McKenzie, 1986; Meek, 1988; Taylor, 1983).

GUIDED READING

This teaching strategy gives students the opportunity to read a wide variety of texts; to problem solve while reading for meaning; to use strategies on complete, extended text; and to attend to words in texts. Guided reading requires that a teacher's selection of text, guidance, demonstration, and explanation be made explicit to the reader (Clay, 1991a, 1991b; Holdaway, 1979; Lyons, Pinnell, & DeFord, 1993; McKenzie, 1986; Meek, 1988; Routman, 1991; Wong, Groth, & O'Flavahan, 1994). This strategy offers students the chance to develop as individual readers while participating in a socially supported activity, and gives teachers ongoing opportunities to observe individuals as they process new texts (cf. Clay, 1991a; Fountas & Pinnell, 1996).

EXPLICIT WORD STUDY

Cunningham and Allington (2003) discuss activities that help students build basic understanding about words and letter-sound patterns; ensure that students develop an instant and automatic ability to read and write high-frequency words; focus on the important skill of cross-checking meaning with letter-sound knowledge; and establish learning patterns for decoding and spelling. Vocabulary development also fits into this category of explicit word study.

EXPLICIT STRATEGY INSTRUCTION

Skills become strategies when readers become cognizant of their performance limitations, intentionally weigh their options, and willfully execute compensatory procedures (Alexander & Jetton, 2000). Readers must be able to determine which strategies to use, depending on the content and difficulty of the text (Alexander & Jetton, 2000).

ORAL READING

Raskinski and Hoffman (2003) suggest four strands that support the potential role of oral reading in instruction: (1) oral reading fluency; (2) teacher responses to oral reading miscues; (3) self-monitoring and miscue analysis; and (3) guided reading and strategy development.

READING ALOUD

Much research (Anderson, Hiebert, Scott, & Wilkinson, 1985; cf. Adams, 1990; Beck & McKeown, 2001; Clark, 1976; Cochran-Smith, 1984; Cohen, 1968; Durkin, 1966; Goodman, Y., 1984; Green & Harker, 1982; Hiebert, 1983; Ninio, 1980; Pappas & Brown, 1987; Schickedanz, 1978; Wells, 1986) supports the reading aloud of high-quality children's and young adult texts as an effective strategy for continually modeling successful reading practices and allowing children to "experience and contemplate literacy work they cannot yet read" (Fountas & Pinnell, 1996, p. 1).

SHARED READING

Fountas and Pinnell (1996) found that shared reading experiences can explicitly demonstrate early strategies for beginning readers. For upper elementary students and adolescent readers (Fountas & Pinnell, 2001), shared reading is more an experience of sharing the cognitive process involved in reading the shared text.

12. Children need the opportunity to read, read, read.

Access, time, modeling, choice, multiple readings, difficulty: these are all factors in providing students with many opportunities to read (Allington, 1977, 1980; Allington & Cunningham, 1996; Cunningham & Allington, 2003; Stanovich, 1986). What is critical is that students do read—lots, for sustained periods, for meaning, and for real and authentic purposes. Pearson (1993) observes, "One is tempted to conclude that some of the best 'practice' for enhancing reading skill occurs when children are given greater opportunity to read everyday materials" (pp. 507–8).

Allington and McGill-Franzen (2003) suggest that effective instruction must ensure that all students engage in extensive, high-success reading activities throughout the school day, and must reliably enhance the volume of voluntary reading students do outside the school day. When students are held accountable for a wide variety of reading experiences (for example, compiling reading logs, participating in sustained, silent reading [SSR], and documenting reading-at-home experiences), positive attitudes toward reading will develop.

Neuman and Celano (2001, 2004) found that children who feel confident in reading will read more challenging materials and for higher-level purposes. They also found that access to literacy materials is not easily and equally accessible to all children and their families (2001, p. 11; cf. Duke, 2000).

Providing time and opportunities for learners to read is a critical aspect in successful reading instruction across the spectrum of development. Advocates of school reform, particularly of secondary schools, concur that students need multiple opportunities for engaged, sustained print encounters in the classroom every day (Alvermann et al., 2002; Langer, 2001; Moore, Bean, Birdyshaw, & Rycik, 1999). The easier the access to interesting print materials, the more frequently adolescents read (McQuillan & Au, 2001). The research literature highlights the importance of access to appropriate materials and opportunities for successful reading experiences to support reading development and growth.

13. Monitoring the development of reading processes is vital to student success.

Monitoring learners' progress calls for a variety of assessment and evaluation strategies. Assessment and instruction are integral processes, each informing the other to meet the individual needs of students. Authentic assessment describes a fusion of instruction and assessment; that is, activities that involve real reading and real writing provide assessment information on literacy (Cooper & Kiger, 2005). Teachers must constantly use keen observation of student growth and development to inform instruction. Also, students must learn to become critically aware of their own reading processes; that is, to become metacognitive, to support their development as competent, engaged, and effective readers. We might see assessment as an ongoing process of gathering information about what students can and cannot do. Evaluation, the next step, takes into account all assessments and observations in order to make a judgment about an individual student. In general, the purpose of assessment is to inform instruction, ultimately to support learning. Purposes for evaluation may include grading and placement.

No one test can serve the needs of instruction and accountability. Ironically, the national focus on accountability may leave little room for assessment linked to instruction that could actually improve literacy outcomes for students who are being left behind (Braunger & Lewis, 2006). Assessment experts emphasize the importance of systematic assessment that is tied to the curriculum and has the strong buy-in of teachers. Research shows a statistically significant relationship between such assessment and students' growth in reading fluency and reading performance (Taylor et al., 1999).

Aspects of reading development to monitor, and selected examples of appropriate tools for each aspect, include

- personal perceptions, attitudes, and interests via interviews (Goodman, Watson, & Burke, 1987; Barr & Syverson, 1999), surveys and personal reading histories (cf. Atwell, 1998; Schoenbach et al., 1999), inventories, and observation.

- comprehension via response, retelling (Brown & Cambourne, 1990), individual reading inventories (cf. Leslie & Caldwell, 2001), interviews, work samples (McDonald, 2001; Schoenbach et al., 1999), conferences, observations, and teacher anecdotal records or student self-evaluations of contributions to a discussion of a text.

- processing words and other text features in at least two ways: (1) concepts of letters, words, and sentences via concepts of print, identification of letter names and sounds, word knowledge, writing, and hearing and recording sounds in words (Clay, 1985, 1991a); (2) errors (miscues) made via error analysis, miscue analysis, and retrospective miscue analysis (Goodman et al., 1987; Goodman & Marek, 1996; Moore & Aspegren, 2001), anecdotal records and observations, and student self-assessment.

- fluency via repeated reading, listening, and oral reading with two texts; and timed reading of short texts. For very young readers, oral reading is the best way to get at fluency. But oral reading fluency is not a reliable indicator of either silent fluency or comprehension. For readers past the period of formal reading instruction, the goal is to increase silent fluency.

- metacognition and reading strategies via think-alouds (Brown, C. S., & Lytle, 1988; Schoenbach et al., 1999); metacognitive logs (Schoenbach et al., 1999; Schoenbach, et al., 2003); metacognitive inventories (Bennett, 2003; Mokhtari & Reichard, 2002); student self-assessment; and anecdotal records and observation.

- environment and instruction via both teacher and student self-assessment and reflection.

Conclusion

To summarize, learning to read and growing as a reader are about access to critical components of time, text, and resources; knowledgeable and supportive teachers; appropriate instruction; demonstrations of how readers, writers, and texts work; other readers; and students' own reading processes.

Our challenge—to bring all students to a higher level of literacy—is daunting. At the same time that our standards for literacy are rising, some learners in U.S. schools struggle to acquire basic skills in reading, and U.S. school populations are more diverse than ever before. How can we meet the needs of individuals and help them all develop a firm command of basic skills and strategies, the ability to construct and negotiate meanings with text, and the knowledge and disposition to be critical, lifelong readers?

As policymakers, educators, parents, or other adults involved in children's education, we all have significant roles to play. The Commission on Reading documents contained in the Appendixes of this book should prove helpful in such endeavors.

References

Adams, M. J. (1990). *Beginning to read: Thinking and learning about print*. Cambridge, MA: MIT Press.

Adams, M. J., & Bruck, M. (1995). Resolving the "great debate." *American Educator, 19*(2), 10–20.

Alexander, P. A., & Jetton, T. L. (2000). Learning from text: A multidimensional and developmental perspective. In M. L. Kamil, P. B. Mosenthal, P. D. Pearson, & R. Barr (Eds.), *Handbook of reading research: Vol. 3* (pp. 285–310). Mahwah, NJ: Erlbaum.

Alfassi, M. (1998). Reading for meaning: The efficacy of reciprocal teaching in fostering reading comprehension in high school students in remedial reading classes. *American Educational Research Journal, 35*(2), 309–32.

Allington, R. L. (1977). If they don't read much, how they ever gonna get good? *Journal of Reading, 21*(1), 57–61.

Allington, R. L. (1980). Poor readers don't get to read much in reading groups. *Language Arts*, *57*(8), 873–75.

Allington, R. L., & Cunningham, P. M. (1996). *Schools that work: Where all children read and write*. New York: Longman.

Allington, R. L., & Johnston, P. H. (2002a). *Reading to learn: Lessons from exemplary fourth-grade classrooms*. New York: Guilford Press.

Allington, R. L., & Johnston, P. H. (2002b). *What do we know about effective fourth-grade teachers and their classrooms?* (CELA research report 13010). Albany, NY: National Research Center on English Learning and Achievement, State University of New York–Albany.

Allington, R. L., & McGill-Franzen, A. (2003). The impact of summer reading setback on the reading achievement gap. *Phi Delta Kappan*, *85*(1), 68–75.

Almasi, J. (1995). The nature of fourth graders' sociocognitive conflicts in peer-led and teacher-led discussion of literature. *Reading Research Quarterly*, *30*(3), 314–51.

Alvermann, D., Boyd, F., Brozo, W., Hinchman, K., Moore, D., & Sturtevant, E. (2002). *Principled practices for a literate America: A framework for literacy and learning in the upper grades*. New York: Carnegie Corporation.

Anderson, R. C., Hiebert, E., Scott, J., & Wilkinson, I. (1985). *Becoming a nation of readers: The report of the Commission on Reading*. Washington, DC: National Academy of Education.

Anderson, R.C., & Nagy, W. (1992, Winter). The vocabulary conundrum. *American Educator*, *16*, 14–18, 44–47.

Anderson, R. C., & Pearson, P. D. (1984). A schema-theoretic view of basic processes in reading comprehension. In P. D. Pearson, R. Barr, M. L. Kamil, & P. Mosenthal (Eds.), *Handbook of reading research: Vol. 1* (pp. 255–92). New York: Longman.

Anderson, R. C., Wilkinson, I., & Mason, J. (1991). A microanalysis of the small-group guided reading lesson: Effects of an emphasis on global story meaning. *Reading Research Quarterly*, *26*(4), 417–41.

Applebee, A. N., & Langer, J. A. (1983). Instructional scaffolding: Reading and writing as natural language activities. *Language Arts*, *60*(2), 168–75.

Applebee, A. N., Langer, J., Nystrand, M., and Gamoran, A. (2003). Discussion-based approaches to developing understanding: Classroom instruction and student performance in middle and high school English. *American Educational Research Journal, 40*(3), 685–730.

Atwell, N. (1998). *In the middle: New understandings about writing, reading, and learning* (2nd ed.). Portsmouth, NH: Boynton-Cook.

Barr, M. A., & Syverson, M. A. (1999). *Assessing literacy with the Learning Record: A handbook for teachers, grades 6–12.* Portsmouth, NH: Heinemann.

Beck, I. L., & Juel, C. (1995). The role of decoding in learning to read. *American Educator, 19*(2), 8, 21–25, 39–42.

Beck, I. L., & McKeown, M. G. (2001). Text talk: Capturing the benefits of read-aloud experiences for young children. *Reading Teacher, 55*(1), 10–20.

Beck, I. L., McKeown, M. G., Hamilton, R. L., & Kucan, L. (1997). *Questioning the author: An approach for enhancing student engagement with text.* Newark, DE: International Reading Association.

Bennett, M. B. (2003). From practice to preaching: Helping content area teachers teach comprehension. *Voices from the Middle, 11*(1), 31–34.

Braunger, J., & Lewis, J. P. (1997). *Building a knowledge base in reading.* Portland, OR: Northwest Regional Educational Laboratory.

Braunger, J., & Lewis, J. P. (2006). *Building a knowledge base in reading* (2nd ed.). Newark, DE: International Reading Association; Urbana, IL: National Council of Teachers of English.

Brown, A., & Palinscar, A. (1989). Guided, cooperative learning and individual knowledge acquisition. In L. Resnick (Ed.), *Knowing, learning, and instruction: Essays in honor of Robert Glaser.* Hillsdale, NJ: Erlbaum.

Brown, C. S., & Lytle, S. L. (1988). Merging assessment and instruction: Protocols in the classroom. In S. M. Glazer, L. W. Searfoss, & L. M. Gentile (Eds.), *Reexamining reading diagnosis: New trends and procedures* (pp. 94–102). Newark, DE: International Reading Association.

Brown, H., & Cambourne, B. (1990). *Read and retell: A strategy for the whole-language/natural learning classroom.* Portsmouth, NH: Heinemann.

Bruce, D. J. (1964). The analysis of word sounds by young children. *British Journal of Educational Psychology, 34,* 158–70.

Bruner, J. S. (1975). The ontogenesis of speech acts. *Journal of Child Language*, 2(1), 1–19.

Bus, A. G., & van Ijzendoorn, M. H. (1999). Phonological awareness and early reading: A meta-analysis of experimental training studies. *Journal of Educational Psychology*, 91(3), 403-14.

Caine, R. N., & Caine, G. (1991). *Making connections: Teaching and the human brain*. Alexandria, VA: Association for Supervision and Curriculum Development.

Caine, R. N., & Caine, G. (1997). *Education on the edge of possibility*. Alexandria, VA: Association for Supervision and Curriculum Development.

Cambourne, B. (2001). What do I do with the rest of the class? The nature of teaching-learning activities. *Language Arts,* 79(2), 124–35.

Cambourne, B. (2002). Holistic, integrated approaches to reading and language arts instruction: The constructivist framework of an instructional theory. In A. Farstrup & S. Samuels (Eds.), *What research has to say about reading instruction* (3rd ed., pp. 25–47). Newark, DE: International Reading Association.

Cantrell, S. C. (1999). Effective teaching and literacy learning: A look inside primary classrooms. *Reading Teacher*, 52(4), 370–78.

Carnine, D., & Grossen, B. (1993). Phonics instruction: Comparing research and practice. *Teaching Exceptional Children*, 25(2), 22–25.

Chall, J. (1983). *Learning to read: The great debate* (updated ed.). New York: McGraw-Hill.

Clark, M. (1976). *Young fluent readers: What can they teach us?* London: Heinemann.

Clay, M. M. (1979). *Reading: The patterning of complex behaviour* (2nd ed.). Auckland, NZ: Heinemann.

Clay, M. M. (1985). *The early detection of reading difficulties: A diagnostic survey with recovery procedures*. Auckland, NZ: Heinemann.

Clay, M. M. (1991a). *Becoming literate: The construction of inner control*. Portsmouth, NH: Heinemann.

Clay, M. M. (1991b). Introducing a new storybook to young readers. *Reading Teacher*, 45(4), 264–73.

Cochran-Smith, M. (1984). *The making of a reader*. Norwood, NJ: Ablex.

Cohen, D. (1968). The effects of literature on vocabulary and reading achievement. *Elementary English, 45*(2), 209–13, 217.

Cooper, J. D. (1993). *Literacy: Helping children construct meaning*. Boston: Houghton Mifflin.

Cooper, J. D., & Kiger, N. D. (2005). *Literacy assessment: Helping teachers plan instruction* (2nd ed.). Boston: Houghton Mifflin.

Cunningham, P. M. (1992). What kind of phonics instruction will we have? In C. K. Kinzer & D. K. Leu (Eds.), *Literacy research, theory, and practice: Views from many perspectives*. 41st Yearbook of the National Reading Conference (pp. 17–31). Chicago: National Reading Conference.

Cunningham, P. M., & Allington, R. L. (2003). *Classrooms that work: They can all read and write* (3rd ed.). Boston: Allyn & Bacon.

Dahl, K. L., Sharer, P. L., Lawson, L. L., & Grogan, P. (1999). Phonics instruction and student achievement in whole language first-grade classrooms. *Reading Research Quarterly, 34*(3), 312–41.

DeFord, D. (1981). Literacy: Reading, writing, and other essentials. *Language Arts, 58*(6), pp. 652–58.

Doise, W., & Mugny, G. (1984). *The social development of the intellect*. (A. St. James-Emler & N. Emler, Trans.). New York: Pergamon Press.

Dowhower, S. L. (1991). Speaking of prosody: Fluency's unattended bedfellow. *Theory into Practice, 30*(3), 165–75.

Duke, N. K. (2000). For the rich, it's richer: Print experiences and environments offered to children in very low- and very high-socioeconomic status first-grade classrooms. *American Educational Research Journal, 37*(2), 441–78.

Duke, N. K., & Pearson, P. D. (2002). Effective practices for developing reading comprehension. In A. Farstrup & S. Samuels (Eds.), *What research has to say about reading instruction* (3rd ed., pp. 205–42). Newark, DE: International Reading Association.

Durkin, D. (1966). *Children who read early: Two longitudinal studies*. New York: Teachers College Press.

Durkin, D. (1974–1975). A six-year study of children who learned to read in school at the age of four. *Reading Research Quarterly, 10*(1), 9–61.

Eeds, M., & Wells, D. (1989). Grand conversations: An exploration of meaning construction in literature study groups. *Research in the Teaching of English, 23*(1), 4–29.

Ehri, L. C. (1991). The development of the ability to read words. In R. Barr, M. Kamil, P. Mosenthal, & P. D. Pearson (Eds.), *Handbook of reading research: Vol. 2* (pp. 383–417). New York: Longman.

Ehri, L. C., & Wilce, L. (1980). The influence of orthography on readers' conceptualization of the phonemic structure of words. *Applied Psycholinguistics, 1*(4), 371–85.

Fisher, C., & Adler, M. A. (1999). *Early reading programs in high poverty schools: Emerald Elementary beats the odds* (CIERA Report 3-009). Ann Arbor: Center for the Improvement of Early Reading Achievement, University of Michigan.

Fisher, D., Flood, J., & Lapp, D. (2003). Material matters: Using children's literature to charm readers (or why Harry Potter and the Princess Diaries matter). In L. M. Morrow, L. B. Gambrell, & M. Pressley (Eds.), *Best practices in literacy instruction* (2nd ed., pp. 167–86). New York: Guilford Press.

Flood, J., Lapp, D., Flood, S., & Nagel, G. (1992). Am I allowed to group? Using flexible patterns for effective instruction. *Reading Teacher, 45*(8), 608–16.

Foorman, B., Francis, D. J., Fletcher, J. M., Mehta, P., & Schatschneider, C. (1998). The role of instruction in learning to read: Preventing reading failure in at-risk children. *Journal of Educational Psychology, 90*(1), 37–55.

Fountas, I. C., & Pinnell, G. S. (1996). *Guided reading: Good first teaching for all children.* Portsmouth, NH: Heinemann.

Fountas, I. C., & Pinnell, G. S. (2001). *Guiding readers and writers, grades 3-6: Teaching comprehension, genre, and content literacy.* Portsmouth, NH: Heinemann.

Gambrell, L. (1996). What research reveals about discussion. In J. F. Almasi & L. B. Gambrell (Eds.), *Lively discussions! Fostering engaged reading* (pp. 39–51). Newark, DE: International Reading Association.

Gee, J. (1996). *Social linguistics and literacies: Ideology in discourse* (2nd ed.). Bristol, PA: Taylor & Francis.

Goodman, K. (1996). *On reading.* Portsmouth, NH: Heinemann.

Goodman, Y. (1984). The development of initial literacy. In H. Goelman, A. Oberg, & F. Smith (Eds.), *Awakening to literacy* (pp. 102–9). Exeter, NH: Heinemann.

Goodman, Y. M., & Marek, A. M. (1996). *Retrospective miscue analysis: Revaluing readers and reading*. Katonah, NY: Richard C. Owen.

Goodman, Y. M., Watson, D. J., & Burke, C. L. (1987). *Reading miscue inventory: Alternative procedures*. Katonah, NY: Richard C. Owen.

Goswani, U. (2000). Phonological and lexical processes. In M. L. Kamil, P. B. Mosenthal, P. D. Pearson, & R. Barr (Eds.), *Handbook of reading research: Vol. 3* (pp. 251–67). Mahwah, NJ: Erlbaum.

Green, J., & Harker, J. (1982). Reading to children: A communicative process. In J. A. Langer & M. T. Smith-Burke (Eds.), *Reader meets author: Bridging the gap* (pp. 196–221). Newark, DE: International Reading Association.

Greenleaf, C. L., Schoenbach, R., Cziko, C., & Mueller, F. (2001). Apprenticing adolescent readers to academic literacy. *Harvard Educational Review, 71*(1), 79–129.

Guthrie, J. T., & Davis, M. H. (2003). Motivating struggling readers in middle school through an engagement model of classroom practice. *Reading and Writing Quarterly, 19*(1), 59–85.

Guthrie, J. T., Van Meter, P., Hancock, G. R., Alao, S., Anderson, E., & McCann, A., (1998). Does concept-oriented reading instruction increase strategy use and conceptual learning from text? *Journal of Educational Psychology, 90*(2), 261–78.

Guthrie, J. T. & Wigfield, A. (2000). Engagement and motivation in reading. In M. L. Kamil, P. B. Mosenthal, P. D. Pearson, & R. Barr (Eds.), *Handbook of reading research: Vol. 3* (pp. 403–22). Mahwah, NJ: Lawrence Erlbaum Associates.

Guthrie, J. T., Wigfield, A., & VonSecker, C. (2000). Effects of integrated instruction on motivation and strategy use in reading. *Journal of Educational Psychology, 92*(2), 331–41.

Halliday, M. A. K. (1973). *Explorations in the functions of language*. London: Arnold.

Halliday, M. A. K. (1975). *Learning how to mean: Explorations in the development of language*. London: Arnold.

Hiebert, E. (1983). An examination of ability grouping for reading instruction. *Reading Research Quarterly, 18*(2), 231–55.

Hiebert, E. (1998). *Text matters in learning to read* (CIERA Report No. 1-001). Ann Arbor, MI: Center for the Improvement of Early Reading Achievement, University of Michigan.

Hoffman, J. V., Roser, N. L., Salas, R., Patterson, E., & Pennington, J. (2000). *Text leveling and little books in first-grade reading* (CIERA Report No. 1-010). Ann Arbor: Center for the Improvement of Early Reading Achievement, University of Michigan.

Holdaway, D. (1979). *The foundations of literacy*. Sydney, AU: Ashton Scholastic; Exeter, NH: Heinemann.

International Reading Association (IRA). (2000). *Excellent reading teachers: A position statement of the International Reading Association*. Newark, DE: International Reading Association. Retrieved June 7, 2005, from http://www.reading.org/resources/issues/position_excellent.html

International Reading Association (IRA). (2002). *What is evidence-based reading instruction? A position statement of the International Reading Association*. Newark, DE: International Reading Association. Retrieved June 22, 2008, from http://www.reading.org/resources/issues/positions_evidence_based.html

Ivey, G., & Baker, M. I. (2004). Phonics instruction for older students? Just say no. *Educational Leadership, 61*(6), 35–39.

Johnson, D., & Johnson, R. (1979). Conflict in the classroom: Controversy and learning. *Review of Educational Research, 49*(1), 51–69.

Juel, C. (1988). Learning to read and write: A longitudinal study of 54 children from first through fourth grades. *Journal of Educational Psychology, 80*(4), 437–47.

Juel, C. (1991). Beginning reading. In R. Barr, M. L. Kamil, P. Mosenthal, & P. D. Pearson (Eds.), *Handbook of reading research: Vol. 2* (pp. 759–88). New York: Longman.

Juel, C., & Minden-Cupp, C. (2000). Learning to read words: Linguistic units and instructional strategies. *Reading Research Quarterly, 35*(4), 458–92.

Kamil, M. (2003). *Adolescents and literacy: Reading for the 21st century*. Washington, DC: Alliance for Excellent Education.

Keene, E. O., & Zimmermann, S. (1997). *Mosaic of thought: Teaching comprehension in a reader's workshop.* Portsmouth, NH: Heinemann.

Kucer, S. (2005). *Dimensions of literacy: A conceptual base for teaching reading and writing in school settings* (2nd ed.). Mahwah, NJ: Erlbaum.

Kucer, S., & Tuten, J. (2003). Revisiting and rethinking the reading process. *Language Arts, 80*(4), 284–90.

Langer, J. A. (1993). Discussion as exploration: Literature and the horizon of possibilities. In G. E. Newell & R. K. Durst (Eds.), *Exploring texts: The role of discussion and writing in the teaching and learning of literature* (pp. 25–43). Norwood, MA: Christopher-Gordon.

Langer, J. A. (2001). Beating the odds: Teaching middle and high school students to read and write well. *American Educational Research Journal, 38*(4), 837–80.

Langer, J. A. (2002). *Effective literacy instruction: Building successful reading and writing programs.* Urbana, IL: National Council of Teachers of English.

Leslie, L., & Caldwell, J. (2001). *Qualitative reading inventory, 3.* New York: Longman.

Lie, A. (1991). Effects of a training program for stimulating skills in word analysis in first-grade children. *Reading Research Quarterly, 26*(3), 234–50.

Lyons, C., Pinnell, G. S., & DeFord, D. (1993). *Partners in learning: Teachers and children in reading recovery.* New York: Teachers College Press.

Maehr, M. L. (1976). Continuing motivation: An analysis of a seldom considered educational outcome. *Review of Educational Research, 46*(3), 443–62.

Mann, V. (1986). Phonological awareness: The role of reading experience. *Cognition, 24,* 65–92.

McDonald, J. P. (2001). Students' work and teachers' learning. In A. Lieberman & L. Miller (Eds.), *Teachers caught in the action: Professional development that matters* (pp. 209–35). New York: Teachers College Press.

McKenzie, M. (1986). *Journeys into literacy.* Huddersfield, UK: Schofield & Sims.

McKeown, M. G., Beck, I. L., Omanson, R. D. & Pople, M. T. (1985). Some effects of the nature and frequency of vocabulary instruction on the knowledge and use of words. *Reading Research Quarterly, 20*(5), 522–35.

McQuillan, J., & Au, J. (2001). The effect of print access on reading frequency. *Reading Psychology, 22*(3), 225–48.

Meek, M. (1988). *How texts teach what readers learn.* Stroud, UK: Thimble Press.

Milligan, J. L., & Berg, H. (1992). The effect of whole language on the comprehending ability of first grade children. *Reading Improvement, 29*(3), 146–54.

Mokhtari, K., & Reighard, C. (2002). Assessing students' metacognitive awareness of reading strategies. *Journal of Educational Psychology, 94*(2), 249–59.

Moore, D., Bean, T., Birdyshaw, D., & Rycik, J. (1999). Adolescent literacy: A position statement. *Journal of Adolescent & Adult Literacy, 43,* 97–112.

Moore, G. (1986). Effects of spatial definition of behavior setting on children's behavior: A quasi-experimental field study. *Journal of Environmental Psychology, 6,* 205–31.

Moore, R. A., & Aspegren, C. M. (2001). Reflective conversations between two learners: Retrospective miscue analysis. *Journal of Adolescent & Adult Literacy, 44*(6), 492–503.

Morais, J., Bertelson, P., Cary, L., & Alegria, J. (1986). Literacy training and speech segmentation. *Cognition, 24*(1–2), 45–64.

Morrow, L. M., Gambrell, L. B., & Pressley, M. (Eds.) (2003). *Best practice in literacy instruction* (2nd ed.). New York: Guilford Press.

Moustafa, M. (1997). *Beyond traditional phonics: Research discoveries and reading instruction.* Portsmouth, NH: Heinemann.

Moustafa, M., & Land, R. E. (2002). The reading achievement of economically-disadvantaged children in urban schools using *Open Court* vs. comparably disadvantaged children in urban schools using non-scripted reading programs. In *Urban Learning, Teaching, and Research* (2002 yearbook, pp. 44–53). Washington, DC: American Educational Research Association. Retrieved May 21, 2005, from http://instructional1.calstatela.edu/mmousta/The_Reading_Achievement_of_Economically_Disadvantaged_Children_in_Urban_Schools_Using_Open_Court.pdf

Mugny, G., & Doise, W. (1978). Socio-cognitive conflict and structure of individual and collective performances. *European Journal of Social Psychology, 8,* 181–92.

Nagy, W. E., Anderson, R. C., & Herman, P. A. (1987). Learning word meanings from context during normal reading. *American Educational Research Journal, 24*(2), 237–70.

Nagy, W. E., & Scott, J. A. (2000). Vocabulary processes. In M. L. Kamil, P. B. Mosenthal, P. D. Pearson, & R. Barr. (Eds.), *Handbook of reading research: Vol. 3* (pp. 269–84). Mahwah, NJ: Erlbaum.

National Council of Teachers of English & International Reading Association (1996). *Standards for the English language arts.* Urbana, IL: National Council of Teachers of English; Newark, DE: International Reading Association.

National Institutes of Health. National Institute of Child Health and Human Development (NICHD). (2000). *Report of the National Reading Panel. Teaching children to read* (NIH Publication No. 00-4769). Washington, DC: Government Printing Office. [http://www.nichd.nih.gov/publications/nrp/smallbook.cfm]

Neuman, S. B., & Celano, D. (2001). Access to print in low-income and middle-income communities: An ecological study of four neighborhoods. *Reading Research Quarterly, 36*(1), 8–26.

Neuman, S. B., & Celano, D. (2002). *The importance of the library for vulnerable young children.* Final report to the William Penn Foundation. Philadelphia: William Penn Foundation.

Neuman, S. B., & Celano, D. (2004). Save the libraries! *Educational Leadership, 61*(6), 82–85.

Ninio, A. (1980). Picture book reading in mother-infant dyads belonging to two subgroups in Israel. *Child Development, 51*(2), 587–90.

Opitz, M. (1998). *Flexible grouping in reading, grades 2-5.* New York: Scholastic.

Palinscar, A., & Brown, A. (1984). Reciprocal teaching of comprehension-fostering and comprehension-monitoring activities. *Cognition and Instruction, 1*(2), 117–75.

Pappas, C., & Brown, E. (1987). Learning to read by reading: Learning how to extend the functional potential of language. *Research in the Teaching of English*, 21(2), 160–77.

Paris, S. G., Lipson, M. Y., & Wixon, K. K. (1983). Becoming a strategic reader. *Contemporary Educational Psychology*, 8(3), 293–316.

Paris, S. G., Wasik, B. A., & Turner, J. C. (1991). The development of strategic readers. In R. Barr, M. L. Kamil, P. B. Mosenthal, & P. D. Pearson (Eds.), *Handbook of reading research: Vol. 2* (pp. 609–40). New York: Longman.

Pearson, P. D. (1993). Focus on research: Teaching and learning reading: A research perspective. *Language Arts*, 70(6), 502–11.

Pearson, P. D. (1996). Foreword. In E. McIntyre & M. Pressley (Eds.), *Balanced instruction: Strategies and skills in whole language*. Norwood, MA: Christopher-Gordon.

Perfetti, C., Beck, I., Bell, L., & Hughes, C. (1987). Phonemic knowledge and learning to read are reciprocal: A longitudinal study of first grade children. *Merrill-Palmer Quarterly*, 33(3), 283–319.

Pressley, M. (1998). *Reading instruction that works: The case for balanced teaching*. New York: Guilford Press.

Pressley, M. (2000). What should comprehension instruction be the instruction of? In M. L. Kamil, P. B. Mosenthal, P. D. Pearson, & R. Barr (Eds.), *Handbook of reading research: Vol. 3* (pp. 546–61). Mahwah, NJ: Erlbaum.

Pressley, M. (2002). Metacognition and self-regulated comprehension. In A. Farstrup & S. Samuels (Eds.), *What research has to say about reading instruction* (3rd ed., pp. 291–309). Newark, DE: International Reading Association.

Pressley, M., Allington, R. L., Wharton-McDonald, R., Block, C. C., & Marrow, L. M. (Eds.) (2001). *Learning to read: Lessons from exemplary first-grade classrooms*. New York: Guilford.

Pressley, M., Rankin, J. L., & Yokoi, L. (1996). A survey of the instructional practices of primary teachers nominated as effective in promoting literacy. *Elementary School Journal*, 96(4), 363–84.

RAND Reading Study Group. (2002). *Reading for understanding: Toward an r&d program in reading comprehension*. Santa Monica, CA: RAND.

Rankin-Erickson, J. L., & Pressley, M. (2000). A survey of instructional practices of special education teachers nominated as effective teachers of literacy. *Learning Disabilities Research & Practice, 15*(4), 206–25.

Raphael, T. (1986). Teaching question answer relationships, revisited. *Reading Teacher, 39*(6), 516–22.

Rasinski, T. V. (2004). Creating fluent readers. *Educational Leadership, 61*(6), 46–51.

Rasinski, T. V., & Hoffman, J. V. (2003). Oral reading in the school literacy curriculum. *Reading Research Quarterly, 38*(4), 510–22.

Read, C., Zhang, Y., Nie, H., & Ding, B. (1986). The ability to manipulate speech sounds depends on knowing alphabetic writing. *Cognition, 24*(1–2), 31–44.

Richardson, J. S. (2000). *Read it aloud! Using literature in the secondary content classroom.* Newark, DE: International Reading Association.

Rosenblatt, L. M. (1978). *The reader, the text, and the poem: The transactional theory of the literary work.* Carbondale, IL: Southern Illinois University Press.

Rosenblatt, L. M. (1995). *Literature as exploration* (5th ed.). New York: Modern Language Association. (Original work published 1938)

Routman, R. (1991). *Invitations: Changing as teachers and learners K–12.* Portsmouth, NH: Heinemann.

Rumelhart, D. E. (1980). Schemata: The building blocks of cognition. In R. J. Spiro, B. C. Bruce, & W. F. Brewer (Eds.), *Theoretical issues in reading comprehension: Perspectives from cognitive psychology, linguistics, artificial intelligence, and education* (pp. 38–58). Hillsdale, NJ: Erlbaum.

Ryder, R. J., Burton, J. L., & Silberg, A. (2003). *Results of direct instruction reading program evaluation: First through third grade, 2001-2003.* Milwaukee: University of Wisconsin–Milwaukee.

Sacks, C. H., & Mergendoller, J. R. (1997). The relationship between teachers' theoretical orientation toward reading and student outcomes in kindergarten children with different initial reading abilities. *American Educational Research Journal, 34*(4), 721–39.

Scherer, M. M. (Ed.). (1997). How children learn [Theme issue]. *Educational Leadership, 54*(7), 6.

Schickedanz, J. (1978). Please read that story again! Exploring relationships between story reading and learning to read. *Young Children*, 33(5), 48–55.

Schoenbach, R., Braunger, J., Greenleaf, C., & Litman, C. (2003). Apprenticing adolescents to reading in subject-area classrooms. *Phi Delta Kappan*, 85(2), 133–38.

Schoenbach, R., Greenleaf, C., Cziko, C., and Hurwitz, L. (1999). *Reading for understanding: A guide to improving reading in middle and high school classrooms*. San Francisco: Jossey-Bass.

Scholes, R. J. (1998). The case against phonemic awareness. *Journal of Research in Reading*, 21(3), 177–88.

Schumm, J. S., Moody, S. W., & Vaughn, S. (2000). Grouping for reading instruction: Does one size fit all? *Journal of Learning Disabilities*, 33(5), 477–88.

Smith, F. (1994). *Writing and the writer* (2nd ed.) Hillsdale, NJ: Erlbaum.

Smith, F. (2004). *Understanding reading* (6th ed.). Mahwah, NJ: Erlbaum.

Snow, C., and Biancarosa, G. (2003). *Adolescent literacy and the achievement gap: What do we know and where do we go from here?* New York: Carnegie Corporation.

Snow, C., Burns, M. S., & Griffin, P. (1998). *Preventing reading difficulties in young children*. Washington, DC: National Academy Press.

Stahl, S. (1998). Four questions about vocabulary knowledge and reading and some answers. In C.R. Hynd (Ed.), *Learning from text across conceptual domains* (pp. 73–94). Mahwah, NJ: Erlbaum.

Stanovich, K. (1986). Matthew effects in reading: Some consequences of individual differences in the acquisition of literacy. *Reading Research Quarterly*, 21(4), 360–407.

Stanovich, K. (1991). Word recognition: Changing perspectives. In R. Barr, M. Kamil, P. Mosenthal, & P. D. Pearson (Eds.), *Handbook of reading research: Vol. 2* (pp. 418–52). New York: Longman.

Strickland, D. S. (1988). *Teaching phonics today: A primer for educators*. Newark, DE: International Reading Association.

Swanson, H. L., Trainin, G., Necoechea, D. M., & Hammill, D. D. (2003). Rapid naming, phonological awareness, and reading: A meta-analysis of the correlation evidence. *Review of Educational Research*, 73(4), 407–40.

Sweet, A. P. (1993). *State of the art: Transforming ideas for teaching and learning to read* (Report No. OR 93-3046). Washington, DC: U.S. Department of Education, Office of Educational Research and Improvement.

Taylor, B. M., Pearson, P. D., Clark, K. F., & Walpole, S. (1999). *Beating the odds in teaching all children to read* (CIERA Report No. 2-006). Ann Arbor: Center for the Improvement of Early Reading Achievement, University of Michigan.

Taylor, D. (1983). *Family literacy: Young children learning to read and write*. Exeter, NH: Heinemann.

Teale, W. (1982). Toward a theory of how children learn to read and write naturally. *Language Arts*, 59(6), 555–70.

Teale, W. (1984). Reading to young children: Its significance for literacy development. In H. Goelman, A. Oberg, & F. Smith (Eds.), *Awakening to literacy* (pp. 110–21). Exeter, NH: Heinemann.

Tierney, R.J., & Shannahan, T. (1991). Research on the reading-writing relationship: Interactions, transactions, and outcomes. In R. Barr, M. L. Kamil, P. B. Mosenthal, & P. D. Pearson (Eds.), *Handbook of reading research: Vol. 2* (pp. 246–89). New York: Longman.

Treiman, R., & Baron, J. (1981). Segmental analysis ability: Development and relation to reading ability. In T. G. Waller & G. E. MacKinnon (Eds.), *Reading research: Advances in theory and practice: Vol. 3* (pp. 159–97). New York: Academic Press.

Troia, G. A. (1999). Phonological awareness intervention research: A critical review of the experimental methodology. *Reading Research Quarterly*, 34(1), 28–52.

Tumner, W., & Nesdale, A. (1985). Phonemic segmentation and beginning reading. *Journal of Educational Psychology*, 77, 417–27.

Vygotsky, L. S. (1978). *Mind in society: The development of higher psychological processes*. Cambridge, MA: Harvard University Press.

Wells, C. G. (1986). *The meaning makers: Children learning language and using language to learn*. Portsmouth, NH: Heinemann.

Wharton-McDonald, R., Pressley, M., & Hampston, J. M. (1998). Outstanding literacy instruction in first grade: Teacher practices and student achievement. *Elementary School Journal*, 99, 101–28.

Wilhelm, J. (2001). *Improving comprehension with think-aloud strategies*. New York: Scholastic Professional Books.

Wilkinson, I. A. G., & Townsend, M. A. R. (2000). From rata to rimu: Grouping for instruction in best practice New Zealand classrooms. *Reading Teacher*, 53(6), 460–71.

Winner, H., Landerl, K., Linortner, R., & Hummer, P. (1991). The relationship of phonemic awareness to reading acquisition: More consequence than precondition but still important. *Cognition*, 40(3), 219–49.

Wong, S., Groth, L., & O'Flavahan, J. (1994). *Characterizing teacher-student interaction in Reading Recovery lessons* (National Reading Research Center Report No. 17). National Reading Research Project of the Universities of Georgia and Maryland. Athens, GA: University of Georgia.

Xue, Y., & Meisels, S. J. (2004). Early literacy instruction and learning in kindergarten: Evidence from the Early Childhood Longitudinal Study—Kindergarten Class of 1998–1999. *American Educational Research Journal*, 41(1), 191–229.

Yaden, D., & Templeton, S. (Eds.). (1986). *Metalinguistic awareness and beginning literacy: Conceptualizing what it means to read and write*. Portsmouth, NH: Heinemann.

Yatvin, J., Weaver, C., & Garan, E. (2003). Reading First: Cautions and recommendations. *Language Arts*, 81(1), 28–33.

CHAPTER FIVE

What Young Children Teach Us about Literacy Learning

CATHERINE MADERAZO AND PRISCA MARTENS
Towson State University

Two-year-old Elliot sits at his mother's computer and begins to type his name. Instead of typing *E-L-L-I-O-T*, he studies the keyboard looking for his favorite letters, *Z* and *X*, and then numbers *1* and *1*, and finally a *Q*. "What does that say?" his mother asks. "Elliot," he answers confidently. For the next two years, when Elliot is asked to log in at a website to play a game, sign a card, or write using the computer or paper, he writes his name *ZX11Q*.

At age two, Elliot is a knowledgeable and experienced reader and writer who understands that the print he creates represents his meaning. Since his name is important to him, he invents a special, personal way to spell it, using close to the number of letters in *Elliot*. He uses <Z> and <X>, which are his favorite letters, two numeral 1s that resemble the double <l>, and a <Q> that is similar to the <O> but, perhaps in his eyes, more elaborate. (Note: the symbol < > indicates the letter written.) When he is three and a half years old, he begins adding *Elliot* to his signature (see Figure 5.1), indicating that he knows the difference between his signature and the name by which others know him. His family, friends, preschool teacher, and classmates all read and accept his signature, understanding that Elliot is using the multiple perspectives from which he sees the world to assert his identity and place his mark on it.

Elliot is Catherine Maderazo's son, but he represents all young learners becoming literate in our complex world. Young children have much to teach us about literacy and how they learn to

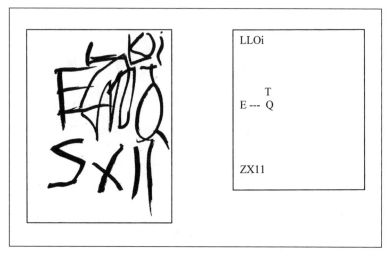

FIGURE 5.1. *Elliot (age four) signs a Mother's Day card with both his name* Elliot *and* ZX11Q.

read and write. As *kidwatchers* (Goodman, Y., 1996), we recognize the importance of learning from children by letting children be our informants (Harste, Woodward, & Burke, 1984; Martens, 1996a). This perspective is particularly critical when the majority of what matters and informs reading instruction are outside measures of what constitutes reading and reading well. In Elliot's situation, *ZX11Q* is unrelated to *Elliot.* Educators must continue to listen to and learn from readers themselves about what literacy is, and what each reader, like Elliot, is capable of doing with print and text, in the name of literacy.

In 2004, the Commission on Reading of the National Council of Teachers of English (NCTE) developed guidelines for reading: *On Reading, Learning to Read, and Effective Reading Instruction: An Overview of What We Know and How We Know It* (see Appendix A for complete document). This document synthesizes evidence-based perspectives of reading, reading development, and quality literacy practices as sociocultural, cognitive, and linguistic processes. Within these guidelines the Commission makes the case that what we know about reading is rooted in what we have observed and studied readers doing with text, their thinking about literacy, and their perceptions of what it means to be literate.

In this chapter we illustrate and discuss five literacy lessons that demonstrate what young children know about literacy and how they come to know it (Goodman, Y., & Martens, 2007; Whitmore, Martens, Goodman, Y., & Owocki, 2004; Commission on Reading, 2004). The language stories that illustrate each literacy lesson are intentionally drawn from our children, Leo and Elliot Maderazo, and Sarah and Matthew Martens. Because of our relationships with and close proximity to our children, and our knowledge of literacy processes, we have the advantage of using our inherent "enlightened subjectivity" as parents (Bissex, 1980, p. vi) to document aspects of our children's literacy learning that other researchers studying these same children would not see. Since our children are no more or less "gifted" than other children, we are confident that the language stories and literacy lessons we share are similar to those of all young children. We conclude the chapter by exploring how these literacy lessons inform the instruction that engages children as thoughtful, motivated early readers and writers who understand, enjoy learning, and believe in their abilities (Guthrie & Wigfield, 2000).

Literacy Lesson One

Children develop an understanding of literacy through their early experiences and interactions with significant others and engaging texts.

> At age three, Leo's world centers on trains. He plays with wooden trains, goes to the nearby park to ride the train, watches Thomas the Tank Engine videos, and draws trains (see Figure 5.2). His favorite books include *Chugga, Chugga, Choo-Choo* (Lewis & Kirk, 1999), *Freight Train* (Crews, 1992), *Trains* (Barton, 1986), and a rebus story *I'm Taking a Trip on My Train* (Neitzel & Parker, 1999). As a preschooler, Leo also willingly listens to *Busy Trains* (Lippman, 1981), a Golden Book picture book with detailed illustrations and lengthy informational text. He falls asleep thinking about trains and wakes up every morning talking about diesels and steam engines.

FIGURE 5.2. *Leo (age four) draws a picture of "The Little Train."*

Motivated by his passion for trains, Leo's first reading experiences are with familiar books about trains that connect what he knows to new information and new possibilities. Looking at pictures, observing real trains, and talking about trains with parents and others expands his knowledge and thinking. As he learns about his world through stories and close interaction with others, he deepens his understanding of books and reading. Leo simultaneously learns language, learns about language, and learns through language (Halliday, 1980). Gradually he begins to use the pictures in the story, the patterned text, and his memory to talk through and read the story (Matlin, 1984; Mikkelsen, 1985). It is his knowledge of trains, his experience with the books, and his belief that he *can* read that gives him control over the text.

From birth all children, regardless of ethnicity and language, are immersed in a constant stream of rich and diverse literacy and language practices, seamlessly woven into various daily cultural and social contexts (Barratt-Pugh, 2000; Paratore, 2002; Taylor & Dorsey-Gaines, 1988). They listen to stories, draw and write, play with print, and attempt to read books that interest them. They observe Mom reading the mail and writing grocery lists, and see Dad reading recipes as he cooks dinner or writing notes on reports from work. They interact with siblings and other children, writing thank-you notes for gifts, reading directions for the newest video game, and doing homework. In their communities, young children see people reading labels in the grocery store and writing to sign in at the doctor's office.

Children learn what literacy is and what literate people do by observing and participating in the functions literacy serves in their sociocultural environment (Goodman, Y., 1984; Goodman, Y., & Martens, 2007). As children engage in these literacy practices with the more experienced experts in their world, they learn how to *mean* (Halliday, 1975). Their participation brings them into the "literacy club" (Smith, 1997) as members who are socialized and knowledgeable about language (Halliday, 1975) and literacy, and about the functions, uses, and forms of literacy (Taylor, 1993). The same conditions that facilitate learning to talk also facilitate literacy development: a social context, immersion in language and literacy, demonstration/modeling, opportunities for approximation, responsibility for their own learning, opportunity to practice in a risk-free environment, and feedback from more knowledgeable others (Cambourne, 1988; Morrow, 1997). Even though all children learn through these conditions, they follow an infinite variety of paths as they grow as readers and writers (Taylor, 1993), motivated by human interaction (Taylor, 1998), oral language, and rich literacy experiences that convince them that reading and writing are worthwhile acts that they can and want to "do" (Cambourne, 1988). Like Leo, their unique development, experiences, interests, and knowledge bases provide the foundation for their growth as readers and writers. They transition to school with an understanding of what literacy is, an awareness of its potential, and a concept of their personal identities as literate beings.

Literacy Lesson Two

Children invent reading and writing for authentic purposes to represent personal meanings in their sociocultural community.

Before school, Sarah's older brother Matthew (age six and a half) is busy creating a birthday card for his first-grade teacher, Miss

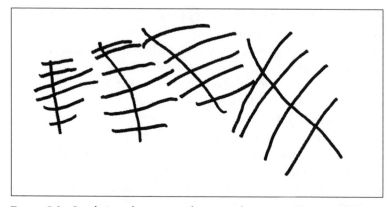

FIGURE 5.3. *Sarah (age three years, four months) writes "Hap-py Birth-day" using the syllabic hypothesis, matching each syllable to one mark, left to right.*

Cartwright. Sarah (age three years, four months) grabs paper and a marker and says, "I want to make a card for Miss Cartwright too." She gets to work, then hands her card to Matthew and announces, "Here, it says 'Hap-py Birth-day,'" pointing to one mark for each syllable she said (see Figure 5.3).

Sarah is inventing how to write. She made her first written marks at age two and a half by drawing horizontal or straight lines, which she asked others to read, or read herself using labels such as "Peter" or "people." While she was the only person who could read her lines, the lines demonstrated her "basic understanding of written marks as cultural objects which have a sign potential" (Harste et al., 1984, p. 108). Sarah then began writing <o>s, adding the curves that, with lines, are the salient features of her language. In her birthday card for Miss Cartwright (see Figure 5.3) she invents a way to directly connect her personal meaning with the language she reads, and writes by matching one mark on her paper to each word or syllable of her meaning. Ferreiro (1984) referred to this "matching" as the *syllabic hypothesis* and the beginning of children's understanding of phonics as the relationship between oral and written language. Although she does not control the graphic form, Sarah knows the purpose of written language and focuses on understanding how letter patterns relate to sound patterns (Ferreiro, 1991; Goodman, K., 1993).

Inventions are children's best guesses as to how reading and writing work, based on their knowledge of and experience with language and the world. Inventions allow young children to communicate and participate as active members of their democratic society. As children perceive authentic purposes for literacy, they invent the written language they need (Goodman, K., 1986).

◆ Leo (age four) invented how to address an envelope, including his house number followed by three horizontal lines as the return address, "To Mom and Dad" as the recipients, and a decorative stamp he drew.

◆ Before a trip to the grocery, Elliot (age three) added his own page to the list of items he believed were needed: *Transformers*, or *TRM/A/RFOR/NS/E*.

◆ After a family discussion about responsibilities around the house, Sarah (age five years, two months) created a chart with jobs such as dusting (*DICD*), make your bed (*MAkBAD*), and clean room (*KLENYUM*), followed by boxes for each day of the week.

Because they invent authentic meaningful language, children's inventions naturally include all the systems of language: syntax (grammar), semantic-pragmatic (meaning in a situational or cultural context), and graphophonics (visual and sound cues) (Goodman, K., 2003). Based on others' responses to and comprehension of their inventions (or lack of it), children revise their hypotheses and invent again, gradually moving their personal inventions closer to the conventions of their sociocultural communities.

Inventing Reading

Children's inventions are not limited to writing; children also invent how to read. Sarah's reading inventions included signs and logos in the community (Toys-R-Us and K-Mart signs) and at home (Frys, a grocery chain, on a shopping bag and Walt Disney in a newspaper ad). For Leo and Elliot, growing up in a suburb meant driving to school past signs for restaurants and shops that the boys associated with food and toys (Starbucks, In and Out,

Einstein Bagels, KB Toys). When Leo was three, after driving by a Red Lobster restaurant, he would repeat the words *red lobster* and talk daily about having dinner there. He remembered the restaurant's location, and television ads reminded him of wanting to go there with his grandparents for a special family dinner.

From the time Leo, Elliot, and Sarah could hold and manipulate books on their own, they have read, telling the story and sounding like the book. Their use of "book language" signifies their understanding of the unique structure of stories that differs from everyday oral language or environmental print (Harste et al., 1984). To predict and construct a meaningful story, they integrate meaning from the illustrations, from their knowledge of the language in books, and from their experiences with language, the world, and books (Matlin, 1984). Rather than merely the memorization of books, these readings are the children's syntheses of the meanings they are constructing (Martens, 1996a, 1996b; Mikkelsen, 1985). The readings position them as "critics" who have deeply processed the texts and outgrown themselves to know more than they knew (Frye, 1984).

Although Leo, Elliot, and Sarah were not the first to "invent" reading and writing, their inventions are "firsts" for them, just as the inventions of other readers and writers are their own firsts. These firsts make inventions powerful for the learner. Duckworth (1987), a Piagetian scholar, states,

> I see no difference in kind between wonderful ideas that many other people have already had, and wonderful ideas that nobody has yet happened upon. That is, the nature of creative intellectual acts remains the same, whether it is an infant who for the first time makes the connection between seeing things and reaching for them . . . or an astronomer who develops a new theory of the creation of the universe. In each case, new connections are being made among things already mastered. (p. 14)

Literacy Lesson Three

Children refine their reading and writing inventions as they draw on their experiences, personal knowledge, and interests in meaningful literacy events.

der KABI   VAK U l
Dear Grandpa. Thank you fo-

R V   Kd   Ad BZL.
r   the candy and puzzle.

I L U SARAH
I love you Sarah

FIGURE 5.4. *Sarah's (age four years, seven months) thank-you note to her grandfather.*

Sarah (age four years, seven months) wrote the thank-you note to her grandfather shown in Figure 5.4 one year and three months after the writing sample in Figure 5.3, and before she started receiving formal instruction in reading and writing in kindergarten. As she continued to invent during this time, she continually revised her inventions, based on others' responses and her transactions with the reading and writing in her world. While not "conventional," Sarah's inventions in her note show increasing similarities to the written language in her sociocultural community. They reveal that she uses her experiences as an observer and participant in literacy events to develop deeper conceptualizations of literacy.

Sarah's note also shows how her inventions support her developing knowledge of phonics and punctuation. Although parts of her note may appear to be random letters, her efforts to understand how written language works and make sense of letter and sound patterns (phonics) are evident in her inventions.

◆ She represents the /p/ (voiceless phoneme) [Note: the symbol / / indicates the sound of the designated letters] in *Grandpa* and *puzzle* with <B> (/b/ is a voiced phoneme) because /p/ and /b/ are both articulated on the lips. Similarly, she represents the /g/ in *Grandpa* with <K> because /g/ (voiced phoneme) and /k/ (voiceless phoneme) are both articulated in the throat. The /k/ in *candy* she also represents with <K>.

◆ *Grandpa* has two <a>s but they have different sounds. Sarah represents the first with <A> and the second with <I>. The first is in the accented syllable and has a sound similar to the /a/ in *Thank* and *and*, while the second is a *schwa* sound, which Sarah consistently represents in her written inventions with <I>.

◆ Sarah uses <V> to represent the <th> letter and sound patterns in *Thank* and *the*, which she is also consistent about in her inventions. At this time she pronounced /th/ as /f/: she pronounced her brother Matthew's name as *Mafew* and said she was *free* years old. Since /f/ and /v/ are articulated similarly, she represented /th/ with /v/.

◆ She uses the letter names <U> for *you*, <e> in *Dear*, and <D> in *candy*. She also uses the sounds of some letter names, such as <d> in *Dear* and *and*, <R> in *Dear* and *for*, <K> in *Thank*, and <Z> and <L> in *puzzle*.

◆ She invents a placeholder, <l>, to represent the /f/ in *for*.

◆ She uses her personal logo *ILU* for *I love you*, which she did consistently for over a year at this time. Her logo functioned for her as hearts or *XOXOXO* do for other writers.

◆ She writes the <S> in her name backwards from a conventional perspective but not from her invention perspective. Her "backwards" <S> is written left to right, following the direction of our writing system and the remainder of her name. She had a lot to remember: write her name from left to right across the page, but form her first letter from right to left.

Sarah began inventing phonics—that is, how the visual system of language relates to the sound system (Goodman, K., 1993)—well over a year before writing this letter to Grandpa. She continues to refine her inventions as she gains experience as a reader and writer. Her phonics inventions are based on how she perceives the significant phonemes she hears (Goodman, K., 2003). They are logical and systematic, and reveal how she is making sense of reading and writing to meet her personal functions and purposes (Martens, 1996a).

Refining through Punctuation

Sarah's note in Figure 5.4 also demonstrates that the refining of her written language includes inventing how to use punctuation.

Authors use spacing and punctuation to share information about meaning or language structure not contained in the words of the written text (Martens & Goodman, Y., 1996). Spacing and punctuation disambiguate writing for readers (Hall & Robinson, 1996). Leo (age four) began disambiguating his writing by using dots similar to periods between words. Elliot (age three years, five months) drew vertical lines between words. Sarah began disambiguating her writing not through spacing but through punctuation. Her first use of punctuation was periods. She was aware of their function of marking "the end" or "stop," as she said, from her personal transactions and experiences with books and other written language, and from hearing Matthew comment about his writing.

Sarah continues to use periods very deliberately and limits them to specific places that mark "the end" of something. She never places periods in the middle of words or phrases. In her thank-you note in Figure 5.4, for example, Sarah includes two periods: to designate the end of the greeting, and the end of the content or body of her note. Children, like all authors, want their writing to make sense to their readers, and they invent ways that support their readers' understandings, gradually refining these inventions also.

Refining through Story

As children continue to read and comprehend and make sense of their world (Smith, 2003), they draw on their experiences with story, with their personal interests, and with their knowledge of language and the world as they continue to refine their inventions. Figure 5.5 presents a page from Leo's (age six) story, titled "NASA's Missing," a multi-page book he has written about astronauts. In this illustration one of the astronauts is talking into his walkie-talkie. Leo works for two hours at the table until he finishes the story and the astronauts save the ship and the earth. Then he staples the pages together and reads the story to his family with a dramatic voice, explaining the action in the pictures.

When Leo wrote the story, Catherine immediately connected the events in it to Leo's collection of books on space and astronauts, and to a Fisher Price Rescue Hero video episode where

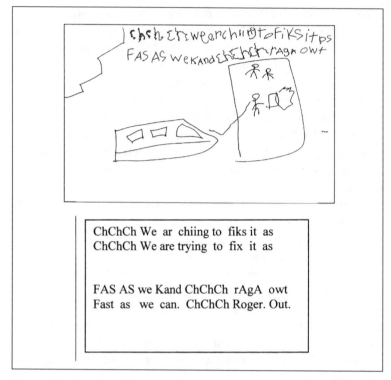

FIGURE 5.5. Leo (age six) writes the story "NASA's Missing" (excerpted page).

one of the characters finds himself in similar peril, floating away from the space station. Leo uses his knowledge, his experiences, and his imagination to invent a book about space with a dramatic problem that is resolved by the presence of walkie-talkies and a group of astronauts working together to fix the space station. Leo's book reveals his awareness that a story has characters, setting, and plot—including conflict and resolution—and shows that he understands stories need to be cohesive.

Leo's inventions also demonstrate his developing knowledge of phonics. He writes *chiing* for trying, for example, because /ch/ and /tr/ are articulated similarly on the front roof of the mouth. His <ks> for /x/ in *fix* and <ow> for /ou/ in *out* are alternate spellings for those sounds. And Leo spells four words conventionally: *we, to, it, as*. Though he omits the silent <e> in *are*, he demonstrates his attention to the visual aspects of spelling in his writing <ar> (Goodman, K., 1993). We don't "hear" the <a>. Leo shows his understanding that spelling is much more than learning sounds and letters.

Refining Reading Inventions

As children continue to read and transact with books and other written texts, they also refine their reading inventions. When Sarah invents the syllabic hypothesis in writing, she applies it to reading as a way of matching the oral story meaning to the written text in a book. For example, at age three years, four months, while reading *Time for School, Little Dinosaur* (Herman, 1990), she points to the sign that says *BUS* and comments, "I know what that says. 'Bus' [pointing to the <B>], 'Bus' [pointing to the <U>], 'Bus' [pointing to the <S>]." As she gains experience, she draws on her knowledge of language and books to read and connect with the printed text by using familiar language such as *I, no, mommy,* or other key words as landmarks. She makes her finger and voice reach the landmarks at the same time, rereading to perfect the timing if they didn't.

> Leo (age three years, three months) invents a similar strategy for refining his reading. He loves trains, and he uses his knowledge and experience with trains, train toys, and books about trains when he attempts to read a new text about them. One of his favorite books is *This Train* (Collicutt, 2001) (see excerpt in Figure 5.6). Leo reads with expression, drawing out *e-lec-tric-i-ty* and *downnnnnhillll* while moving his eyes back and forth between the illustrations and the text. He integrates text cues, his knowledge of the book language, and his personal language to predict the verb phrase *is going* on pages 8–9 for "is." On page 21, instead of following the language pattern on page 20, he predicts *by night.* At the end of page 23, after a mighty "All Aboard!" he shuts the book and smiles.

Leo, Elliot, and Sarah, like all young readers, are experienced language users. They know how language sounds and that it makes sense. In reading, they invent how to match that knowledge with the print on the page, that is, how to integrate the meaning they understand with letter patterns and sound patterns

	This Train by Paul Collicutt
	downnnnnhillN
pp. 7–8	This train goes uphill. This train goes downhill.
	is going *is going*
pp. 8–9	This train is in the country. This train is in the city.
	a *e-lec-tric-i-ty*
pp. 14–15	This train runs on steam. This train runs on electricity.
pg. 20	This train travels in the day.
	by
pg. 21	This train travels in the night.
pp. 22–23	This train is at the station... All Aboard!

FIGURE 5.6. *Excerpt from Leo's (age three years, three months) oral reading of* This Train.

(graphophonics) they see. Through their inventions they grow as effective young beginning readers, intelligently discovering how reading works (Goodman, D., Flurkey, A., & Goodman, Y., 2007).

Children's inventions and their continual revisions of them do not indicate mistakes or gaps in learning. Rather than being haphazard or arbitrary, their inventions are windows into the children's brilliant minds. As they revise their inventions, children reveal their thoughtful logic and their reflection on the "conventional" reading and writing surrounding them (Whitmore et al., 2004). Their inventions are evidence of their personal inquiries and wonderings, their working to make sense of reading, writing, and the world, and their desire to be active participants in their sociocultural communities.

Literacy Lesson Four

Children use multiple methods to represent their meanings in their written language, and their written language reflects their understandings of reading and writing.

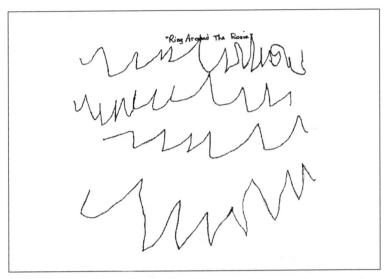

FIGURE 5.7. *Sarah's (age three years, three months) songwriter.*

While straightening up Sarah's room one afternoon, Prisca found on the floor a number of papers with rows of wavy lines (see Figure 5.7). Thinking Sarah (age three years, three months) was inventing cursive writing, Prisca asked her what she had written. Sarah replied, "That's my songwriter." "Your songwriter?" Prisca responded. "Yes, this is 'Ring around the Rosie,'" Sarah answered. Then she took her songwriter, held it in front of herself, and sang "Ring around the Rosie." When Sarah finished, Prisca added the song title to the paper. Sarah wrote and sang from her songwriter in church, at home, or in the car for several months.

Young children are immersed in an environment filled not only with rich and purposeful written language, but with multiple other ways to sign and communicate meaning. They observe or participate in reading and singing hymns in church and Sunday school, doodling while talking on the telephone, and measuring with tablespoons and cups to follow a recipe. Logos include both art and writing; commercials weave musical jingles and text on the television screen; and signs advertise product and price in a variety of colors and fonts. In addition to written language, then, children are surrounded by a wide variety of ways that meaning is represented. It's not surprising that children also invent ways to represent their meanings in these other symbol systems.

Although her family is not immersed in music, Sarah hears it on the car radio, on television, or in church, and she perceives music as another way to communicate meaning. Because the music she hears and sings and the language she reads and writes "sound" different and have different functions and purposes, she represents them with different surface texts. Presumably, the wavy lines of her songwriter reflect the connected ascending and descending flow of melody. The use of different symbol systems indicates her understanding that meaning is represented in different ways at different times, depending on the purpose (Harste et al., 1984).

Children frequently communicate meaning through their artwork, sometimes to support their written text, and other times with only the drawing representing the meaning. They write numerals to indicate their age, how many members are in their family, or the allowance they'd like to receive. They dance and they play alone or with friends. Leo made a sign for his brother that contained a circle with a line drawn through it. In the center was Elliot's face. The message: *No Brother!* Elliot created a wish list on the family refrigerator with numbered pictures of items he would like to have. Leo, Elliot, and Sarah show their ability to communicate beyond written language, and their individual range of communication systems is their meaning potential (Harste et al., 1984).

Children also invent alternate ways to embed meaning in their written texts. While oral language is supported by gestures, intonation, volume, facial expressions, voice speed, situational context, and so on, written language is limited by two-dimensional space, allowing only for grammatical structures and marks that support and clarify the meaning for readers (Martens & Goodman, Y., 1996). Children, like all readers and writers, invent fonts, graphics, and punctuation marks to enhance and emphasize their meanings for their readers. In Figure 5.5, for example, Leo uses wavy lines for *ChChCh* to indicate to his readers that the walkie-talkie is emitting a crackling sound. Rather than use words to describe that, he invents a font.

At age eight, Matthew knew how to needle, tease, and upset Sarah. One afternoon, when Sarah (age five years, two months) had had enough of Matthew's teasing, the sign in Figure 5.8 appeared on her bedroom door. Sarah's sign stretched across three pieces of different colored construction paper horizontally taped together, with the text *DOTBIKME* spread top to bottom and end to end across all three pages, and *KABAt* written in smaller letters at the top of the middle page. Sarah was frustrated. Matthew wasn't listening to her oral language. To emphasize her meaning in written language, she used colored paper and different colored markers, created a fancy font for *KABAt*, and "yelled" *DOTBIKME* as loudly as she could—with her text, primarily in capital letters, bounded only by the edges of the paper. She included a period following *At* but no punctuation after *ME,* possibly because there was no room on the page. In her other writing, Sarah occasionally included hearts, rainbows, or fonts she invented to enhance her meaning. Sarah's sign shows her continual refinement of her written language inventions. For example, she used the conventional spelling of *me* and the sounds of the letter names <K>, <t>, <D>, <O>, and <B>. Her use of <B> for /p/ and <A> for /ee/ in *Keep*; <A> for /ou/ in *Out*; and <K> for /g/ in *BUG* are all related to the similar articulation of those sounds. She continued to represent the *schwa* sound in *BUG* with <I>.

Children understand that meanings are not limited to the letters in written language. They are socialized not only to the ways we use print in our society, but to the richness of these multiple methods of communicating; and they effortlessly and seamlessly weave these together to represent their meanings. Understanding the variety of ways in which meaning is constructed in reading and writing in their sociocultural communities is central to children's literacy development (Anstey & Bull, 2006). Literacy is much richer and more complex than the verbocentric views often found in schools (Harste et al., 1984). It is a tapestry of the multiple ways we weave our meanings into the fabric of our lives and the lives of others.

Literacy Lesson Five

Children draw on their experiences with and interests in technology, media, and popular culture to grow as readers and writers.

FIGURE 5.8. *Sarah's (age five years, two months) sign on her bedroom door.*

When Elliot is a toddler (age three), Hot Wheels celebrates its thirty-fifth year making toy cars with an elaborate concept—*Highway 35*. Thirty-five new cars, numbered 1 to 35, in five distinct teams, are sold that year: Wave Rippers, Scorchers, Dune Ratz, Street Breed, and Road Beasts. These teams of drivers with histories and personalities compete in a series of five races on futuristic, gravity-defying tracks. From videos, cards, websites, and products, Elliot soon learns all the names of the drivers, cars, teams, and regions they represent, and even the smallest details of the World Race itself. Figure 5.9 shows a poster he placed in his room. The car and the words become a type of trademark whenever he writes or draws; the logos and pictures of cars are on his backpack, clothing, shoes, and snacks. The websites are bookmarked on the computer in a folder marked *Elliot.* He knows how to launch the Internet and open his folder. He scrolls down to find the icon he is looking for. Hot Wheels becomes part of his identity, his access to peers, and what it means to be literate in a fast-changing world.

Elliot first learns about the World Race when Catherine buys him a special edition Hot Wheels car, linked to the World Race website. What begins as joint meaning making between Elliot and his family, learning through exploration and interaction, evolves into a shared knowledge and language embedded in popular culture. Elliot's schema for World Race and Hot Wheels expands while collecting the different cars and following the biographies and storylines of the characters and races; he is actively engaged in making sense of this world and his place in it.

Elliot's language and literacy learning is embedded in two rapidly expanding and changing worlds: a world brimming with

FIGURE 5.9. *Elliot (age four) draws a Hot Wheel car (HOTWHEESL).*

popular culture (new products, new video and computer games, media, and collector cards), and a world of information technology or "new literacies" (navigating the Internet for information and connections). His play on the computer brings together both worlds through rapid delivery of information, images, and connections to assist him in making sense of how his world works and defining his place in it. Elliot's identity, although influenced by his experience and interaction with World Race, continues to evolve with new interests, interactions, and engagements in multiple layers of activity around popular culture and information technology.

Elliot's experiences and interactions with the Internet, embedded in popular culture, add dimension to his early reading and writing experiences, simultaneously teaching him about his world and about the possibilities of reading and writing. Reading is what he does to get to where he wants to be, to do what he wants to do, and to learn something new. As Elliot learns to read his world, he learns about himself, his family, and his environment. As his interest evolves it will include new worlds, and literacy will be further embedded in the social and symbolic stuff of childhood (Dyson, 2003a). Young readers and writers entering school are sophisticated and savvy. They bring with them the expectation that literacy is something they use to learn, to do, to communicate, and to connect. That is the world they are born into, and the world of which they are natives.

What Young Readers and Writers Teach Us about Literacy Teaching

As the examples of Leo, Elliot, Matthew, and Sarah in this chapter demonstrate, children are readers and writers long before they enter school. They arrive ready to learn, with varying degrees of knowledge and experience with literacy. Knowledgeable, kidwatching teachers intentionally work to know who their students are as readers and writers, and to build on and deepen what the children know and do (Goodman, Y., 1996). They work to engage children in meaningful literacy experiences and strengthen their identities as readers and writers. They encourage and value the children's literacy inventions, with their multiple forms and functions embedded in popular culture and technology, recognizing the role of inventions in learning, even though those inventions are not "conventional." They scaffold early readers and writers, particularly building on their meaning-making systems (Smith, 2003) and drawing in their personal interests.

We write this chapter at a time when early readers must negotiate and navigate between two very different perspectives of literacy: their literacy-rich and multimodal world, and the reality of reading instruction and assessment of reading skills and performance. We are seeing curricula move away from developmentally appropriate experiences and materials (Neuman & Roskos, 2005) to an increasing emphasis on early assessment of children's knowledge of reading skills with interventions for reading failure or language delays. In the midst of this stress and pressure, we encourage teachers to be kidwatchers, who watch and learn from children engaged in literacy as a valid means of planning instruction, assessing learning, and showing growth. Teachers who know children and what they can do will be better able to engage in reading instruction that is evidence-based, theoretically sound, and aligned to what is known and has been known about reading and learning to read (Commission on Reading, 2004).

The value of living with children—whether as a parent, significant other, or teacher—is in sharing their experiences, hearing their stories, and valuing their histories. We hope for all children what we hope for our own: that they are in the company of knowledgeable teachers who know the value of the lessons young children can teach us, as individuals and in groups, about literacy learning.

References

Anstey, M., & Bull, G. (2006). *Teaching and learning multiliteracies: Changing times, changing literacies.* Newark, DE: International Reading Association.

Barratt-Pugh, C. (2000). The socio-cultural context of literacy learning. In C. Barratt-Pugh & M. Rohl (Eds.), *Literacy learning in the early years* (pp. 1–26). Philadelphia, PA: Open University Press.

Bissex, G. (1980). *Gnys at wrk: A child learns to write and read.* Cambridge, MA: Harvard University Press.

Cambourne, B. (1988). *The whole story: Natural learning and the acquisition of literacy in the classroom.* Auckland, NZ: Ashton Scholastic.

Cole, A. (2004). *When reading begins: The teacher's role in decoding, comprehension, and fluency.* Portsmouth, NH: Heinemann.

Commission on Reading of the National Council of Teachers of English (2004). *On reading, learning to read, and effective reading instruction: An overview of what we know and how we know it.* Retrieved June 16, 2008, from http://www.ncte.org/about/policy/guidelines/118620.htm.

Duckworth, E. (1987). *"The having of wonderful ideas" & other essays on teaching & learning.* New York: Teachers College Press.

Dyson, A. H. (2003a). *The brothers and sisters learn to write: Popular literacies in childhood and school cultures.* New York: Teachers College Press.

Dyson, A. H. (2003b). "Welcome to the jam": Popular culture, school literacy, and the making of childhoods. *Harvard Educational Review, 73*(3), 328–61.

Farstrup, A. E., & Samuels, S. J. (Eds.). (2002), *What research has to say about reading instruction* (3rd ed.). Newark, DE: International Reading Association.

Ferreiro, E. (1984). The underlying logic of literacy development. In H. Goelman, A. Oberg, & F. Smith (Eds.), *Awakening to literacy* (pp. 154–73). Exeter, NH: Heinemann.

Ferreiro, E. (1991). Literacy acquisition and the representation of language. In C. Kamii, M. M. Manning, & G. Manning (Eds.), *Early literacy: A constructivist foundation for whole language* (pp. 31–55). Washington, DC: National Education Association.

Frye, N. (1984). Literacy and linguistic scholarship in a postliterate world. *PMLA, 99*(5), 990–95.

Goodman, D., Flurkey, A., & Goodman, Y. (2007). Effective young beginning readers. In Y. Goodman & P. Martens (Eds.), *Critical issues in early literacy: Research and pedagogy* (pp. 1–16). Mahwah, NJ: Erlbaum.

Goodman, K. (1986). *What's whole in whole language?* Portsmouth, NH: Heinemann.

Goodman, K. (1993). *Phonics phacts.* Portsmouth, NH: Heinemann.

Goodman, K. (2003). Reading, writing, and written texts: A transactional sociopsycholinguistic view. In A. Flurkey & J. Xu (Eds.), *On the revolution of reading: The selected writings of Kenneth S. Goodman* (pp. 3–45). Portsmouth, NH: Heinemann.

Goodman, Y. (1984). The development of initial literacy. In H. Goelman, A. Oberg, & F. Smith (Eds.), *Awakening to literacy* (pp. 102–9). Exeter, NH: Heinemann.

Goodman, Y. (1996). Kidwatching: Observing children in the classroom. In S. Wilde (Ed.), *Notes from a kidwatcher: Selected writings of Yetta M. Goodman* (pp. 219–27). Portsmouth, NH: Heinemann.

Goodman, Y., & Martens, P. (Eds.). (2007). *Critical issues in early literacy: Research and pedagogy.* Mahwah, NJ: Erlbaum.

Guthrie, J. T., & Wigfield, A. (2000). Engagement and motivation in reading. In M. L. Kamil, P. B. Mosenthal, P. D. Pearson, & R. Barr

(Eds.), *Handbook of reading research: Vol. 3* (pp. 403–22). New York: Erlbaum.

Hall, N., & Robinson, A. (Eds.). (1996). *Learning about punctuation*. Portsmouth, NH: Heinemann.

Halliday, M. A. K. (1975). *Learning how to mean: Explorations in the development of language*. London: Arnold.

Halliday, M. A. K. (1980). Three aspects of children's language development: Learning language, learning through language, learning about language. In Y. Goodman, M. Haussler, & D. Strickland (Eds.), *Oral and written language development research: Impact on the schools* (pp. 7–19). Newark, DE: International Reading Association.

Harste, J., Woodward, V., & Burke, C. (1984). *Language stories and literacy lessons*. Portsmouth, NH: Heinemann.

Kamii, C., Manning, M. M., & Manning, G. (Eds.). (1991). *Early literacy: A constructivist foundation for whole language*. Washington, DC: National Education Association.

Leu, D. J. (1998a). Caity's question: Literacy as deixis on the Internet. *Reading Online*. [Article reprinted from *Reading Teacher, 51*(1), 62–67.] [Online serial]. Available: http://www.readingonline.org/electronic/RT/caity.html

Leu, D. J. (1998b). Sarah's secret: Social aspects of literacy and learning in a digital information age. *Reading Online.* [Article reprinted from *Reading Teacher, 50*(2), 162–65.] [Online serial.] Available: http://www.readingonline.org/electronic/RT/sarah.html

Martens, P. (1996a). *I already know how to read: A child's view of literacy*. Portsmouth, NH: Heinemann.

Martens, P. (1996b). Inventing how to read: Sarah's story. *Kansas Journal of Reading, 12*, 8–18.

Martens, P., & Goodman, Y. (1996). Invented punctuation. In N. Hall and A. Robinson (Eds.) *Learning about punctuation* (pp. 37–53). Portsmouth, NH: Heinemann.

Matlin, M. (1984). *Transitions into literacy: A working paper* (Occasional Paper No. 10). Tucson: University of Arizona, College of Education, Program in Language and Literacy.

Mikkelsen, N. (1985). Sendak, "Snow White," and the child as literary critic. *Language Arts, 62*(4), 363–73.

Morrow, L. M. (1997). *Literacy development in the early years: Helping children read and write* (3rd ed.). Boston: Allyn and Bacon.

Neuman, S. B., & Roskos, K. (2005). Whatever happened to developmentally appropriate practice in early literacy? *Young Children*, 60(4), 22–26. Retrieved June 27, 2008, from http://journal.naeyc.org/btj/200507/02Neuman.asp

Paley, V. G. (2004). A child's work: The importance of fantasy play. Chicago: University of Chicago Press.

Paratore, J. (2002). Home and school together: Helping beginning readers succeed. In A. Farstrup & S. J. Samuels (Eds.), *What research has to say about reading instruction* (3rd ed., pp. 48–68). Newark, DE: International Reading Association.

Piaget, J. (1970). Piaget's theory. In P. H. Mussen (Ed.), *Carmichael's manual of child psychology* (pp. 703–32). New York: John Wiley & Sons.

Smith, F. (1997). *Reading without nonsense* (3rd ed.). New York: Teachers College Press.

Smith, F. (2003). *Unspeakable acts and unnatural practices: Flaws and fallacies in "scientific" reading instruction.* Portsmouth, NH; Heinemann.

Smith, F. (2004). *Understanding reading* (6th ed.). Mahway, NJ: Erlbaum.

Taylor, D. (1993). *From the child's point of view.* Portsmouth, NH: Heinemann.

Taylor, D. (1998). *Family literacy: Young children learning to read and write* (2nd ed.). Portsmouth, NH: Heinemann.

Taylor, D., & Dorsey-Gaines, C. (1988). *Growing up literate: Learning from inner-city families.* Portsmouth, NH: Heinemann.

Whitmore, K., Martens, P., Goodman, Y., & Owocki, G. (2004). Critical lessons from the transactional perspective on early literacy research. *Journal of Early Childhood Literacy*, 4(3), 291–325.

Children's Literature References

Barton, B. (1986). *Trains*. New York: Harper Collins.

Collicutt, P. (2001). *This train*. New York: Farrar, Straus & Giroux.

Crews, D. (1992). *Freight train*. (Reissue). New York: Mulberry Books.

Herman, G. (1990). *Time for school, Little Dinosaur*. New York: Random House.

Lewis, K., & Kirk, D. (1999). *Chugga, chugga, choo-choo*. New York: Hyperion.

Lippman, P. J. (1981). *Busy trains*. New York: Random House.

Neitzel, S., Parker, N.W. (1999). *I'm taking a trip on my train*. New York: Greenwillow.

CHAPTER SIX

Childhood Reading and Literacy Engagements: Curricular Concerns, Contexts, and Challenges

RITA S. BRAUSE
Fordham University

SOYONG LEE
The City College of New York, City University of New York

ARLENE A. MOLITERNO
Fordham University

In the current political climate, the No Child Left Behind (NCLB) legislation causes frequent administration of standardized tests while providing financial support for the use of scripted curricula. Teachers are faced with obstacles and dilemmas that challenge their teaching of reading in a way that is respectful both of students and of the social, communicative nature of language, while also being law-abiding. A major dilemma in this context is reconciling current knowledge of literacy development and effective literacy instruction as documented in recent British initiatives associated with the National Literacy Strategy (NLS) (Barber, 1997; Beard, 2000; Stannard & Huxford, 2007). This nationwide curriculum emphasizes the explicit teaching of the multiple language systems that contribute to each individual's creation and interpretation of authentic texts. The NLS includes the establishment of a Literacy Hour in every classroom. The time is intended to provide teacher-led literacy/comprehension instruction and student interpretations of high-quality narrative and expository texts. Attention is focused on three different text levels as each contributes to understanding, creating, and interpreting texts. Teachers' direct and explicit support and "interventions" are emphasized to remedy the absence of instruction documented in observations of classrooms with high-poverty students (see Durkin [1978–1979] for a historic link to this phenomenon). Along with direct instruction in language, the NLS curriculum mandates specific activities to support literacy development and empowerment.

The new literacies movement (Barton & Hamilton, 1998; Gee, 2005; Street & Lefstein, 2007) validates the pervasiveness of literate behaviors in real-world activities (even beyond alphabetic texts) while supporting the inclusion, if not substitution, of these activities for current classroom practice. Goodwin (2005), Meyer and Manning (2007), and Smith (2004) advocated the development of a personal practical theory of literacy to guide each teacher's classroom practice. This chapter seeks to support that evolution, drawing on the documents recently prepared by the Commission on Reading of the National Council of Teachers of English (NCTE).

In this chapter, we seek to contribute to our profession's knowledge, focusing on classroom teachers' understanding of effective literacy and reading engagements in schools by

- ◆ characterizing dominant reading instruction paradigms while emphasizing the model we believe is most effective and useful (a meaning-based, socioculturally responsive model for constructing and negotiating meaning in text)

- ◆ providing guidelines for organizing classroom literacy learning with students that build on their vast range of interests and proficiencies

- ◆ describing opportunities for using a wide array of symbol systems and modalities, including drama and drawing, while engaging with text

Curriculum Concepts

Current knowledge of reading and literacy development highlights the importance of language-rich contexts in our students' achievements with literacy. These contexts are characterized by complex linguistic systems, which are integral to authentic text creation. The proficient learner strategically accesses and understands these elements in spoken and written text. As teachers, we are charged with creating effective settings, which includes the selection of quality texts and the support for students' interpretation and subsequent creation of similar quality texts. We use terms such as *authentic text, quality texts,* and *language-rich environments* without consciously being aware of the characteristics of the texts used in these settings, particularly as they are distinguished from texts that are controlled for vocabulary and sentence structure, for example. Table 6.1 notes representative elements of authentic, quality texts focusing on the total text, sentence, and word levels.

Learning to read (alphabetic texts and visual images) is a lifetime endeavor. There is no point at which anyone has finished

TABLE **6.1.** Representative Linguistic Elements in Authentic Texts

Text Focus	Total Text	Phrases, Sentences, and Structural Organization	Words and Symbolic Conventions
Text Qualities	<u>Cohesion</u> Order of presentation of information [Chronological order, flashback]; Repetitive use of specialist vocabulary; Consistent tone [mysterious, authoritative] <u>Genre or language register</u> Story schema, academic essay <u>Language style</u> Familiar vs. mechanistic	<u>Grammatical patterns</u> S-V-O [I see a big dog.] V-S-O [Is George's home nearby?] <u>Physical presentation of text</u> Headings, tables, graphics <u>Text organization</u> Chapters, table of contents <u>New and old information</u> Established information vs. new perspectives,	<u>Common letter features</u> Letter recognition Left-to-right progression Sound-symbol Correspondences <u>Word/vocabulary</u> High-frequency words One and multi-syllabic words Spelling-meaning connection <u>Graphic presentation</u> Punctuation marks
Linguistic Terms	Semantic and pragmatic functions	Syntactic forms	Lexical and graphophonic elements

learning to read or write, because there is an infinite array of choices we can use in any context and multiple systems we can adopt to interpret them. In addition, we are mindful of how meaning is influenced by the unique context in which each text is found. The explosion in knowledge about language makes us aware of the complexity integral to the processes of teaching and learning. In this context, we acknowledge that an individual's disposition to learn in a particular context predicts the success of an engagement, in part.

Effective instructional contexts build on careful *kidwatching* advanced by Goodman (Owocki & Goodman, 2002). Using this stance, we know that prior to school entrance, children are productively engaged, learning to navigate and negotiate the communities in which they live. During the years preceding kindergarten enrollment, they have become effective at using oral language to accomplish a diverse array of activities. Their learning resulted from a combination of observation and incidental, contextually sensitive scaffolding by more knowledgeable others such as parents, caretakers, and older siblings. The learning has been personally meaningful in contributing to the flow of their lives.

School entrance frequently initiates children into a new setting, one in which direct, large-group instruction dominates. And the activities that are scheduled may be remote from the learner's real-world experiences. The support system changes dramatically, with the learner's role becoming one of responding to others' directives rather than being at the center of the activity. It is this context we label as *Learning-to-Read* activities. In contrast, *Reading-to-Learn* settings provide instruction about the code systems that occurs simultaneously as the child engages in real-world actions.

Learning-to-Read and Reading-to-Learn

Table 6.2 notes dominant characteristics of two curricular approaches: Learning-to-Read and Reading-to-Learn. The former focuses on symbol-sound correspondences and accuracy in decoding controlled texts, and the latter focuses on purposeful ac-

TABLE 6.2. Learning-to-Read vs. Reading-to-Learn

	Learning-to-Read	Reading-to-Learn While Learning-to-Read
Primary Focus of Instruction	◆ Separation/ discrete isolation of predetermined, sequentially organized curriculum (phonemic awareness, phonics, vocabulary, spelling, reading, writing, comprehension, word study) ◆ Factual comprehension of discrete facts and details	◆ Integrated, multidisciplinary, conceptual/ ideational/ inquiry/ thematic curriculum focus (presidential election, bird study, author study) ◆ Multiple interpretations and perspectives on events in literature and life
Instructional Emphasis	◆ Publisher-created scripted lessons (decoding words) ◆ Skill-based focus to practice skills in isolation for use at a later date (finding the main idea, listing details) ◆ Daily completion of teacher-provided assignments (work sheets, exercise pages)	◆ Student-experience based, locally crafted activities (recognize words and write using invented spelling in early drafts) ◆ Focus on strategies, processes for inferring information, making connections, predicting ◆ Long-term (1 week +) development of collaboratively designed projects and products (dramatic presentation of *The Enormous Turnip)*
Instructional Processes	◆ Teacher-directed instruction (I-R- E) ◆ Cooperative, teacher-assigned exercises ◆ Practice to prepare for a future, authentic use	◆ Scaffolded independent and small group authentic interactions ◆ Collaborative and locally negotiated projects ◆ Activities to produce locally established objectives
Evidence of Student Achievement	◆ Responses in spoken and written contexts to teacher-posed questions ◆ Scores on standardized tests	◆ Student initiation and exploration of authentic, academic inquiries ◆ Anecdotal records and portfolio contents

cessing of authentic texts to communicate effectively. We intentionally dichotomize this presentation, acknowledging that while most settings include elements of both, there is usually a stronger emphasis on one.

We believe, along with many other researchers (Gee, 2005; Halliday, 1975; Harste, Woodward, & Burke, 1984; Holdaway, 1979; Kucer, this volume; Kutz, 1997; Pahl & Rowsell, 2005), that classrooms in which Reading-to-Learn is the focus are more effective settings for developing both literacy proficiencies and responsible, independent learners, hallmarks of a literate people. In this section we explain research-based differences in these settings, with the subsequent parts of this chapter providing specific ideas for implementing the Reading-to-Learn model in childhood classrooms.

Learning-to-Read

Guided in large measure by the highly controversial National Reading Panel (NRP) report (National Institutes of Health, 2000), much Learning-to-Read classroom literacy instruction is separate from the rest of the curriculum and organized around five topics: phonics, phonemic awareness, vocabulary, fluency, and comprehension. Students focus on decoding isolated lists of letters and words as prelude to pronouncing words in larger contexts (Chall, 1967, 1996). There is no research base connecting the effectiveness of these materials on student learning and literacy development (Manzo, 2007) for this curriculum. Rather, major book publishers create multi-grade text series or "systems," providing a "teacher-proof curriculum." Scripted lessons are dominated by three-part interchanges: (1) *Initiate* question ("What is this letter? [pointing to a letter]"). (2) This question is followed by student *Response* ("A"). (3) And then the teacher *Evaluates* ("Good.") this response. This I-R-E interchange (Cazden, 2002; Kutz, 1997; Snow, Griffin, & Burns, 2005) typifies Learning-to-Read rhythms. The primary (both first and dominant) focus in these teacher-centered classrooms is on the accurate decoding of words (Beck, 1997; Fry, 1975, 1987; Levy, Abello, & Lysynchuk, 1997; Thorndike, 1913).

DIBELS testing reifies the importance of sound-symbol knowledge, despite the fact that this is the least effective way to promote successful, independent readers (Chittenden & Salinger, 2001; Chomsky, 1972; P. Cunningham, 2005a, 2005b; Goodman, K., 2006; Kucer, 2005; Smith, 2004). When language is simplified and controlled, students experience the antithesis of a language-rich environment, depriving them of the contexts that we know promote literacy development and literate behaviors (Barton & Hamilton, 1998; Compton-Lily, 2003; Maderazo & Martens, this volume). Children whose school literacy engagements are restricted to encoding and decoding leveled and controlled texts (Bear et al., 2007; Fountas & Pinnell, 1999; Fry, 1975; McGraw-Hill, 2007) have difficulty "pulling it all together" when they encounter increasingly complex content (Chittenden & Salinger, 2001; Dahl & Freppon, 1995). In this context, the validity of "readability formulas" is called into question (Cunningham, J. W., Spadorcia, Erickson, Koppenhaver, Sturm, & Yoder, 2005; Hart & Risley, 1995). Yet these are the materials specifically created to facilitate student literacy development. The problems is that these materials, and the instructional approaches they support, are antithetical to developing the literacy proficiencies they purport to promote.

Many teachers hold the belief that reading is a skill that is practiced and learned independently of other aspects of the curriculum. In some extreme settings, reading and language arts time is organized around five topics: phonemic awareness, phonics, vocabulary, comprehension, and fluency. Texts are used to reinforce the concept of regularities and exceptions to rules, for example, connecting alphabetic symbols (spelling) with their pronunciation (sound). In addition, vocabulary is promoted as grade-level word lists for memorization. Brief passages are read to locate main ideas and details. Topics and themes represented in the words and texts are irrelevant in these contexts. The first goal is to learn to break the code. After students give evidence of near-perfect matching of sounds and symbols, they use additional leveled or graded texts to practice these skills, seeking to achieve fluency and accuracy in their comprehension of the facts presented in the text. There is no interrogation of accuracy of sources, diverse perspectives, or contradictory information. Much like stringing beads on a necklace, these facts and ideas are isolated, with little focus on a "big picture" of a concept or phenomenon.

Reading-to-Learn

> Engagement is the key; merely completing reading activities is not synonymous with learning. . . . Classrooms in which students are actively engaged in learning for a large proportion of the time demonstrate higher achievement in reading and writing than do classrooms in which students are not so engaged. (Blair, Rupley, & Nichols, 2007, p. 436)

In Reading-to-Learn settings (Gallas, 1994; Lindfors, 1999; Rogovin, 1998a, 1998b; Wells, 1986), students are actively engaged, accessing texts and creating texts that promote their development of personally meaningful interpretations. They record and share perspectives and interpretations as they access and use multiple symbol systems (Britton, 1993; Chomsky, 1969; Duckworth, 2006; Halliday, 1975, 1980; Halliday & Hasan, 1976; Heath, 1983). Students negotiate the validity of multiple interpretations/understandings/meanings in a variety of contexts, constantly mindful and responsive to the different experiences, dispositions, and personal motivations in accomplishing class-initiated projects. In the process, students are at the center of learning engagements, with each student acquiring personally relevant information and strategies (along with sound-symbol correspondences), and building on personally evolving understandings.

At the heart of all activities when in a Reading-to-Learn setting is increasing students' repertoire of effective, appropriate communication strategies (functions/purposes/audiences, contexts, and styles) (Britton, 1993; Compton-Lily, 2003; Heath, 1983; Wells, 1986). Reading-to-Learn uses small, collaborative settings through the daily integration of all language-based activities: reading, writing, speaking, listening, representing, and visualizing. Sample topics include how communities develop, ways of understanding life in a metropolitan area, and how traditions are created (Beach, 2007; Holdaway, 1979). Researchers have found that students in classrooms with the most effective teachers spend significant time in small-group work. They use more authentic texts in contrast to vocabulary and sentence structure–controlled textbooks (Blair et al., 2007; Cambourne, 1995; Harste, 2000; Harste et al., 1984; Lindfors, 1999; Taylor, Pearson, Clark, & Walpole, 2000), and they recognize the value of choosing words carefully (Johnston, 2004).

Students who read authentic texts ultimately create more complex, meaningful texts than do those immersed in learning basic skills (Dahl & Freppon, 1995). Reading-to-Learn students seek to obtain the gist of a story and events, with meaning and understanding being at the heart of their enterprise. They use authentic, naturally occurring texts (trade books, biographies, research reports, novels) in language-rich environments that support their evolving development of more sophisticated linguistic repertoires essential for success in academic contexts. Typically they are engaged in reading stories, conversing and debating, and writing essays to share elaborated messages with community members (Cox, Fang, & Otto, 1997). These activities enable Reading-to-Learn students to become active, effective participants in the community and society, prepared to engage in and promote morally responsive actions (Barton & Hamilton, 1998; Duckworth, 2006; Freire & Macedo, 1987; Heath, 1983).

Instruction in these settings focuses on developing a large repertoire of strategies while interpreting and communicating ideas, experiences, and feelings with diverse audiences and for multiple purposes. Think-aloud protocols and extended conversations and discussions addressing the processes an individual used to arrive at a particular inference or generalization are effective scaffolding experiences that typify a Reading-to-Learn agenda. In the process, students become more aware of their own strategies, enabling them to become increasingly independent as learners. The empowerment of students in these settings is palpable.

Our Professional Challenge

In the current, highly charged political climate, with politicians seeking to drive educational practice, we as professional educators need to decide which path we will follow: the easy road of "going along to get along" or the more challenging road of enacting our personally powerful professional philosophy. Ultimately, we each individually decide how we will organize our classrooms. In the following sections, we describe literacy engagements that occur in Reading-to-Learn, language-rich settings that effectively support students' literacy development. These ideas are offered for contemplation in creating effective classroom contexts for consequential literacy instruction and learning.

Literacy Engagements in the Reading-to-Learn Setting

Within the Reading-to-Learn setting, children experience literacy engagements that simultaneously involve the complex tasks of learning language, learning about language, and learning through language (Halliday, 1980; International Reading Association/National Council of Teachers of English [IRA/NCTE], 2008). The International Reading Association (IRA) and NCTE (IRA/NCTE, 2008) describe the concept of literacy engagements. They note that when children learn language, they use language and other sign systems as ways of making meaning. When children learn *about* language, they come to understand how language works (they acquire linguistic knowledge). When children learn *through* language, they use reading and writing, as well as speaking and listening, as tools for exploration, for learning, or for critiquing the world. Short, Kaufman, Kaser, Kahn, and Crawford (1999) described classroom literacy engagements as "multifaceted events involving curricular invitations and the arrangement of materials, space, time, and people" (p. 377). Thus, literacy engagements that occur within classroom contexts include specific linguistic content to be learned, specific texts to be read, specified time allotments, and teacher-initiated instructional interactions. Teachers create these contexts by reading aloud to children; engaging in shared reading and writing; using guided reading; facilitating literature circles, book clubs and buddy reading; and providing individualized literacy experiences. Table 6.3 provides examples of literacy engagements that occur in the Reading-to-Learn classroom. These literacy engagements are appropriate for the whole class, small groups, or individual students.

TABLE 6.3. Sample Literacy Engagements in the Reading-to-Learn Setting

Sample Literacy Engagements in the Reading-to-Learn Setting
➤ Reading and writing poetry, songs, rhymes, tongue twisters, and morning messages; using invented spelling in daily journal writing; reading the room and word wall; making language play a part of the curriculum using air writing, finger painting, sand writing, or creating letters with clay while supporting phonological awareness and teaching letter formations
➤ Using choral reading, echo reading, and buddy reading; using chants, songs, and rhymes as texts; reading a wide variety of texts, including those created by the students to explore personal experiences, while demonstrating and enacting fluent reading; using think-alouds during these activities to make strategy use transparent
➤ Writing about, talking about, drawing, or acting out a story; drawing a story map or graphic organizer; identifying the presentation order of events with pictures or sentence strips; making a book; reading and retelling a story with scribes; creating stories with different presentation orders (chronological, flashback, or stream-of-consciousness); summarizing text information orally or in writing; synthesizing information as a narrative or in a graphic organizer to help children identify main ideas, story sequence, and story details (who, what, when, where, how)
➤ Interpreting character traits and actions orally or in writing; creating a character map; writing a diary entry; comparing with characters in other stories; attending to the variety of ways that authors offer this information; using drama with strategies such as voices in the head
➤ Identifying (orally or in writing) implied main ideas and figurative language as these contribute to a cohesive text; finding evidence in the text to support one's interpretation; using reader response journals to document these analyses; creating new texts that include these techniques
➤ Talking, drawing, writing, or role playing (using puppets) about mood or emotional reactions (characters' reactions, personal reactions, reactions of others; different point of view); retelling or rewriting a story from the point of view of different characters; creating original texts using different narrative voices
➤ Relating the text (either orally or in writing) to personal experiences (text-to-self connection), to other texts (text-to-text connection), or to the world (text-to-world); using real-life photos related to the experience; distinguishing (orally or in writing) between essential and tangential information, and between fact and opinion; recording data in a graphic organizer or in a narrative form
➤ Identifying and interpreting propaganda techniques and perceived bias in texts written from a variety of perspectives; writing or rewriting stories from different perspectives; engaging in debates with students taking different sides of an issue; using multicultural children's literature to compare Cinderella stories from various cultures.

Authentic literacy experiences (similar to those presented in Table 6.3) require that children engage in meaningful activities with quality texts for real purposes (Cullinan, 1992; Halliday, 1975; Smith, 1978; Teale & Sulzby, 1986; Wells, 1986). These classroom reading and writing experiences serve the very same purposes as reading and writing do in the real world: to communicate, to make meaning, to learn, and to enjoy the experience.

In the Reading-to-Learn classroom, it is the interplay of authentic texts with meaningful literacy engagements that supports children's learning how to read and write. Berardo (2006) described authentic texts as those that are written for native speakers and contain "real" language, in contrast to non-authentic texts that are specifically designed for language-learning purposes (for example, basal readers and phonics workbooks). He observed that the language found in non-authentic texts is artificial and typically concentrates on something that has to be taught. Authentic texts are the ones that children will encounter in the real world and that reflect how language is really used. Examples of authentic texts that support literacy engagements are fiction and nonfiction texts, magazines, newspapers, primary source documents, films, books on tape, Internet-based sources, and multimedia games (Labbo, 2005; Malloy & Gambrell, 2006). In an ever-changing society, learning to manipulate multiple "real world" discourses, including the discourses of media and technology (the Internet, instant messaging, email), is essential.

As with other skills and competencies acquired in life, the more time children engage in meaningful reading and writing, the more proficient they become. In typical elementary classrooms, 90–120 minutes each day are devoted exclusively to reading/writing instruction. In Reading-to-Learn settings, literacy blocks and workshops are supplemented with opportunities for children to engage in authentic reading and writing throughout the school day and beyond. Research (Freppon & Dahl, 1998; Gallas, 2003; Rogovin, 1998a) suggests that effective classroom teachers are those who consistently weave reading and writing activities (literacy engagements) into all aspects of the school day. Such teachers understand that text creation, analysis, and interpretation are integral components of learning in all subject areas, including math, science, social studies, music, art, and physical education.

Reading and writing for learning in the content areas involves practices such as writing explanations for mathematics or science reasoning, creating diary entries from various historical perspectives, reading and writing poems or lyrics for celebrating events (such as Flag Day or Election Day), and writing reflective papers on works of art. Literacy engagements can even extend to physical education, where children read about and play athletic games representing diverse cultures, or perhaps engage in folk dance activities.

In creating multiple opportunities for literacy engagement in the Reading-to-Learn classroom, teachers intentionally group students in a variety of ways. Grouping options include large-group (or whole-class), small-group, and individual activities. The practice of varying the types of groups used for instruction is called *flexible grouping*. Flexible grouping allows teachers to differentiate instruction for learners who typically differ in background knowledge, experiences, interests, and literacy proficiencies. Teachers group and regroup to create instructional contexts of different sizes, of different compositions, and for different purposes based on students' proficiencies, interests, or needs (Chapman, 1995). Research supports the use of small-group instruction (especially for reading) in the primary grades, as small groups generally result in higher levels of pupil engagement (Taylor et al., 2000). Grouping options work together with varied teaching strategies (such as those suggested in Table 6.3) in providing different levels of support for student learning (Opitz, 1999). In the Reading-to-Learn classroom, small-group and individual (one-on-one) literacy engagements are either led by the teacher or supported by peers, thus providing sufficient support for student learning.

Contexts for Literacy Engagements in the Reading-to-Learn Setting

Teachers create these contexts by reading aloud to children; engaging in shared reading and writing; using guided reading; facilitating literature circles, book clubs, and paired reading; and providing independent literacy experiences. These contexts foster engagements that promote meaningful conversations about texts and how language works (Harste, 2000). The following section describes literacy contexts that support learning to read and write and are characteristic of Reading-to-Learn classroom settings.

Reading aloud is a teacher-led instructional context used with the whole class or with small groups of children. When reading aloud, the teacher reads from a text at a level more difficult than that at which the children can read on their own, and engages them in conversations and meaningful talk before, during, and after reading. Fountas and Pinnell (2006) and Hoyt (2007) used the term *interactive read-aloud* because both teachers and children are active participants as they read, reflect, discuss, and respond to texts in meaningful ways. The interactive nature of the read-aloud is also evident when children read with their peers in small- or large-group contexts. Within the context of reading aloud, children experience opportunities to engage with and respond to texts.

Shared reading and *shared writing* contexts are created with the whole class and small groups. In shared reading, the teacher and children (or a group of children) read together in unison from a shared text. In shared writing, the teacher and children (or a group of children) write a text or story together. Shared reading and writing create a context for supportive literacy engagements.

Guided reading is a term used to describe a context characterized by small-group, teacher-led instruction (Fountas & Pinnell 1996, 2006; Schwartz, 2005). During guided reading, teachers demonstrate "how to read" and provide scaffolding to support the emerging skills of primary grade students. Fountas and Pinnell (2006) suggest that teachers use guided reading with small groups of children (five to six students) who read at the same level and have similar reading needs. Each student reads his or her own text silently or aloud, and the teacher provides mini-lessons to demonstrate effective reading strategies. Mini-lessons engage children in conversations about the type of book that will be read, such as a novel, biography, or folktale. Mini-lessons can also support children's efforts to interpret texts by demonstrating how to summarize a passage or how to make analogies while reading; or by engaging children in conversations about word use or grammatical aspects of the text. As teachers closely observe children during guided reading, they note the strengths reflected in each student's performance, and determine the additional types of reading engagements or mini-lessons children will need to support developing literacy.

Literature circles, book clubs, and *paired reading* create instructional contexts characterized by shared reading and writing, collaborative responses to texts, discussions of common interests, and shared learning. Four to six children may compose a literature circle or book club, while two students work together in paired reading. Literature circles, book clubs, and paired reading provide unique opportunities for small groups of children to discuss a specific text in depth as the children talk about the story events, the characters, the author's craft, and personal experiences related to the story. Schlick Noe and Johnson (1999) suggested that literature circles allow children to think critically and reflect as they read, discuss, and respond to books. They noted that as children collaborate and discuss a text, meaning is constructed with other readers and understandings of the text are reshaped. Literature circles, book clubs, and paired reading are characterized by self-selection of literature, reader response, student responsibility and ownership, and flexibility and fluidity— meaning that literature circles never look the same way twice.

Independent literacy experiences create a context that allows children to have intensive and extended engagements with authentic texts. As children self-select texts, choose their own topics for writing, and independently embrace literacy engagements, they become increasingly proficient readers and writers. Teacher conferences support individual learning by providing one-on-one support and a venue for teachers to demonstrate effective reading and writing strategies; assess individual progress; teach to a specific need; or suggest subsequent texts to read or write.

Explicit Demonstrations and Scaffolding

Showing children how to read and write is an essential component of literacy instruction within Reading-to-Learn classrooms. All learning begins with implicit or explicit demonstrations, sometimes with running commentary (seeing another brainstorm ideas for a story, creating a story map while reading, or identifying an author's style by comparing two stories) and "thinking aloud" about one's processes (Cambourne, 1995).

As illustrated in the literacy engagements presented in Table 6.3, teachers and others demonstrate reading strategies. These include how to

select appropriate texts.

ask and answer questions from the text.

clarify a purpose for reading.

activate relevant prior knowledge.

make predictions about the text.

recognize text structure.

create summaries (oral, written, and visual).

monitor one's comprehension.

use fix-up strategies when one fails to comprehend (Neufield, 2005; Pardo, 2004).

By sharing their own writing and discussing their craft with their students, teachers can also demonstrate writing in profound and meaningful ways (Graves & Kittle, 2005). Such intentional and explicit demonstrations serve to make reading and writing processes and strategies visible to children.

Explicit demonstrations of reading and writing must be accompanied by instruction that supports or scaffolds learning (Vygotsky, 1978). Scaffolding is usually described as coaching, modeling, and supporting the learner as he or she attempts to engage in personally meaningful reading and writing. Teacher scaffolding can take the form of thought-provoking hints or suggestions; or the teacher can actually perform parts of the task that students cannot yet perform on their own (Anderson, Armbruster, & Roe, 1990; Taylor, Pearson, Peterson, & Rodriguez, 2003). Scaffolding also includes affirmations and supportive gestures such as finger pointing, gentle touches, and smiles, along with specific thinking-aloud behaviors. Younger children and novice readers and writers need more of such encouragement than do fluent readers.

Clark and Graves (2005) suggested that scaffolding instruction should be highly flexible and adaptable so that the level of support changes as children become increasingly active and proficient readers and thinkers. Teachers must assess student learning to determine the appropriate amount of support needed to further literacy learning (Knipper & Duggan, 2006), and to know what to teach next and how to teach it (Guskey, 2003). Teachers also need to know when to remove or reduce support as children learn to read and write independently.

The literacy engagements presented in Table 6.3 identify opportunities for meaningful instruction and explicit scaffolding experiences so that teachers can meet the needs of each developing learner. Classroom teachers will find that the IRA/NCTE website www.readwritethink.org is an excellent resource on literacy engagements. The extensive lesson plan database allows teachers to search in a variety ways, including by grade level, literacy strand (learning language, learning about language, learning through language), and type of literacy engagement. Research on instruction that promotes multi-modal engagements is discussed in the next section.

Supporting Literacy through Multiple Modes of Engagement

When we encounter texts, we are charged with interpreting others' words (Bakhtin, 1981). Successful interpretation of others' words in the form of written language requires experience and effort. Indeed, the content and form of the written word come in many different ways; and children's background knowledge, or their social and cultural experiences with text, may or may not be conducive to the types of negotiation and interpretation called for in a particular text. So as children encounter text in school, they learn strategies—ways of interacting with and comprehending text—that may help them extend their ways of understanding a text.

Writing and talking are the most popular ways of engaging with text experienced in schools. Typically, we ask children to read a book, talk about it either with the teacher or with their peers, and then produce written work that responds to the text in different ways. While these two popular modes of engagement do provide children with ways of deepening their understanding of text, research on childhood literacy suggests that we need to move beyond talking and writing, to support multiple modes of engagement for literacy development (Dyson, 2001a, 2001b; Gallas, 1994; Harste, 2000; Hoyt, 1992; Kress, 2000; Short, Kaufman, & Kahn, 2000; Siegel, 1995). This is especially true in the Reading-to-Learn context. To do so, researchers claim that educators should observe and investigate children's social and cultural experiences, and should use resources that emerge as entry points for productive, focused, and negotiated interpretations of written text. We know that children bring different social and cultural assets to school, and when teachers build on such resources for literacy development, it opens up space for diverse modes of engagement and interpretation of text (Au, 1979; Ballenger, 1999; Compton-Lily, 2003; Heath, 1983; Ladson-Billings, 1994).

The need to provide children with multiple modes of engagement, and to support their cultural and linguistic resources in literacy development, is echoed by those who take a semiotic perspective on literacy development. As Siegel (2006) explained in a review of research on multimodal transformations, Harste et al. (1984) were the pioneers in bringing a semiotic perspective to the study of children's literacy development. According to these scholars, the resources that children utilize in reading and writing go far beyond the alphabet system. Children use all kinds of signs and symbol systems, such as pictures, gestures, and numbers, in the process of making meaning when reading and writing.

Different children bring different kinds of symbol systems to school, depending on the kinds of communicative events that they have experienced. Especially in contemporary times, with the advancement of technology, we see a wider range of representational modes reinforcing the idea that children's development of writing is only one part of the child's development of signs (Vygotsky, 1978), and thus there is more to literacy and literacy learning than the conventional acts of reading and writing alphabetic text on paper. Some children who speak a language other than English use signs and symbol systems from their first language as entry points and as a basis for developing understandings of the English language (Genishi, Stires, & Yung-Chan, 2001; Moll, Saez, & Dworin, 2001). Studies have also shown that children who speak a vernacular dialect considered "nonstandard" benefit from instruction that enables them to codeswitch, choosing the language variety appropriate to the communicative context (Baugh & Hymes, 2002; Delpit & Dowdy, 2002; Dyson, 2006; Labov, 1972; Perry, 1996; Smitherman, 2002; Wheeler & Swords, 2004).

Short et al. (1999) claimed that when children use different symbol systems in relationship to literacy, they develop "multiple ways of knowing" (p. 170). The process of taking understanding of one sign/symbol system and applying it within a different sign/symbol system encourages readers to examine the boundaries and potentials of each system (Siegel, 1995).

In a study of the role of multiple sign systems in responding to literature, Short et al. (2000) reported that the range of symbol systems in addition to reading and writing provide children with the opportunity to think more broadly, to consider other ideas, to connect memories, and to think through feelings as they relate to the text. Engaging in interpretation of the text using multiple sign systems led the children to think of themselves as creators of meaning.

Against such a background, then, it seems only just to investigate different modes of communication and think about ways in which educators may bring such modes of learning back to the teaching of childhood literacy. In the following sections, we discuss such different modes of engagement in detail.

Oral Language and Reading

Research into the relationship between oral language and literacy development suggests, in part, that children use oral language to contextualize, edit, clarify, and question meanings represented through writing, a symbol system fairly new to their repertoire of means to communicate (Britton 1993; Clay, 1998; Dyson, 1989;

Halliday, 1980; Vygotsky, 1978; Wells, 1986). Children do so in a number of different ways.

In a study of kindergarten, first-grade, and second-grade children during read-alouds, Sipe (2002) reported that there are mainly five different ways in which children respond to and engage in text orally during read-alouds. They (1) dramatize the story spontaneously, both in verbal and nonverbal ways; (2) talk back to the characters of the story; (3) suggest alternatives in plots, characters, or settings; (4) insert themselves in the story and assume the roles of the story characters; and (5) take over the text and manipulate the story for their own purpose.

Children also use oral language to participate in identifying and understanding ideologies represented in texts. Dyson (1989), for instance, explained that this process is inherently social, and young children use oral language as a tool to mediate and explore—to gain membership into, and in a similar vein, gain distance from—ideologies that are not clearly spelled out in stories.

Hoyt (1992) proposed the use of *reader's theater* as a way of engaging children's oral language in reading. Children create a script from a piece of literature and use their expressive voices to capture the listener. Unlike drama, reader's theater does not involve any action. The readers use the various aspects of reading—reading rate, intonation, loudness of voice—to emphasize meaning and to make the characters and text come alive. Children are challenged to transmediate what is in text to expressive oral language.

The importance of oral language as a resource in providing depth and breadth to interpretations of text, and in gaining an ideological sense of the particularities of texts, cannot be overstated (Dyson, 1989). However, many children who are learning English as a second language in our classrooms do not have adequate opportunities to use oral language as a resource in developing reading and writing (Lee, 2006). When a classroom teacher does not speak the child's first language (which is often the case in U.S. classrooms), English language learners lack opportunities to discuss texts with more knowledgeable others in a language in which they are proficient. In the classroom, peers who speak the child's first language may fill this gap (Fassler, 2003). In the home, practices that encourage parents to read and discuss texts in their native language with their children have been effective in helping children both read in a second language and affirm their identity as readers and writers (Lee, 2006). As Kucer explained in Chapter 3 of this volume, researchers have found the ability to read and write in the first language to be a supportive resource in developing reading and writing in the second language (Cummins, 1991; Jimenez, Garcia, & Pearson, 1995). Thus, for children who are learning English as a second language, continued engagement with literacy using their first language adds to the development of literacy in the second language.

Dramatic Enactments

Drama, as defined by Heathcote (1984), is a complex system made up of different semiotic resources. Drama provides a space where children employ diverse symbol systems and resources to stretch their understandings of text through critical reflection and action. In contrast to many of today's "back-to-basics" and scripted literacy programs that focus on discrete, isolated bits of skills and information as the basis for understanding texts, connecting drama with literacy events has the potential to engage students in multiple semiotic systems, thereby tapping into more natural ways of making meaning.

How, then, does a teacher use drama to engage students in meaningful reading? In her work with Latino/Latina students and Latino/Latina literature, Medina (2004) proposed both the use of multicultural realistic fiction and a list of questions to engage students dramatically. She reminded us that the potential of drama in the childhood classroom relies on its power to move beyond literal interpretations and dramatization of text. She suggested that teachers consider questions such as the following in preparation for dramatic enactments:

> What is the text saying? What is missing? Which perspectives, events, and social issues surrounding the text that are present or implied could become part of the classroom dialogue? How do the students and I relate to the experience in the text? Do I need to learn and provide more information before we read the text? Would it be generative for students to look at the experience from an insider character or an outsider? What are some of the

tensions and possibilities presented in the text that provide a context for a powerful drama? (p. 281)

Drama activities should not be for just "fun and play" (Medina & Campona, 2006, p. 326). Rather, they should provide students with alternative and multiple avenues for negotiating and understanding texts. Medina and Campona also suggested the use of frozen images without talk or movement. They stated that "by looking at a frozen moment, the participants in the drama can analyze a particular event more deeply. Students also have the opportunity to conceptualize bodily visual representations, extending traditional written and spoken curricular engagements" (p. 340).

Mental imaging—creating clear pictures in our minds of what we are reading—is another key strategy in engaging students in reading texts. Mental imaging or "visualization" helps readers store information for later retrieval (McMaster, 1998). Ross and Roe (1977) found that engaging in certain drama games, or dramatization of a certain part of a text after reading, stretched the students' mental imaging and also motivated them to apply visualization to other parts of the story. *Voice in the head* is a strategy that encourages students to reflect on what a character is thinking or feeling at a particular time in the story (Neelands, 1990). Students enact the scene and speak the character's thoughts and feelings aloud. In Macy's (2004) study of drama and reading in an elementary classroom, she found students effectively applying voice in the head to understand the novel *Hatchet* (Paulsen, 1987). The following is an excerpt from her study.

> The teacher, Kelti has led the group to the point in *Hatchet* where Brian is sitting in the chaos after the tornado. Kelti asks the students to think about what Brian would be thinking at this point. She passed the hatchet to the first student.
>
> CHERI: [Receives the hatchet from Kelti] Why does this have to happen?
>
> VIOLA: I do not have nothing. I still have the hatchet.
>
> PAUL: I am scared. I am frightened. There is nothing that I can eat except for the raspberries. All my things are wet. My clothes are soggy. I haven't washed in days. What am I going to do? (p. 246)

In addition to voice in the head, Macy suggests a number of strategies, such as soundscape, caption making, giving witness, and interviews. (For detailed descriptions of the strategies, see Macy, 2004.)

Visual Arts

Semiotic systems such as visual arts, mathematics, music, and body movements are systems we use on a daily basis to express our thoughts and communicate with others. A number of studies have explored the value of visual representation in literacy development. Ernst (1994) found in her study of visual media and literacy that art was a "creative process to offer children broad avenues for expression and understanding" (p. 102) especially in the language arts. Kress (2000), however, noted that within the context of school, visual images are often ignored or overlooked as a mode of conveying ideas and reflecting on literary experiences. Such findings are problematic considering the fact that children use visual representation as a mode of communication long before they begin to use written symbol systems such as the alphabet. The wide use of visual representations in today's communication systems also attests to its effectiveness as a tool for communication.

Carger (2004) proposed the use of art in picture books and storybooks and putting art at the center of literacy events. This is a move away from conceptualizing art as an extension activity to reading and writing. In her study of art and literacy with bilingual children, she found that children engaged in genuine conversations and developed critical literacy skills in responding to art-related questions in picture books, as they talked about artists' motives and techniques of drawing. Carger suggests that teachers plan a variety of art experiences using media to which children do not routinely have access. She urges linking those media to picture books and poetry, and setting clear expectations regarding the use of art materials.

Typically, the visual arts are not accessible to all children. Hoyt (1992) claimed that visual arts are often reserved for children who are gifted or for those in enrichment programs. However, especially children who have difficulty with conventional forms of reading and writing may benefit most from connecting literacy with images. Hoyt adds that exploring images in books and expressing understandings of texts through images enables children to organize their thinking and rehearse for expression through writing. *Sketch to Stretch* (Siegel, 1984, cited in Hoyt, 1992) is an activity that encourages children to use visual images, namely sketches, to express their understandings of text. In this activity, children are given a limited amount of time to quickly sketch an impression of what they just read, without a lot of detail. Children then share their sketches with their peers or teacher and explain how the sketch reflects their understandings of the text. In the process, children clarify the content, reflect on their understandings, and edit or extend their original sketch.

In a study of children's language and the use of pictures, Gray (2006) found that setting up separate centers for certain semiotics within a classroom may segregate and limit the learners from naturally moving from one semiotic system to another; therein lies the challenge for many teachers. Gray posits that children and adults alike spontaneously and naturally draw from multiple semiotic systems in communication, and often this leads to use of more than one semiotic system at a time. She explained that Gardner's proposal of multiple intelligences (1983) as it relates to education, and especially to the understanding of semiotics, seeks to encourage educators and learners to think musically or to draw on basic structural aspects of music, and to use such understandings to further other curricular concepts—not necessarily to separate them out into activities.

Conclusion

In this chapter we have considered research related to content and processes integral to effective instruction in childhood literacy. Our purpose was to provide teachers and other educators with research-based principles and practices that encourage them to view literacy development in the childhood grades from a position that focuses on the contextual features, as well as the conceptual features, of instruction. Throughout, we have emphasized the importance of contextual factors such as flexible student grouping; uninterrupted time for reading and writing; use of quality authentic texts and authentic assessment measures; and scaffolding and demonstrations in instruction. We have stated that using diverse semiotic systems, selecting texts that use rich language, and providing space for children's appropriation of multiple discourses is appropriate, respectful, and essential. Current federal law mandating the use of direct instruction and a back-to-basics approach to reading instruction establish trajectories for development that ignore much current research. The rigid and inflexible nature of prescribed reading programs ignores the communicative and situated nature of literacy, and fails to provide space for child agency (Barton & Hamilton, 1998; Compton-Lily, 2003; Heath, 1983). This chapter, in concert with the other chapters in this book, provides a solid foundation on which to design effective contemporary literacy engagements.

References

Anderson, R. C., Armbruster, B. B., & Roe, M. (1990). Improving the education of reading teachers. *Daedalus, 119*(2), 187–210.

Au, K. H. (1979). Participation structures in a reading lesson with Hawaiian children: Analysis of culturally appropriate instructional events. *Anthropology and Education Quarterly, 11*(2), 91–115.

Bakhtin, M. (1981). Discourse in the novel. In M. Holoquist (Ed.), *The dialogic imagination: Four essays* (pp. 259–422). Austin: University of Texas Press.

Ballenger, C. (1999). *Teaching other people's children*. New York: Teachers College Press.

Barber, M. (1997). *A reading revolution: How we can teach every child to read well*. Preliminary Report of the Literacy Task Force. London, UK: Literacy Task Force.

Barton, D., & Hamilton, M. (1998). *Local literacies: Reading and writing in one community*. New York: Routledge.

Baugh, J., & Hymes, D. (2002). *Beyond Ebonics: Linguistic pride and racial prejudice*. New York: Oxford University Press.

Beach, R. (2007). *Teachingmedialiteracy.com*. New York: Teachers College Press.

Bear, R., Dole, J., Echevaris, A., Hasbrouck, G., Paris, S., Shanahan, T., & Tinajero, P. (2007). *McGraw Hill Reading Series*. New York: McGraw Hill.

Beard, R. (2000). Research and the National Literacy Strategy. *Oxford Review of Education*, 26(3/4), 421–36.

Beck, I. L. (1997). *Questioning the author: An approach to enhancing student engagement with text*. Newark, DE: International Reading Association.

Berardo, S. A. (2006). The use of authentic materials in the teaching of reading. *Reading Matrix*, 6(2), 60–69.

Blair, T. R., Rupley, W. H., & Nichols, W. D. (2007). The effective teacher of reading: Considering the "what" and "how" of instruction. *Reading Teacher*, 60(5), 432–38.

Britton, J. N. (1993). *Language and learning* (2nd ed.). Portsmouth, NH: Boynton/Cook. (Original work published 1972)

Cambourne, B. (1995). Toward an educationally relevant theory of literacy learning: Twenty years of inquiry. *Reading Teacher*, 49(3), 182–90.

Carger, C. L. (2004). Art and literacy with bilingual children. *Language Arts*, 81(4), 283–93.

Cazden, C. (2002). *Classroom discourse: The language of teaching and learning* (2nd ed.). Portsmouth, NH: Heinemann.

Chall, J. S. (1967). *Learning to read: The great debate*. New York: McGraw-Hill.

Chall, J. S. (1996). *Stages of reading development* (2nd ed.). Fort Worth, TX: Harcourt-Brace.

Chapman, M. (1995). Designing literacy learning experiences in a multiage classroom. *Language Arts*, 72(6), 416–28.

Chittenden, T., & Salinger, M. (2001). *Inquiry into meaning: An investigation of learning to read* (Rev. ed.). New York: Teachers College Press.

Chomsky, C. (1969). *The acquisition of syntax in children from 5–10*. Cambridge, MA: MIT Press.

Chomsky, C. (1972). Stages in language development and reading exposure. *Harvard Educational Review, 42*(1), 1–33.

Clark, K. F., & Graves, M. F. (2005). Scaffolding students' comprehension of text. *Reading Teacher, 58*(6), 570–80.

Clay, M. (1998). *By different paths to common outcomes.* York, ME: Stenhouse.

Compton-Lily, C. (2003). *Reading families: The literate lives of urban children.* New York: Teachers College Press.

Cox, B. E., Fang, Z., & Otto, B. S. (1997). Preschoolers' developing ownership of the literate register. *Reading Research Quarterly, 32*(1), 34–53.

Cullinan, B. (Ed.). (1992). *Invitation to read: More children's literature in the reading program.* Newark, DE: International Reading Association.

Cummins, J. (1991). Interdependence of first and second-language proficiency in bilingual children. In E. Bialystok (Ed.), *Language processing in bilingual children* (pp. 70–89). Cambridge, UK: Cambridge University Press.

Cunningham, J. W., Spadorcia, S. A., Erickson, K. A., Koppenhaver, D. A., Sturm, J. M., & Yoder, D. E. (2005). Investigating the instructional supportiveness of leveled texts. *Reading Research Quarterly, 40*(4), 410–27.

Cunningham, P. (2005a). "If they don't read much, how they ever gonna get good?" *Reading Teacher, 59*(1), 88–90.

Cunningham, P. (2005b). *Phonics they use: Words for reading and writing,* (4th ed.). Boston: Pearson, Allyn & Bacon.

Dahl, K., & Freppon, P. A. (1995). A comparison of innercity children's interpretations of reading and writing instruction in early grades in skills-based and whole language classrooms. *Reading Research Quarterly, 30*(1), 50–74.

Delpit, L., & Dowdy, J. K. (Eds.). (2002). *The skin that we speak: Thoughts on language and culture in the classroom.* New York: New Press.

Duckworth, E. (2006). *"The having of wonderful ideas" and other essays on teaching and learning* (3rd ed.). New York: Teachers College Press.

Durkin, D. (1978–1979). What classroom observation reveals about reading comprehension instruction. *Reading Research Quarterly, 14*(4), 481–533.

Dyson, A. H. (1989). *Multiple worlds of child writers: Friends learning to write.* New York: Teachers College Press.

Dyson, A. H. (2001a). Where are the childhoods in childhood literacy? An exploration in outer (school) space. *Journal of Early Childhood Literacy, 1*(1), 9–39.

Dyson, A. H. (2001b). Writing and children's symbolic repertoires: Development unhinged. In S. B. Neuman & D. Dickinson (Eds.), *Handbook on early literacy research* (pp. 126–41). New York: Guilford Press.

Dyson, A. H. (2006). On saying it right (write): "Fix-its" in the foundations of learning to write. *Research in the Teaching of English, 41*(1), 8–42.

Ernst, K. (1994). *Picturing learning: Artists and writers in the classroom.* Portsmouth, NH: Heinemann.

Fassler, R. (2003). *Room for talk: Teaching and learning in a multilingual kindergarten.* New York: Teachers College Press.

Fountas, I. C., & Pinnell, G. S. (1996). *Guided reading: Good first teaching for all children.* Portsmouth, NH: Heinemann.

Fountas, I. C., & Pinnell, G. S. (1999). *Matching books to readers: Using leveled books in guided reading, K-3* (L. Bridges, Ed.). Portsmouth, NH: Heinemann.

Fountas, I. C., & Pinnell, G. S. (2006). *Teaching for comprehending and fluency: Thinking, talking, and writing about reading, K–8.* Portsmouth, NH: Heinemann

Freppon, P. A., & Dahl, K. L. (1998). Balanced instruction: Insights and considerations. *Reading Research Quarterly, 33*(2), 240–51.

Friere, P., & Macedo, D. (1987). *Literacy: Reading the word and the world.* South Hadley, MA: Bergin & Garvey.

Fry, E. (1975). The readability principle. *Language Arts, 52*(6), 847–51.

Fry, E. B. (1987). The varied uses of readability measurement today. *Journal of Reading, 30*(4), 338–43.

Gallas, K. (1994). *The language of learning: How children talk, write, dance, draw, and sing their understanding of the world.* New York: Teachers College Press.

Gallas, K. (2003). *Imagination and literacy: A teacher's search for the heart of learning.* New York: Teachers College Press.

Gardner, H. (1983). *Multiple intelligences.* New York: Basic Books.

Gee, J. P. (1996). *Social linguistics and literacies: Ideology in discourse* (2nd ed.). Bristol, PA: Taylor & Francis.

Gee, J. P. (2005). *An introduction to discourse analysis theory and method* (2nd ed.). New York: Routledge.

Genishi, C., Stires, S. E., & Yung-Chan, D. (2001). Writing in an integrated curriculum: Prekindergarten English language learners as symbol makers. *Elementary School Journal, 101*(4), 399–416.

Goodman, K. (Ed.). (2006). *The truth about DIBELS: What it is, what it does.* Portsmouth, NH: Heinemann.

Goodwin, P. (Ed.). (2005). *The literate classroom* (2nd ed.). London: Fulton.

Graves, D. H., & Kittle, P. (2005). *Inside writing: How to teach the details of craft.* Portsmouth, NH: Heinemann.

Gray, E. C. (2006). Children's use of language and pictures in classroom inquiry. *Language Arts, 83*(3), 227–37.

Guskey, T. R. (2003). How classroom assessments improve learning. *Educational Leadership, 60*(5), 6–11.

Halliday, M. A. K. (1975). The functional bases of language. In B. Bernstein (Ed.). *Class, codes and control, Vol. 2: Applied studies towards a sociology of language.* London: Routledge & Kegan Paul.

Halliday, M. A. K. (1980). Three aspects of children's language development: Learning language, learning through language, and learning about language. In Y. Goodman, M. Haussler, & D. Strickland (Eds.), *Oral and written language development research: Impact on the schools* (pp. 7–19). Newark, DE: International Reading Association.

Halliday, M. A. K., & Hasan, R. (1976). *Cohesion in English.* London: Longman.

Harste, J. (2000). Supporting critical conversations in classrooms. In K. M. Pierce (Ed.), *Adventuring with books: A booklist for pre-K–grade 6* (12th ed., pp. 507–44). Urbana, IL: National Council of Teachers of English.

Harste, J., Woodward, V., & Burke, C. (1984). *Language stories and literacy lessons.* Portsmouth, NH: Heinemann.

Hart, B., & Risley, T. (1995). *Meaningful differences in the everyday experience of young American children.* Baltimore, MD: P. H. Brookes.

Heath, S. B. (1983). *Ways with words: Language, life and work in communities and classrooms.* Cambridge: Cambridge University Press.

Heathcote, D. (1984). *Dorothy Heathcote: Collected writings on education and drama* (L. Johnson & C. O'Neill, Eds.). London: Hutchinson.

Holdaway, D. (1979). *The foundations of literacy.* Sydney, AU: Ashton-Scholastic; Exeter, NH: Heinemann.

Hoyt, L. (1992). Many ways of knowing: Using drama, oral interactions, and the visual arts to enhance reading comprehension. *Reading Teacher, 45*(8), 580–84.

Hoyt, L. (2007). *Interactive read-alouds: Linking standards, fluency, and comprehension.* Portsmouth, NH: Heinemann.

International Reading Association/National Council of Teachers of English [IRA/NCTE]. (2008). *Read, write, think: Literacy engagements.* Retrieved February 22, 2008, from http://www.readwritethink.org/literacy/index.html

Jimenez, R., Garcia, G., & Pearson, P. D. (1995). Three children, two languages, and strategic reading: Case studies in bilingual/monolingual reading. *American Educational Research Journal, 32*(1), 67–93.

Johnston, P. (2004). *Choice words: How our language affects children's learning.* Portland, ME: Stenhouse.

Knipper, K. J., & Duggan, T. J. (2006). Writing to learn across the curriculum: Tools for comprehension in content area classes. *Reading Teacher, 59*(5), 462–70.

Kress, G. (2000). Multimodality. In B. Cope & M. Kalantzis (Eds.), *Multiliteracies: Literacy learning and the design of social futures* (pp. 182–202). London: Routledge.

Kucer, S. B. (2005). *Dimensions of literacy: A conceptual base for teaching reading and writing in school settings* (2nd ed.). Mahwah, NJ: Erlbaum.

Kutz, E. (1997). *Language and literacy: Studying discourse in communities and classrooms.* Portsmouth, NH: Boynton/Cook.

Labbo, L. D. (2005). Books and computer response activities that support literacy development. *Reading Teacher, 59*(3), 288–92.

Labov, W. (1972). *Language in the inner city: Studies in the Black English vernacular.* Philadelphia: University of Pennsylvania Press.

Ladson-Billings, G. (1994). *The dreamkeepers: Successful teachers of African American children.* San Francisco: Jossey-Bass.

Lee, S. (2006). Using children's text to communicate with parents of English-language learners. *Young Children, 61*(5), 18–25.

Levy, B. A., Abello, B., Lysynchuk, L. (1997). Transfer from word training to reading in context: Gains in reading fluency and comprehension. *Language Disability Quarterly, 20*(3), 173–88.

Lindfors, J. W. (1999). *Children's inquiry: Using language to make sense of the world.* New York: Teachers College Press.

Macy, L. (2004). A novel study through drama. *Reading Teacher, 58*(3), 240–49.

Malloy, J. A., & Gambrell, L. B. (2006). Approaching the unavoidable: Literacy instruction and the Internet. *Reading Teacher, 59*(5), 482–84.

Manzo, K. K. (2007, August 29). Federal reading research overlooks popular texts. *Education Week* (p. 8).

McGraw-Hill. (2007). *Fox in a box: Diagnostic literacy assessment system.* New York: McGraw-Hill.

McMaster, J. (1998). "Doing" literature: Using drama to build literacy classrooms. *Reading Teacher, 51*(7), 574–84.

Medina, C. L. (2004). Drama wor(l)ds: Explorations of Latina/o realistic fiction. *Language Arts, 81*(4), 272–83.

Medina, C. L., & Campona, G. (2006). Performing identities through drama and teatro practices in multilingual classrooms. *Language Arts, 83*(4), 332–41.

Meyer, R. J., & Manning, M. (2007). *Reading and teaching*. Mahwah, NJ: Erlbaum.

Moll, L., Saez, R., & Dworin, J. (2001). Exploring biliteracy: Two student case examples of writing as a social practice. *Elementary School Journal, 101*(4), 435–50.

National Institutes of Health. National Institute of Child Health and Human Development. (NICHD). (2000). *Report of the National Reading Panel. Teaching children to read* (NIH Publication No. 00-4769). Washington, DC: Government Printing Office.

Neelands, J. (1990). *Structuring drama work: A handbook of available forms in theatre and drama* (T. Goode, Ed.). Cambridge: Cambridge University Press.

Neufield, P. (2005). Comprehension instruction in content area classes. *Reading Teacher, 59*(4), 302–12.

Opitz, M. F. (1999). *Flexible grouping in reading, grades 2–5*. New York: Scholastic.

Owocki, G., & Goodman, Y. (2002). *Kidwatching: Documenting children's literacy development*. Portsmouth, NH: Heinemann.

Pahl, K., & Rowsell, J. (2006). *Literacy and education: Understanding the new literacy studies in the classroom*. London: Chapman.

Pardo, L. S. (2004). What every teacher needs to know about comprehension. *Reading Teacher, 58*(3), 272–80.

Paulsen, G. (1987). *Hatchet*. New York: Bradbury Press.

Perry, T. (1996). *Teaching Malcolm X*. New York: Routledge.

Rogovin, P. (1998a). *Classroom interviews*. Portsmouth, NH: Heinemann.

Rogovin, P. (1998b). *Classroom interviews in action* [videotape]. Portsmouth, NH: Heinemann.

Ross, E. P., & Roe, B. D. (1977). Creative drama builds proficiency in reading. In N. H. Brizedine & J. L. Thomas (Eds.), *Learning through dramatics: Ideas for teachers and librarians* (pp. 44–51). Phoenix, AZ: Oryx.

Schlick Noe, K. L., & Johnson, N. J. (1999). *Getting started with literature circles*. Norwood, MA: Christopher-Gordon.

Schwartz, R. M. (2005). Decisions, decisions: Responding to primary students during guided reading. *Reading Teacher, 58*(5), 436–43.

Serafini, F. (2003). Informing our practice: Modernist, transactional, and critical perspectives on children's literature and reading instruction. *Reading Online, 6* (6). Retrieved December 3, 2006, http://www.readingonline.org/articles/art_index.asp?HREF=serafini/index.html

Shanahan, T. (2006). Copernicus. *AMC reading system: Vol. 1* (p. 130). Parsippany, NJ: Pearson Education.

Short, K., Kaufman, G., & Kahn, L. (2000). "I just need to draw": Responding to literature across multiple sign systems. *Reading Teacher, 54*(2), 160–71.

Short, K., Kaufman, G., Kaser, S., Kahn, L. H., & Crawford, K. M. (1999). Teacher-watching: Examining teacher talk in literature circles. *Language Arts, 76*(5), 377–85.

Siegel, M. (1984). Sketch to stretch. In O. Cochran (Ed.), *Reading, writing, and caring* (p. 178). Katonah, New York: Richard C. Owen.

Siegel, M. (1995). More than words: The generative power of transmediation for learning. *Canadian Journal of Education, 20*(4), 455–75.

Siegel, M. (2006). Rereading the signs: Multimodal transformations in the field of literacy education. *Language Arts, 84*(1), 65–77.

Sipe, L. R. (2002). The construction of literary understanding by first and second graders in oral response to picture storybook read-alouds. *Reading Research Quarterly, 35*(2), 252–75.

Smith, F. (1978). *Reading without nonsense.* New York: Teachers College Press.

Smith, F. (2004). *Understanding reading* (6th ed.). Mahwah, NJ: Erlbaum.

Smitherman, G. (1994). "The blacker the berry, the sweeter the juice": African American student writers and the national assessment of educational progress. In A. H. Dyson & C. Genishi (Eds.), *The need for story: Cultural diversity in classroom and community* (pp. 80–101). Urbana, IL: National Council of Teachers of English.

Smitherman, G. (2002). Toward a national public policy on language. In L. Delpit & J. K. Dowdy (Eds.), *The skin that we speak: Thoughts on language and culture in the classroom* (pp. 163–78). New York: New Press.

Snow, C., Griffin, P., & Burns, M. (Eds.). (2005). *Knowledge to support the teaching of reading: Preparing teachers for a changing world*. San Francisco: Jossey-Bass.

Stannard, J., & Huxford, L. (2007). *The literacy game: The story of the National Literacy Strategy*. New York: Routledge.

Street, B., & Lefstein, A. (Eds.) (2007). *Literacy: An advanced resource book for students*. London: Routledge.

Taylor, B. M., Pearson, P. D., Clark, K., & Walpole, S. (2000). Effective schools and accomplished teachers: Lessons about primary-grade reading instruction in low-income schools. *Elementary School Journal, 101*(2), 121–66.

Taylor, B. M., Pearson, P. D., Peterson, D. S., & Rodriguez, M. C. (2003). Reading growth in high poverty classrooms: The influence of teacher practices that encourage cognitive engagement in literacy learning. *Elementary School Journal, 104*(1), 3–28.

Teale, B., & Sulzby, E. (1986). *Emergent literacy: Reading and writing*. Norwood, NJ: Ablex.

Thorndike, E. L. (1913). *Educational psychology, Vol. 1: The original nature of man*. New York: Teachers College, Columbia University.

Vygotsky, L. S. (1978). *Mind in society: The development of higher psychological processes*. Cambridge, MA: Harvard University Press.

Wells, C. G. (1986). *The meaning makers: Children learning language and using language to learn*. Portsmouth, NH: Heinemann.

Wheeler, R. S., & Swords, R. (2004). Codeswitching: Tools of language and culture transform the dialectally diverse classroom. *Language Arts, 81*(6), 470–80.

What We Know about the Teaching of Adolescent Reading

KAREN DELBRIDGE

Laramie County School District #1, Cheyenne, Wyoming

In all things, in all subjects, there is a story to be told. It could be a science concept, how to solve a math equation, the history of the United States, or what we know about the teaching of adolescent reading. Like many teachers, I love a good story. While growing up in the South, one of my favorite things to do was sit around the kitchen table with the women in my family and listen to stories. We would all sit and eat banana pudding or some other family dessert, drink sweet tea, and laugh, talk, and tell stories. I found myself running back and forth from the kitchen to the humid outdoors, where the men in my family would sit on the front porch or gather around outside, telling their own legends. Whether from the women or the men, the story was always about life.

Literacy is about learning to read the world, and our world is constantly changing. "Literacy is a set of skills that reflect the needs of the time" (Beers, 2007). When our students come to us with lived experiences, we must remember that those experiences are similar to, and different from, our own. When we think about the teaching of adolescent reading, we must realize that we are helping students to write the story of their own lives while they are learning to read the world. We are one of the many authors who help create the character they will become. When I look over my years of teaching, studying, and researching adolescent literacy, I am reminded of Atticus Finch's advice to his young daughter, Scout, in *To Kill a Mockingbird*: "First of all, if you can learn a simple trick, Scout, you'll get along a lot better with all kinds of folks. You never really understand a person until you consider things from his point of view—until you climb into his skin and walk around in it" (Lee, 1960, p. 30). Atticus was more a teacher of adolescents than he realized. He knew the importance of getting an inside perspective, and he knew that all people just want to be understood. That's how our students are. They want to be heard, they want to be understood, and they want to understand. Through the various texts they read, whether they learn from a character in a book or an expert in a particular field, they are able to "climb into" someone else's skin for a while, and try to consider things from his or her point of view. They want to participate in literacy practices that are suited to their own lives in their world.

In order to help students, we must be willing to look within ourselves and be reflective practitioners. Teachers hold their own subjectivity about why texts are chosen and which viewpoints are heard. The teacher can be the one who allows voices to be heard, or voices to be silenced. Palmer (1998) noted that teaching, like any human activity, emerges from one's inwardness, for better or worse. As we teach, we project the condition of our soul onto our students, onto what we teach and our way of being together. Palmer also said that teaching holds a mirror to the soul. "If I am willing to look in that mirror and not run from what I see, I have a chance to gain self-knowledge—and knowing myself is as crucial to good teaching as knowing my students and my subject" (p. 2). Being reflective about who we are and questioning where we're going is crucial to educating our students and impacting our schools. Teachers who are really good at what they do are metacognitive, bringing a spirit of inquiry to their teaching. Not only are they reflective about their teaching, but they are always asking questions while expecting the same from students.

Learning *with* adolescents is what makes teaching spectacular. As teachers, we must know and understand why we teach reading the way we do. In order to understand how to teach adolescents, we must not only look within ourselves, but we must learn to listen to sound research and listen to the students we teach. They have their own story to tell us about how best to teach them. Alvermann (2006) recommended that we remain open to the possibility that listening to students for guidance in adapting our instruction is both feasible and worthwhile.

Reading to Construct Meaning

Literacy is a dynamic interaction of the social and cognitive realms, with textual understandings growing from a student's knowledge of his or her world to knowledge of the external world (Commission on Reading, 2004a; Langer, 2002). We know that adolescent literacy is the idea that adolescents already possess knowledge and skills, and they want to participate in literacy practices that are suited to their own lives (National Council of Teachers of English, 2006). Since literacy is about learning to read the world, then we must assist our students in exploring how to read the changing world and participate in the different situations in their lives.

When I talk to middle and high school teachers about teaching reading, one of the problems I see is that reading is defined so differently. Some believe a good reader knows how to decode words, while others believe a good reader is able to remember what is read. According to the Commission on Reading (2004a),

> Reading is a complex, purposeful, social and cognitive process in which readers simultaneously use their knowledge of spoken and written language, their knowledge of the topic of the text, and their knowledge of their culture to construct meaning. Reading is not a technical skill acquired once and for all in the primary grades, but rather a developmental process. A reader's competence continues to grow through engagement with various types of texts and wide reading for various purposes over a lifetime. (p. 1)

Each student views our world in a different way. When we are teaching our students how to read, we must realize that students come from different places, have different backgrounds, and have different experiences. If literacy is culturally framed and defined, adolescents will be able to identify the meaning of texts and create their own personal interpretations. In addition, they should gain an awareness of how texts may challenge their own beliefs (Elkins & Luke, 1999; Ferdman, 1990). Most adolescents do not need further instruction in phonics. Phonics instruction has not been seen to improve reading comprehension in older students (Commission on Reading, 2004a; National Institutes of Health, 2000). In instances where older students need additional assistance to construct meaning within text, instruction should be "targeted and embedded in authentic reading experiences" (Commission on Reading, 2004a, What Current Research Is Showing Teachers, para. 3). Adolescents need to be able to monitor for meaning, use and create schemata, ask questions, determine importance, infer, use sensory and emotional images, and synthesize (Keene, 2007). Adolescent literacy education is the roundtable where teachers shape identities and citizens, cultures and communities (Elkins & Luke, 1999).

Not only do we want our adolescents to read and construct meaning, but we want them to be able to communicate effectively in different situations. We want them to use their knowledge of spoken and written language, their knowledge of the topic of the text, and their knowledge of their culture to construct meaning. The words of a human language exist to allow people to take and communicate various perspectives on experience. Language is about communicating perspectives and experiences in the world (Gee, 2000). According to Probst (2007), if students are to participate in conversations effectively and productively, they must develop the predispositions, habits, and standards that will make such participation possible. The conversations students have about their reading, which focus on the strategies they use and their language knowledge, help adolescents build confidence in their reading and become better readers (Commission on Reading, 2004a, 2004b; Goodman & Marek, 1996).

The sociocultural view of literacy demands that reading, writing, and speaking be looked upon as not one thing, but as many different socioculturally situated reading, writing, and speaking practices (Gee, 2000). Students must not only participate in these practices, but they must ultimately take responsibility for their own discourse (Probst, 2007). Street's study (1995) examined the socializing of literacy and how people perceive themselves and others. He looked at the sense of tradition that people hold, and he found that literacy may not come from only the home culture. This discovery has so much to do with how students approach text, the connections they make, and the questions they ask.

We act and speak according to the situations we are in. For instance, our students are going to perform differently in class than they do at a football game. Barton and Hamilton (1998) believe that people react differently in situations on the basis of social aspect and the way they were enculturated into literacy. They regard literacy as not limited to only reading and writing, but as situated within a particular context or community.

A few years ago, I worked with an eighth grade student named Pedro, who was reading *Buried Onions* (Soto, 1997). One day in class he connected the story to his family heritage. He said that it reminded him of going to the ranch in Mexico, and how his aunts work for money. Pedro discussed the lack of jobs and his aunts' struggle to make money on their farms trying to raise their own crops. These family interactions represent a part of Pedro's culture and lived experiences. He was bringing the knowledge of his culture to help construct meaning.

Lave and Wenger (1991) emphasized the significance of shifting the "focus from the individual as learner to learning as participation in the social world" (p. 43). They stated that the view or theory of social practice claims that learning, thinking, and knowing arise from the socially and culturally structured world. Participation is based on situated negotiation or renegotiation of meaning in the world; thus, understanding and experience are in constant interaction.

Research on literacy from a social and cultural practice suggests that literacy is not limited to only reading and writing, but it is situated. Literacy practices are what people *do* with literacy, and the ways that people act and behave are connected to structure and power. The culture of the family, school, and community becomes a significant way that students are educated. The ways in which students make meaning of the text, whether narrative or informational, is related through their own experiences. When students are given greater control over conversations, interpretation, and topics, their engagement is enhanced while relationships are built within the classroom community.

Students need to be offered opportunities to read diverse texts in all content areas in order to see themselves within the text. The text can serve as a tool to help students think critically about issues they face on a daily basis. When they are given opportunities to discuss these texts, students become more aware of how they are situated in the world outside of school. In the process, they gain the opportunity to take social action that will serve various communities in their world.

Accessing Knowledge

Reading instruction that is effective will help learners make sense of language (Commission on Reading, 2004b). Whatever the text may be, students bring prior experiences and background knowledge to that text, and teachers must find a way to assist students in activating that prior knowledge. When we activate prior knowledge, comprehension improves because learners connect new information and experiences to prior experiences. Robb (2003) stated that prior knowledge is stored in the brain in frameworks called *schema* or *schemata*. Schema theory argues that our minds organize memories and determine when those memories are activated. Schemata shape the meanings we construct as we read (Ruddell & Unrau, 2004). A reader uses past experiences and knowledge, and then interacts with and constructs meaning from new information in texts (Anderson, 1984; Minsky, 1975; Robb, 2003). Rosenblatt (1982) indicated that thought and feeling are legitimate components of literacy interpretation. Whether a text is informational or literary, it will demand a response from its reader, building on the meaning that the reader brings to the learning situation. Rosenblatt also noted that sometimes students will have an efferent and aesthetic response to a text. Vacca and Vacca (2005) explained that an *efferent* response occurs when a student focuses attention on the ideas and information encountered in a text. An *aesthetic* response to text is "driven by personal feelings and attitudes that are stirred by the reader's transactions with the text" (p. 20). In a study of adolescents, emotion was a powerful connection for students. This kind of response led to the ways that students evaluated text, and thus seemed to move students to think, believe, and even act differently than they did before (Delbridge, 2006).

Galda and Beach (2004) argued that response to literature is a cultural activity. They demonstrated how dissimilarities in responses can reflect differences in students' sociocultural experiences when related to socioeconomic class. They concluded that the meaning of a student's response was grounded in "cultural and historical worlds, activity systems, and tools, and suggested the value of instruction based on developmentally appropriate inquiry about the worlds or systems portrayed in literature as well as students' own related experiences" (p. 863).

Research on student response has focused on how various texts affect response, how experiences affect response, and the context in which response is generated. Research on text consists primarily on the content of the text and focuses on the authenticity and stance of the author (Galda & Beach, 2004). Authors of the text can assume a stance toward the societal norms portrayed, either advocating or attacking the characters' sociocultural practices (Sutherland, 1985). Readers then can critique the texts for accuracy and authenticity: whether the social norms portrayed actually represent a culture (Cai, 1997).

Renee, an eighth grader, was good at critiquing texts for accuracy. In class one day, she took a stance against an author. She felt that the author was stereotyping a group of people. She said, "I use to live in Fresno, and I could not believe what I was reading because I never saw any of that. My stepfamily is of that culture, and nobody did anything wrong just because of who they were. I mean, they were given chances. I thought it [the book] was stereotyping people. Like it was putting out there that they weren't very smart, weren't capable of going through life without getting in a lot of trouble, and it made me feel wrong. It was just wrong, and I could not see how someone could judge someone by the way they look."

Readers have expectations of how characters within a text should behave, and they are sometimes unsure of what to expect when they approach an informational text. When students do have expectations, these are shaped by the cultures in which they live. Encisco (1994) connected response to cultural practices. Students might resist or reject a text that does not reflect their cultural expectations. These responses can also take the form of resisting the social norms perceived to be operating within the classroom structure. Renee was critiquing the accuracy and authenticity of the social norms in the text—whether they actually represented the culture. She disagreed and presented reasons for her feelings.

Students approach a text with a certain amount of lived experience. They are able to comprehend texts when they use prior knowledge to construct meaning (Beers, 2003; Robb, 2003). Prior knowledge reflects the experiences, conceptual understandings, attitudes, and values that a student brings to a text; thus it is important to determine what connections to personal knowledge and experience the students are making. Renee brought her lived experiences from Fresno and her family. In a situation like Renee's, reading becomes a conversation of the reader's prior knowledge and meanings of the text that work together to create a greater sense of things (Wilhelm, 1997). Teaching students to monitor their learning, look for information, interpret literature, and draw upon their own experiences enhances their motivation (National Council of Teachers of English, 2006; Guthrie et al., 1996). Making meaning from texts is critical to reading comprehension, and focused discussion about various academic texts can help students learn to read better at the same time that they comprehend and learn more about a specific field (Applebee, Langer, Nystrand, & Gamoran, 2003; National Council of Teachers of English, 2006).

Strategic Instruction

During our time of teaching, we can probably think of a student who has occasionally liked to remind us how much he or she hates reading. I had one student who would try to find an excuse to do anything else other than read. One day I asked him what his favorite sandwich was. He looked at me strangely, so I rephrased the question and asked him, "If you could eat any kind of sandwich, what would it be?" He went on to describe a meatball sandwich with melted cheese and lots of sauce. He described all the stuff inside it. I told him that I looked at reading a lot like a sandwich. The bread is important, but generally what's on the inside is what really makes the sandwich. I don't read for the words; I read for all the really good stuff inside. I told him that we just had not found his sandwich.

Engagement is key to student learning. Abundant research suggests that the isolated skill instruction that students receive may perpetuate low literacy achievement rather than improving competence and engagement in complex reading tasks (Allington, 2001; Alvermann & Moore, 1991; Brown, 1991; Commission on Reading, 2004b; Heibert, 1991; Hull & Rose, 1989; Knapp & Shields, 1991; Sizer, 1992). Vacca and Vacca (2005) stated that reading is a purposeful activity: students read to achieve some end, and when readers are engaged in the text, they are knowledgeable, strategic, motivated, and socially interactive. Sustained experiences with diverse texts in fiction and nonfiction that offer multiple perspectives on life experiences can enhance motivation (Greenleaf, Schoenbach, Cziko, & Mueller, 2001; Kuhn & Stahl, 2000; National Council of Teachers of English, 2006). And different situations require different reading approaches (Kucer, 2005). When we look at narrative and informational text, we must give students the strategies to approach these different text structures and opportunities to choose these texts. Adolescent readers need opportunities and instructional support to read many diverse texts in order to gain experience, build fluency, and develop a range as readers (Commission on Reading, 2004a; Greenleaf et al., 2001). Effective instruction is grounded in a professional knowledge of how we read and how we learn to read (Commission on Reading, 2004b).

What does it mean to think deeply or to truly understand something? I like Keene's (2007) dimensions of understanding. She said that when we understand, we concentrate, dwell, struggle, manipulate, explore, discuss, create, feel, and ultimately remember (p. 35). When we think about how our students learn to read for a variety of purposes, we must reflect on how we view comprehension, and how we define it. Beers (2003) noted that comprehension requires purposeful, strategic effort on the reader's part. Comprehension should be about the thinking that we want and expect students to do. So what do we want students to do well? Beers believes that students need to "anticipate the direction of text (predicting), seeing the action of the text (visualizing), contemplating and then correcting whatever confusions we encounter (clarifying), connecting what's in the text to what is in our mind to make an educated guess about what's going on (inferencing)" (p. 45–46).

Giving students strategies to encourage discussion and deepen understanding will assist in reading comprehension. We should scaffold our instruction to support students in the use of comprehension strategies, to bring them to a level of evaluation where they are doing a critical analysis of text that they may not have been able to do previously. Ultimately, we want our students to be responsible for their own learning, so we need to teach students how to be metacognitive. *Metacognition* is simply thinking about one's own thinking (Garner, 1987; Ruddell & Unrau, 2004). It is our awareness about learning that takes place in different settings, and it is our ability to think about and control our own learning (Morrow & Gambrell, 2000; Vacca & Vacca, 2005). Teachers who scaffold instruction to assist students are knowledgeable about where their students are, and are able to organize instruction to meet students' needs.

Reading is a thought process, so when students are evaluating a text, they comprehend the text on different levels. Students read and question at the literal level to obtain information explicitly from the text. *Interpretive* questioning refers to when the student is reading between the lines. Students put information together, observe relationships, and make inferences. *Applied* questioning refers to when a student is reading beyond the lines, using information to reflect, understand viewpoints, express opinions, and form new ideas. Students can also *visualize*, which occurs when the student makes mental pictures or sensory images (Daniels & Zemelman, 2004). When students *synthesize* information, they evaluate, question the author, think critically, and draw additional insights and fresh ideas from the material presented (Vacca & Vacca, 2005). Students must have the freedom to question what they read, to ask why characters are doing what they're doing, to apply those actions to their own life, and then to think beyond the book.

Today's students will read a wide variety of texts, and they must be able to think critically and make judgments about the bias and motivation of the author (Keene & Zimmerman, 2007). We need to give our students strategies to use before, during, and after reading. By giving our students the tools and strategies they need to read various texts, we are preparing them to be successful in any class or situation. We want students to use strategies to help deepen comprehension and gain better insight into the material approached.

I can still remember the moment when I realized that I was not preparing my students to read for a variety of purposes over a lifetime. I was teaching eighth-grade English at the time, and I had a weekly meeting with the science, social studies, and math teachers in my core team. We were discussing student reading, and the science teacher commented that her students weren't understanding the chapter on plate tectonics. She said, "They keep saying that they don't understand." I remember thinking, *What have I done to help my students in the science classroom?* I had been so busy with the instruction of narrative text in my class that I had never considered that many of my students left my class to go to science and read a different structure of text. Our students read for a variety of purposes, and teaching text structure will help them understand what they are reading. The recognition and use of organization are essential processes underlying comprehension and retention when reading is concerned (Herber, 1978; Niles, 1965; Salisbury, 1934; Smith, N., 1964). External text structure is the exterior design of the text: for example, the organization of a textbook chapter into sections with headings and subheadings in bold, and a summary at the end. Internal text structure is the inner design of the text: for example, the organization of information within a chapter using a structure such as problem and solution, comparison and contrast, or cause and effect.

Teachers might consider using graphic organizers to help students see the organizational patterns of text. The use of an anticipation guide could assist in setting the reader up for the text. Then to help with comprehension throughout the reading of the text, students could utilize a reading guide. The reading guide accompanies reading and provides instructional support as students need it. The guide also influences content acquisition and prompts higher-order thinking (Beers, 2003). Both these guides can help students become actively engaged in the text, thus promoting comprehension. Students will be more successful if the teacher is modeling the use of various strategies.

When we talk about scaffolding instruction for our students and offering comprehension strategies to assist the reader, we need to know our students' strengths and weaknesses. We must find ways to assess learning, so we know where our students are in their learning and where their comprehension is breaking down. Assessment is not external to instruction, but is an essential part of teaching (National Council of Teachers of English, 2006). Even though we live in a world of high-stakes testing, we must be constantly aware of our purpose and of the reasons we teach reading the way we do. We also must remember that continuous assessment is key to effective reading instruction. Ongoing assessment happens when we regularly monitor student performance to determine how closely it matches the instructional goal (Deshler, Schumaker, & Woodruff, 2004). Assessment should focus on underlying knowledge in the curriculum and on thinking strategies (Commission on Reading, 2004a; Darling-Hammond & Faulk, 1997; Langer, 2002; Smith, M., 1991). Assessments that inform instruction provide information about what the student is learning and what instruction needs to be changed or adapted to be more effective (Deshler, et al., 2004).

Responsibility

We know that reading is a complex, purposeful, social, and cognitive process in which readers simultaneously use their knowledge of spoken and written language, their knowledge of the topic of the text, and their knowledge of their culture to construct meaning (Commission on Reading, 2004b). We also know that reading is not a technical skill acquired once, but rather a developmental process; and that a reader's competence continues to grow through engagement with various types of texts and wide reading for various purposes over a lifetime. If we know and understand this, then when we look at the content classes our students take, we are reminded of the different experiences they have during the day and the different situations in which they must perform. When we look at this changing world and know that our literacy skills reflect the needs of the time, we cannot help but reflect on our responsibility as teachers to empower our students and deepen their understanding. Teaching reading to adolescents is no longer the sole responsibility of the English or language arts teacher. Teachers of all subjects are assisting students in understanding text within their content areas. All teachers have an influence on shaping the literacy practices within their classrooms. We want our students to be metacognitive, and ultimately to become responsible for their learning. We are not only helping adolescents to write the story of their own lives, but we are also helping them to read the world.

References

Allington, R. L. (2001). *What really matters for struggling readers: Designing research-based programs.* New York: Longman.

Alvermann, D. E. (2006). Youth in the middle: Our guides to improved literacy instruction? *Voices from the Middle, 14*(2), 7–13.

Alvermann, D. E., & Moore, D. (1991). Secondary school reading. In P. D. Pearson, R. Barr, M. L. Kamil, & P. Mosenthal (Eds.), *Handbook of reading research: Vol. 2* (pp. 951–83). New York: Longman.

Anderson, R. (1984). Role of the reader's schema in comprehension, learning, and memory. In R. Anderson, J. Osbourne, & R. Tierney (Eds.), *Learning to read in American schools.* Hillsdale, NJ: Erlbaum.

Applebee, A., Langer, J., Nystrand, M., & Gamoran, A. (2003). Discussion-based approaches to developing understanding: Classroom instruction and student performance in middle and high school English. *American Educational Research Journal, 40*(3), 685–730.

Barsalou, L. W. (1992). *Cognitive psychology: An overview for cognitive scientists.* Hillsdale, NJ: Erbaum.

Barton, D. (1994). *Literacy: An introduction to the ecology of written language.* Oxford: Blackwell.

Barton , D., & Hamilton, M. (1998). *Local literacies: Reading and writing in one community*. London: Routledge.

Beers, K. (2003). *When kids can't read what teachers can do: A guide for teachers 6–12*. Portsmouth, NH: Heinemann.

Beers, K. (2007). Introduction. In K. Beers, R. E. Probst, & L. Rief (Eds.), *Adolescent literacy: Turning promise into practice*. Portsmouth, NH: Heinemann.

Brown, R. G. (1991). *Schools of thought: How the politics of literacy shape thinking in the classroom*. San Francisco: Jossey-Bass.

Bruner, J. (1996). Frames for thinking: Ways of making meaning. In D. Olson & N. Torrance (Eds.), *Modes of thought: Explorations in culture and cognition* (pp. 93–105). Cambridge: Cambridge University Press.

Cai, M. (1997). Reader-response theory and the politics of multicultural literature. In T. Rogers & A. O. Soter (Eds.), *Reading across cultures: Teaching literature in a diverse society* (pp. 199–212). New York: Teachers College Press.

Clark, H. H. (1996). *Using language*. Cambridge: Cambridge University Press.

Commission on Reading of the National Council of Teachers of English. (2004a). *A call to action: What we know about adolescent literacy and ways to support teachers in meeting students' needs*. Retrieved June 17, 2008, http://www.ncte.org/about/policy/guidelines/118622.htm

Commission on Reading of the National Council of Teachers of English. (2004b). *On reading. learning to read, and effective reading instruction: An overview of what we know and how we know it*. Retrieved October 31, 2006, from http://www.ncte.org/about/over/positions/category/read/118620.htm

Daniels, H., & Zemelman, S. (2004). *Subjects matter: Every teachers guide to content-area reading*. Portsmouth, NH: Heinemann.

Darling-Hammond, L., & Falk, B.(1997). Using standards and assessments to support student learning. *Phi Delta Kappan, 79*(3), 190–99.

Delbridge, K. M. (2006). *"They don't know what they are missing!": Eighth grade students reading and responding to multicultural texts*. Unpublished doctoral dissertation, University of Wyoming, Laramie.

Deshler, D. D., Schumaker, J. B., & Woodruff, S. K. (2004). Improving literacy skills of at-risk adolescents: A schoolwide response. In D. S Strickland & D. E. Alvermann (Eds.), *Bridging the literacy achievement gap, grades 4–12* (pp. 86–105). New York: Teachers College Press.

Elkins, J., & Luke, A. (1999). Redefining adolescent literacies. *Journal of Adolescent and Adult Literacy, 43*(3), 212–15.

Encisco, P. E. (1994). Cultural identity and response to literature. *Language Arts, 71*(7), 524–33.

Ferdman, B. M. (1990). Literacy and cultural identity. *Harvard Educational Review, 60*(2), 181–204.

Freire, P. (1970). *Pedagogy of the oppressed.* London: Continuum.

Galda, L., & Beach, R. (2004). Response to literature as a cultural activity. In R. B. Ruddell & N. J Unrau (Eds.), *Theoretical models and processes of reading* (5th ed.) (pp. 852–69). Newark, DE: International Reading Association.

Garner, R. (1987). *Metacognition and reading comprehension.* Norwood, NJ: Ablex.

Gee, J. P. (1990). *Social linguistics and literacies: Ideology in discourses.* London: Falmer Press.

Gee, J. P. (1992). *The social mind: Language, ideology, and social practice.* New York: Bergin & Garvey.

Gee, J. P. (2000). Discourse and sociocultural studies in reading. In M. Kamil, P. B. Mosenthal, P. D. Pearson, & R. Barr (Eds.). *Handbook of reading research: Vol. 3* (pp. 195–207). Mahwah, NJ: Erlbaum.

Goodman, Y., & Marek, A. (1996). *Retrospective miscue analysis: Revaluing readers and reading.* Katonah, NY: Richard C. Owens.

Greenleaf, C., Schoenbach, R., Cziko, C., & Mueller, F. (2001). Apprenticing adolescent readers to academic literacy. *Harvard Educational Review, 71*(1), 79–129.

Greeno, J. G. (1997). Response: On claims that answer the wrong questions. *Educational Researcher, 26*(1), 5–17.

Guthrie, J. T., Poundstone, C. C., Van Meter, P., Rice, M. E., McCann, A. D., Faibish, R. M., Wigfield, A., Hunt, B., Bennett, L., & Mitchell, A. M. (1996). Growth of literacy engagement: Changes in motivations and strategies during concept-oriented reading instruction. *Reading Research Quarterly, 31*(3), 302–32.

Heath, S. B. (1983). *Ways with words: Language, life, and work in communities and classrooms.* Cambridge: Cambridge University Press.

Herber, H. L. (1978). *Teaching reading in content areas* (2nd ed.). Englewood Cliffs, NJ: Prentice-Hall.

Hiebert, E. (1991). *Literacy for a diverse society: Perspectives, policies, and practices.* New York: Teachers College Press.

Hull, G.A., & Rose, M. (1989). Rethinking remediation: Toward a so-cial-cognitive understanding of problematic reading and writing. *Written Communication, 6*(2), 139–54.

Keene, E. O. (2007). The essence of understanding. In K. Beers, R. E. Probst, & L. Rief, (Eds.), *Adolescent literacy: Turning promise into practice.* Portsmouth, NH: Heinemann.

Keene, E. O., & Zimmerman, S. (2007). *Mosaic of thought: The power of comprehension strategy instruction* (2nd ed.) Portsmouth, NH: Heinemann.

Knapp, M. S., & Shields, P. M. (1991). *Better schooling for the children in poverty: Alternatives to conventional wisdom.* Berkeley, CA: McCutchan.

Kucer, S. (2005). *Dimensions of literacy: A conceptual base for teaching reading and writing in school settings* (2nd ed.). Mahwah, NJ: Erlbaum.

Kuhn, M. R., & Stahl, S. A. (2000). *Fluency: A review of developmental and remedial practices* (CIERA Report No. 2-008). Ann Arbor, MI: Center for the Improvement of Early Reading Achievement.

Langer, J. (2002). *Effective literacy instruction: Building successful reading and writing programs.* Urbana, IL: National Council of Teachers of English.

Lave, J., & Wenger, E. (1991). *Situated learning: Legitimate peripheral participation.* New York: Cambridge University Press.

Lee, H. (1960). *To kill a mockingbird.* New York: Warner.

Mellor, B., & Patterson, A. (2000). Critical practice: Teaching "Shakespeare." *Journal of Adolescent and Adult Literacy, 43*(6), 508–17.

Minsky, J. (1975). A framework for representing knowledge. In P. H. Winston (Ed.), *The psychology of computer vision.* New York: McGraw-Hill.

Morrow, L. M., & Gambrell, L. B. (2000). Literature-based reading instruction. In M. L. Kamil, P. B. Mosenthal, P. D. Pearson, & R. Barr (Eds). *Handbook of reading research: Vol. 3* (pp. 563–86). Mahwah, NJ: Erlbaum.

National Council of Teachers of English (2006). *NCTE principles of adolescent literacy reform. A policy research brief.* Urbana, IL: National Council of Teachers of English.

National Institutes of Health. National Institute of Child Health and Human Development. (NICHD). (2000). *Report of the National Reading Panel. Teaching children to read* (NIH Publication No. 00-4769). Washington, DC: Government Printing Office.

Niles, O. (1965). Organization perceived. In H. L. Herber (Ed.), *Developing study skills in secondary schools* (pp. 36–46). Newark, DE: International Reading Association.

Palmer, P. (1998). *The courage to teach.* San Francisco: Jossey-Bass.

Probst, R. E. (2007). Tom Sawyer, teaching, and talking. In K. Beers, R. E. Probst, & L. Rief (Eds.), *Adolescent literacy: Turning promise into practice.* Portsmouth, NH: Heinemann.

Robb, L. (2003). *Teaching reading in social studies, science, and math: Practical ways to weave comprehension strategies into your content area teaching.* New York: Scholastic.

Rosenblatt, L. (1982). The literacy transaction: Evocation and response. *Theory into Practice, 21,* 268–77.

Ruddell, R. B., & Unrau, N. J. (2004). *Theoretical models and processes of reading* (5th ed.). Newark, DE: International Reading Association.

Salisbury, R. (1934). A study of the transfer effects of training in logical organization. *Journal of Educational Research, 28,* 241–54.

Sizer, T. (1992). *Horace's compromise: The dilemma of the American high school.* Boston: Houghton Mifflin.

Smagorinsky, P., & O'Donell-Allen, C. (1998). Reading as mediated and mediating action: Composing meaning for literature through multimedia interpretive texts. *Reading Research Quarterly, 33*(2), 198–226.

Smith, M. I. (1991). Put to the test: The effects of external testing on teachers. *Educational Researcher, 20*(5), 8–11.

Smith, N. B. (1964). Patterns of writing in different subject areas. *Journal of Reading, 7*, 31–37.

Soto, G. (1997). *Buried onions*. San Diego: Harcourt Brace.

Street, B. (1995). *Social literacies: Critical approaches to literacy in development, ethnography, and education*. London: Longman.

Sutherland, R. (1985). Hidden persuaders: Political ideologies in literature for children. *Children's Literature in Education, 16*(3), 143–57.

Vacca R., & Vacca, J. (2005). *Content area reading: Literacy and learning across the curriculum* (8th ed.). Boston: Pearson/Allyn and Bacon.

Wilhelm, J. (1997). *"You gotta BE the book": Teaching engaged and reflective reading with adolescents*. New York: Teachers College Press.

CHAPTER EIGHT

The Paradoxical Situation Created by Test-Driven Schooling for Multilingual Children

MARYLOU M. MATOUSH
Western Carolina University

DANLING FU
University of Florida

Educators across the United States are well aware that the number of English Language Learners (ELLs) who enroll in our schools has increased dramatically in recent years. Statistics published by federal agencies only confirm what our largely monolingual teaching force can see by simply scanning the seats in their classrooms. Although there is some question as to whether reading in a second language is more closely related to first-language literacy or second-language oral abilities (Garcia, 2000) educators also know, without consulting standardized test scores, that those students who are not fully language proficient in English simply cannot take full advantage of classroom instruction in all academic areas. To do so would require that students be able to understand and converse in everyday English and also to read, write, listen, and speak about academic topics in English.

As more and more classroom seats are occupied by second-language learners, one might ask, What do we know about the teaching of reading to the multilingual child that would help not only those educators who are fully trained in accommodating the needs of ELLs, but those who are just beginning to see an influx and may not be sure how to help second-language learners reach their full potential? The answer to such a question begins with what we know about language acquisition.

Conversational Language Acquisition

Language learning requires time. Second-language acquisition, according to Krashen (1992, 1993) is similar to initial language acquisition. Language learners acquire language in the course of using it for authentic purposes as they encounter situations where there is a genuine need to understand or be understood. They gradually develop receptive language and turn what they have heard into expressive language in order to communicate. That's why, like very young children, ELLs can pick up enough language to get by when simply being immersed in a new language environment without formal language lessons. Observant teachers can see this "at-the-point-of-need" social language development occurring in ELLs. Such oral language acquisition is not linear. English second-language learners do not simply stop thinking in their first language and begin to acquire a new, second one in a systematic fashion. Instead, they learn to make connections between the known and the new, often code-switching as they go (Fu & Matoush, 2006). ·

Academic Language Acquisition

Second-language literacy development is not linear (Fu, 2003; Fu & Matoush, 2006; Gebhard, 2002/2003) nor do ELLs all begin at the same place academically. Reading, writing, listening, and speaking in one's first and second languages are related, and multilingual students have multilingual thoughts. ELLs who are literate in their first language have experienced a number of years of schooling in another country. Some come from homes with educated parents who are inclined to introduce their children to abstract academic concepts in their first language. Many who are multilingual in languages other than English may develop sophisticated understandings and multiple perspectives simply because they are multilingual and can make use of any literate knowledge they possess (Collier, 1995; Cummins, 1996; Garcia, 2000; Krashen, 1996; Thomas & Collier, 2003). Such students may find that they have well-developed conceptual understandings that they simply do not have sufficient English to express.

ELLs who may not have been literate in a first language, but who are fortunate enough to be immersed in an enriched English oral language environment, may be better prepared by schooling than those who remain among foreign language speakers or those who are so mobile while in the United States that their English language experiences are fragmented. Research shows that low-income or highly mobile speakers of subordinate languages, many of whom may not have been literate in a first language, are at a particular disadvantage (Tse, 2001) when faced with schooling that focuses on "academic language," something that is more difficult to acquire than "conversational language" (Collier, 1992; Cummins, 1996).

Literacy Acquisition

Bernhardt (2000) argued that the existing research on second-language reading can be described not only as a subcategory of reading research, but as a microcosm reflecting many of the same issues that apply to the field as a whole. However, the body of research on multilingual reading is somewhat limited by the fact that the vast majority of reading research is initiated in English-speaking countries where funds for such research are limited. Bernhardt made a particularly salient point about the effects of attitude about bilingual or multilingual language learning: "In the notoriously monolingual Anglophone world *language* is frequently synonymous with English. . . . This monolingualism, that is English-language monolingualism, is such a dominant dimension in the Anglophone world that it is often difficult to get even the most astute scholars to think about the world in ways other than with an Anglophone view" (p. 791).

Garcia (2000) categorized the relatively small body of research focused on bilingual reading into three interrelated topics: (1) metalinguistic awareness, (2) cross-linguistic transfer, and (3) the relationship between oral language proficiency and reading (p. 828). She reported that there is evidence that metalinguistic awareness, which is the awareness of specific representational properties, is greater among bilingual children up to the age of six than it is among monolingual children; she speculates that the age limit may have more to do with schooling focused on single-language literacy than an actual age limit. Garcia urges researchers to study cross-linguistic transfer in both experimental and natural settings, since bilingual students generally report using similar strategies across two or more languages when reading. And, as previously mentioned, she has raised the question about the comparative role of second-language oral proficiency and first-language literacy with regard to reading in a second language. In other words, there is much left to be discovered, and attitudes toward bilingualism, as opposed to English acquisition, play a significant role in the course of that discovery.

Something else that we know about the teaching of reading to ELLs and the multilingual child is that cultural differences do play a role in literacy development. Background knowledge is essential for comprehension and interpretation. ELLs enter our schools with cultural understandings that do not match those of native-born students or those presumed by textbook publishers. Confusion of a sort that native-born, monolingual teachers may not be able to unravel can easily result from cultural mismatches.

The No Child Left Behind Act and Differential Educational Opportunities for Language and Literacy Learning

The creators of the No Child Left Behind (NCLB) Act posit a noble-sounding goal of ensuring that every child in the United States receives the best possible education. This is a goal that garners universal support and is endorsed by educators and the general public alike. Unfortunately, this noble goal has spawned legislation that is based on the ill-founded assumption that the potential to improve educational outcomes for children such as ELLs lies in the strengthening of standardized testing as a means of fortifying accountability. Unwittingly, the U.S. Congress, by defining standards, assessing age-based, grade-level academic proficiency, and assigning sanctions, has actually made it likely that some students, including many ELLs, who might thrive in more flexible, authentic environments created for language and literacy learning, are relegated to attempting to cope with the foibles of an increasingly rigid, under-funded bureaucratic system that offers little or no genuine space for differentiation. By emphasizing standardization to the degree that the obliteration of diversity is part and parcel of schooling, NCLB's authors have unintentionally created a callous, unjust system riddled by paradoxes. There have been a number of book-length criticisms of the Reading First initiative portion of NCLB, including Allington (2002), Coles (2002), and Garan (2002). It may be that the paradoxes presented by the broader NCLB legislation work against literacy acquisition among ELLs just as profoundly as do the specific difficulties cited by those who addressed the Reading First initiative portion of the NCLB Act. Regardless of whether that is the case, those paradoxes are certainly worth considering.

Paradox #1: Normative Deficits

For the first few years in a new language environment, ELLs, by definition, will have Limited English Proficiency (LEP): they will have not acquired English language proficiency to the same degree as average English speakers. There is a fair amount of research to support the fact that although ELLs can acquire conversational language proficiency in two to three years, it takes five to seven years for them to develop academic language proficiency (Collier, 1987; Cummins, 1981). Yet NCLB requires that ELLs who have attended school in the United States for three or more consecutive years be tested using norm-referenced tests. Despite rhetoric to the contrary and a provision for the granting of a rarely awarded waiver of up to two additional years, through the enactment of this requirement as a part of NCLB, policymakers have virtually ensured that there will be a gap between the test scores of ELLs and their native-speaking peers. By forcing ELLs to be measured against the greater population of native-language speakers, NCLB has successfully labeled normal second-language learners who require five to seven years to acquire academic language proficiency as "below normal," "limited," and "deficited." As a result, "normal" second-language learning has come to be thought of as problematic. Our thinking about ELLs as learners, thinkers, and therefore as potential contributing members of our society, is tainted. The potential for this situation to be exaggerated is particularly insidious in states such as California and New York. In these states ELLs students are required to take at least a portion of the standardized tests that all students take, regardless of their English language proficiency. The results are predictable. Ruiz-de-Velasco and Fix (2000) showed that ELLs and LEP students are apt to score in the lowest twenty-fifth percentile on standardized tests.

This paradoxical situation leads thoughtful educators to raise many questions about a test-driven educational environment. Can standardized testing be considered a valid measure of ELLs' academic knowledge? Are appropriate testing accommodations for language differences even possible without giving ELLs unfair advantages and unjustly slapping the "deficit" label on some other population (Abedi, 2001; Wright, 2006)? What about other factors, such as socioeconomic status; length of time in the United States; age and grade placement upon arrival; level of first-language literacy; level of parental education; degree of mobility once in the United States; and the linguistic differences among the more than 400 languages (Abedi, 2001) that various children bring with them upon entering the United States when they are compared to native English speakers? Do we have enough answers regarding such factors to lump all ELLs into a single category and to glibly speak about "closing the gap" and "deficits" with any degree of validity? This is particularly troubling when even the category itself is both limited and unstable because ELLs are excluded once they become fully language proficient (Abedi, 2001). At the very least, shouldn't the testing of ELLs focus on comparisons with other ELLs rather than with native English speakers? Wouldn't an emphasis on examining situated individual growth over time be more effective in determining how each ELL is actually progressing academically, so that differentiated instruction could result? Such questions beg to be answered.

Paradox #2: Time Spent Normative Testing, Not Teaching

NCLB has spawned a test-frenzied atmosphere. A focus on test results has led to the practice of giving additional standardized tests in preparation for NCLB mandated tests or to a narrow, test-driven curriculum that "runs counter to recent research findings, which call for a richer, more engaged approach to literacy instruction" (Commission on Reading, 2004b, p. 2). There is little time to immerse English second-language learners in rich, authentic language-based learning. Student learning time in test-driven schools is consumed by remedial activities that are largely skill driven rather than language driven. Students practice test taking and then take tests. In 2006, one principal in the New York City schools made these comments about the testing of ELLs:

> There is too much testing without instruction these days. ELLs basically take tests year around. But the test score came to us so late (test taken in February, and result came in October), we even can't plan the lessons according to the needs and we have to write CEP blindly without statistics. We have to do our own assessment, and can't rely on the test result, which took eight months to get to us. ELLs have a tough time, very hard for them. Nothing seems [to be] working. That is why we took [it] upon ourselves to assess our children, but all the mandated tests are in the way and we have no time for instruction. ELLs are bombarded with one test after another, and teachers and children are both stressed out.

An English as a Second Language (ESL) coordinator in the same school system verified the principal's point and then enumerated the tests that are given to ELLs.

> Now [an] ELA (English language arts) test is added to ELLs, which is a standardized test taken by mainstream students. In the past, ELLs don't have to take this test until three years later in our system. Now they have to take it during their first year, because of NCLB, so-called equal treatment for all children. This added test is very inappropriate for ELLs, as we know they won't pass it, why ask them to take it? It is a test taken in a language that ELLs barely know—makes no sense. It is setting up for them to fail. The test results won't help us to understand or know the kids, just a general summary of the numbers, which don't tell anything about the kids. They take the test in January, so it doesn't test what they have learned during the year (six months more in the year) and the test result comes in October so we don't know how to plan our lessons before the school starts. ELLs have to take tests years around as they have to take tests for general ed[ucation] students and also specifically for ELLs. All we do is to prepare them for tests, or assess them—no time to teach them.

No reasonable educator would argue with the idea that teachers need to know where students' strengths and difficulties lie. Yet the value of normative tests is limited for teaching purposes, and consumes time not only on the part of students who have to take such tests, but on the part of school personnel who must spend time mired in test administration or statistical analyses and reporting activities. This is time that might be better spent in authentic language engagement with students, and on focused situated assessment that can then be used differentially to support ELLs at-the-point-of-need.

Paradox #3: Grade-Level Focus and Language-Based Segregation

ELLs represent an extremely diverse group who often cannot thrive in age-determined grade levels. Since meeting grade-level norms is the goal of NCLB legislation, it almost goes without saying that test-driven schooling promotes standardization in terms of grade-level-oriented curricula. Grade-level equivalencies, standard courses of study, standardized spiraling curricula, and concomitant instructional approaches assume the use of more sophisticated language at each grade level, which builds on that of previous grades. Yet ELLs may have entered our schools at an older age, with drastically different background knowledge, or without sufficient language proficiency to profit from early teachings. ELLs may be disadvantaged by a standardized, language-based, grade-level-oriented curriculum.

Ruiz-de-Velasco and Fix (2000) pointed out that "20% of all LEP students at the high school level and 12% of LEP at the middle school level have missed two or more years of schooling since age six. Demonstration project teachers in one California school district estimate that as many as 15% of their high school LEP students could be under schooled. Project estimates ran higher in Maryland schools that received large numbers of refugee students during the late 1980s and early 1990s" (p. 55).

Further, teachers report that under-schooled teens also tend to lack basic study skills that promote classroom learning. One teacher, for example, described new refugee students in a middle school who did not know how to use a pencil and were unaccustomed to sitting in a middle school classroom for extended periods or raising a hand to be recognized (Ruiz-de-Velasco & Fix, p. 55). Fu's (1995) study on refugee teens, reported in *My Trouble is My English*, described Sy, age eleven, who entered his American school with no schooling experience in his native country, and experienced the problem of grade-level placement on a first-hand basis. His ESL teacher reported,

> I was told that when he was in school in Massachusetts, he was first put in the second grade. That must have been awful for him, as he was among tiny small kids. Then he was moved to the sixth grade, and stayed there for a couple of months, and then was move down to the fourth grade. Before he came to us, he was in a third-grade class. Last year, when he came to our school, we put him in a sixth-grade class (he was 13).
>
> In his first year of school in America, Sy was shifted to four different grades (second, sixth, fourth and third). When [Fu] asked him about his first year in school, he told [her]: "I didn't understand anything. I didn't know anything the people said around me." (p. 170)

Sy is undoubtedly not the only ELL who simply could not be categorized or placed easily into an age-based, grade-level system. This diverse group might best be served by nonstandard or ungraded schooling of one sort or another. Paradoxically, NCLB, standardization, and the current emphasis on grade-level learning, while claiming to serve the interests of every child, are nevertheless intended to eliminate rather than accommodate diversity of the sort that ELLs represent; and the sanctions imposed by these mandates preclude the discovery of reforms that might better serve the needs of diverse populations. This legislation has caused age-based, grade-level distinctions to become rigidly fixed and unaccommodating, despite the fact that the learning needs of nonstandard learners, including ELLs, might better be served by more flexible, differentiated ways of organizing schooling.

Age-based, grade-leveled schooling often forces educators to place ELLs in separate programs so that their "deficits" can be "remediated." However, doing so segregates ELLs in such a way that it lessens their access to English-speaking peers who could serve as language models (Gebhard, 2002/2003; Gutierrez, Baquedano-

Lopez & Asato, 2001). Deficit-based programs tend to simplify the cognitive content in order to accommodate language "deficits," although many learners, particularly those who are literate in their first language, need age-appropriate, complex, academic challenges (Gebhard, 2002/2003). "Abundant research suggests that . . . isolated skill instruction . . . may perpetuate low literacy achievement. . . . In addition, prescriptive, skills-based instruction mislocates the problem as the students' failure to learn, rather than the institutions' failure to teach reading as the complex mental and social activity it is" (Commission on Reading, 2004a, p.1, 2004b, p. 1).

A related problem in terms of segregation lies in the fact that according to the 1999–2000 Schools and Staffing Survey (SASS), over half (53 percent) of LEP students attend schools where more than 30 percent of their fellow students are also ELLs. In contrast, only 4 percent of non-LEP students attend a school where more than 30 percent of the student body is LEP (Fix & Passel, 2003, p. 25). These patterns of segregation also appear to be reproducing themselves in the new growth states to which many immigrants moved in the 1990s. In the twenty-two "new growth" states, 38 percent of LEP students attend schools where more than 30 percent of the students are LEP. In the six major immigrant destination states, the percentage is much higher—60 percent of LEP students are in schools where more than 30 percent of the students are LEP (Fix & Passel, 2003, p. 25). Yet the linguistic and cultural segregation situation diminishes the potential for academic success among ELL immigrant students because they are denied easy access to practicing and learning English or familiarizing themselves with mainstream culture. Since new immigrants often reside in communities with similar sociolinguistic characteristics, school is quite possibly the only venue for many ELLs to engage in consistent English language and culture learning.

Paradox #4: Systematic, Sequential, Standardized Schooling

To be accessible to all students, instruction must be designed to accommodate the multimodal acquisition of understandings.

Schooling, particularly test-driven schooling of the sort promoted by NCLB, isn't compatible with at-the-point-of-need language acquisition, upon which language learners thrive. Because standardized tests are language based, seemingly the most expedient way to teach academic concepts is to use academic language to do so. This approach favors those who come from homes where abstract English academic language is already understood, or at least those who were able to learn academic concepts on an at-grade-level basis. Language-based, grade-level instruction may not always be accessible to ELLs. Others who come from homes where academic English is not common are also disadvantaged when instruction is limited to verbal modes.

We know that ELLs' academic English acquisition and literacy development are supported by multimodal opportunities for exploring topics across disciplines and genres because such opportunities enhance understandings by supporting language acquisition with nonverbal, sensual input. Such opportunities include

- ◆ chances to see and create visual representations of language-based communications in picture books, films, brochures, digital stories, posters, websites, televised material, podcasts, and myriad other forms.

- ◆ activities that involve hearing and producing written language orally during read-aloud sessions, shared reading, singing, chanting, choral responding, oral reporting, recordings of books on tape, and so on.

- ◆ experiences that mirror the lived experience or recontextualize written language through drama, reader's theater, reenactments, simulations, films, televised material, and other media that support understanding through various combinations of visual, auditory, and kinesthetic and spatially oriented involvement.

Test-driven schooling favors the use of paper-and-pencil tasks that resemble test taking in English, rather than enrichment through integrated learning and multilingual opportunities of the sort described above. We know that for ELLs, as for other learners, literacy development and academic language acquisition is supported by thematic or interdisciplinary experiences that allow students to be immersed in language experiences across the curriculum. Such teaching enhances language acquisition by immersing students in repeated, yet varied references to and experiences with academic concepts (Hudelson, Poynor, & Wolf, 2003). Paradoxically, test-driven schooling favors the isolation of discipline-based subject matter so that tests can be designed to report growth according to separate disciplines.

Similarly, we know that the use of text sets composed of a variety of types of texts, at a variety of levels, focused on a single topic allow language learners to assemble comprehensible input; piece together background knowledge; and gain vocabulary support from easier or more clearly illustrative texts that enhance understandings of more complex examples of written language pertaining to a topic. In other words, we know that wide reading of text that is written at an appropriate level enhances reading abilities (Allington, 2001). Unfortunately, test-driven schooling favors a grade-level focus, standards-based curriculum alignment, and the publication and purchase of only a narrow range of text for any given grade level. This paradox becomes painfully obvious when one tries to find easy or clearly illustrative texts pertaining to the home countries or cultures of ELLs. A range of texts that can be connected with the background knowledge of many ELLs is simply unavailable. Because children are not deemed developmentally ready to embrace a global perspective until they reach advanced academic levels, standardized curricula at the elementary grades focus on dominant cultural heritage. Further, while increasing numbers of culturally diverse children's books are becoming available, generally they portray only the most populous groups of immigrants. Easy or clearly illustrative English language texts that exemplify the background knowledge that many ELLs bring to this country are limited in number and reading or interest level, and may be difficult if not impossible to obtain. They are certainly not readily available in classrooms across the nation.

In her interviews with students and teachers in several New York City high schools, Fu (2007, in press) found that ELL students expressed that they could understand only 30 percent of the textbooks they were required to read. The teachers claimed that some ELLs could barely understand 10 percent of the textbooks they used in the content areas. The teachers have to use these textbooks, because they contain the topics that are required at each grade level and will be tested. Since the ELL students cannot understand these textbooks, they cannot do the homework or pre-read or post-read a textbook for their study. Therefore many teachers simply go over test items one by one in class, and have students memorize what may be tested, which is how teachers teach and students learn the subjects required at the grade level.

ELLs bring nonstandard linguistic and cultural understandings to their transactions with texts. We know that reading, like any interpretative act, is a transactional act (Rosenblatt, 1976) that should remain tentative and open to provisional reinterpretation (Wells & Chang-Wells, 1992). We know that transactions with any meaningful text involve making connections with what is known, and are enhanced by hearing what others have been thinking about any given text. In other words, reading involves much beyond decoding and comprehending what is written on the page. Reading comprehension and interpretation both require the application of background knowledge during the act of making sense of any text. A test-driven, one-right-answer approach to schooling places all students at a disadvantage when handling this complex task; but this approach may work against ELLs in particular ways when it comes to using their life experiences to interpret text, as their life experiences often differ not only from the norm but from those of the writers and their understandings of language as a communicative medium (Commission on Reading, 2004a, p. 2–3, 2004b, p. 2). Additionally, we know that while ELLs gain in terms of comprehension by listening to native English speakers talk about text (Freeman, D. E., & Freeman, Y. S., 2000), of course there is room for native English speakers to gain new perspectives on text by listening to ELLs. Unfortunately, in a test-driven environment such offerings may be looked upon as deficits rather than contributions, for standardized reading tests often promote correct-answer-oriented comprehension instruction rather than multiperspectival idea exchange.

In short, standardized tests of literacy acquisition are problematic in terms of the quality of literacy learning that test-driven schooling promotes, and these problems are magnified for ELLs and other non-normative learners (Darling-Hammond, 1991;

Falk, 1998; Wiggins, 1993). The use of more authentic assessments would not be as problematic. Examining situated individual growth over time would focus schooling on providing the flexibility to meet diverse needs. The use of authentic assessment techniques would be more amenable to teaching techniques that foster rich, multilingual transactions with text. This type of teaching promotes depth of thinking as opposed to a test-driven focus on accuracy.

Paradox #5: The Reign of Dominant Language and Culture

Neither language nor culture is stagnant. New immigrants bring fresh perspectives with them (Schatler, 1997). Multilingual students have potential to introduce new or culturally different background knowledge and an expanded range of cultural and linguistic meanings that may lead to the creative development of connections. Therefore the assumption that learning as measured in English by standardized tests can or should be the sole goal for ELLs is also paradoxical.

Consider the range of perspectives offered in the following excerpt, reported in *An Island of English* (Fu, 2003), taken from a group discussion that was recorded in Chinese after the class had studied the Vietnam War. It was translated as accurately as possible to retain the original meanings.

> A BOY STARTED FIRST: Except the current war in Afghanistan, the Americans fought all the other wars to help others. For instance, they joined World War II to help Europeans, fought Korean War to help the South Korean and in Vietnam War they helped the south regime in Vietnam and then helped Kuwait fight against Iraq in Gulf War. Only in this Afghanistan war, it is for Americans' own revenge after Sept. 11 terrorist attack.

> SEVERAL STUDENTS AGREED WITH HIM AND ONE ADDED HIS WORDS: Americans love to help others, that is to keep them to be the superpower in the world. Now, we are suffering, and look how the Arabs did to us in New York.

> A GIRL JOINED THE DISCUSSION SOFTLY: I think the American fought all the wars for themselves. In World War II, they joined the

war only after the Pearl Harbor attack. They fought Korean and Vietnam wars to prevent the Communism from gaining power in the world. That is also for their own ideas. Then they fought Gulf War for the oil supply.

ANOTHER GIRL ADDED: In China, we call America the imperialist, because they go to other countries to fight . . .

A BOY CUT IN: You can't say that about the World War II and the war in Afghanistan now. They are the wars for justice, to fight against German Nazi and to fight the Muslin terrorists.

ANOTHER STUDENT JOINED IN: My great uncle died in the Korean War. My grandpa told me that he was killed by Americans.

A GIRL SAID: But my great-aunt told me Americans helped us fight against Japanese during World War II. Japanese killed a lot of Chinese in China.

ANOTHER GIRL TRIED TO PULL THE GROUP BACK TO DISCUSS THE VIETNAM WAR: How about the Vietnam War—the American people were against this war themselves?

A BOY FOLLOWED: But nobody is against our war in Afghanistan. We hate those terrorists and want to kill them all. They killed so many here in our city. And it is hard to find jobs now.

ANOTHER STUDENT JOINED HIS DISCUSSION: Yeah, the first time, American was invaded like this and suffered by the outsiders' attack on its own land. Of course, we have to fight back.

It is interesting to notice how they shifted their positions when they talked about different wars. When they talked about the current war in Afghanistan, they felt more personal[ly] connected by referring it to as "our war" and identified themselves as part of Americans by saying "*we* have to fight back." By living so close to the World Trade Center, they were all deeply affected by the 9/11 attack. Since then, it seems that they have never felt being so American (pp. 35–36).

In test-driven schooling, this range of response may never be heard because the focus is on getting the right answers rather than on a range of responses. This focus may also work to alienate ELLs from their families or force them to feel that they have to choose between the "American way" and the ways of their friends and family. The need to succeed as an English-speaking American, and the relegation of native-language learning to domestic settings, may work to cause separation anxieties if not alienation between ELLs and their families and communities (Rose, 1989).

Language and behavior varies with context. Poolroom or barroom conversation and activity varies from the language and behavior appropriate to a classroom; and each varies significantly from that of a shopping mall, church, back alley, bowling alley, ballroom, or boardroom. To be accepted as a member by any given group, one must speak and act in ways that are deemed acceptable by the other participants engaged in activity in that context (Gee, 1990). Is it absolutely essential that ELL immigrant students in the United States abandon the full range of language and behaviors available to them in order to ensure success in school? It is discomforting to realize that the answer to this question might be *yes*, at least as far as concerns the interface between ELLs and teachers. "Nationwide, only 2.5 percent of teachers with ELLs in their classes have any special preparation to work with them" (Ruiz-de-Velasco & Fix, 2000, p. 14).

The purpose of test-driven schooling appears to be to create learners who resemble the norm. Standardized testing, standardized curricula, and an emphasis on English language learning all work to place schools in the precarious position of actively attempting to obliterate linguistic and cultural variations in our society. Unfortunately, test-driven schooling works to exacerbate negative feelings toward diversity of any sort. As Valenzuela (1999) indicated, teachers' stereotypes and negative attitudes toward minority students diminish newcomers' capacity for learning. When minority students are aware of their teachers' negative stereotypes, then they become defensive and underperform to the extent of feeling happier and more competent if they are not with their teachers (Martinez, 2006).

It is possible that by assuming a test-driven position, schools work against their own goals. While it is undeniably true that English is privileged in the United States, and that success in this country implies English proficiency, Macedo (1999/2000) raised a series of very legitimate questions when he asked,

Although the fields of bilingual education and English as a second language have produced a barrage of studies demonstrating the effectiveness of English acquisition, these research studies fail to raise other fundamental questions: Does cultural subordination affect academic achievement? What is the correlation between social segregation and school success? What role does cultural identity among subordinated students play in linguistic resistance? Does the devaluation of students' culture and language affect reading achievement? Is class a factor in bilingual education? Do material conditions that foster human misery adversely affect academic development? (p. 63)

Do multilingual learners deserve anything less than culturally responsive pedagogy (Gay, 2000; Ladson-Billings, 1994) in which linguistic and cultural differences are seen as assets, rather than as deficits? Is schooling aimed at preparing students to participate in a multiperspectival democracy a thing of the past? Is the goal of developing passionate voice or creative and critical thinking on the part of new immigrants and native-born students alike to be forever subordinated to the regurgitation of the sort of information about topics that can be measured on standardized tests by monolingual, standard students?

Paradox #6: Bureaucratized, Test-Driven, Limited Thinking

The final paradox may well be the one that should receive the most careful thought. In its attempts to ensure accountability and school reform, the U.S. Congress may well have insured that education for ELLs and native-language speakers alike is limited to the degree that new, more profound understandings are prohibited from emerging—or may even be censored. This greatest paradox of all lies in the fact that test-driven schooling is limited not only by what can be easily tested, but by what is deemed to be standard knowledge by the dominant group. In other words, standards-based, test-driven schooling is reproductive, not transformative in nature.

The most important learning issues are not testable. Testing works to narrow the curriculum to reflect test content rather than to expand minds in diverse and infinite ways. The question of whether the sort of knowledge that is measured by standardized tests reflects the sort of knowledge and learning which should be sought and promoted for any population is a legitimate one. One must ask if the bureaucratic need for standardization and accountability is actually compatible with meaningful forms of human learning. Sumida and Meyer (2006) raised this greater question in this way:

> [We] are learning that allowing students to make connections between disciplines as interpretative spaces complicates testing and assessment of learning beyond what exists in quantitative terms. Evaluation is no longer neat and contained within the boundaries of a single domain. A creative and liberated mind is not necessarily measurable. Measurement works effectively on mechanical objects so that they can be replicated. (p. 448)

Sumida and Meyer present this question in a way that certainly applies to bright young multilingual students as well as to native-language speakers. It is unconscionable to think of the minds of any group of students in terms of "mechanical objects," yet that is exactly the direction in which test-driven bureaucratization of thinking is leading us, for it ignores the fact that learning is best supported when creative and critical thinking situated in and applied to real-world contexts are promoted (Bruner, 1960; Cohen & Barnes, 1993; Falk, 1998; Fosnot, 1989; Piaget, 1970; Vygotsky, 1978) and assessments allow students to demonstrate what they know and understand (Eisner, 1991). The development of diverse, thoughtful citizens who can negotiate understandings within a diverse, democratic society should, after all, be valued more highly than the standardized development of test takers trained to suit bureaucratic quantitative goals.

References

Abedi, J. (2001). *Assessment and accommodations for English language learners: Issues and recommendations* (CRESST Policy Brief 7). Los Angeles: University of California, National Center for Research on Evaluation, Standards, and Student Testing.

Allington, R. (2001). *What really matters for struggling readers: Designing research-based programs.* New York: Longman.

Allington, R. (Ed). (2002). *Big brother and the national reading curriculum: How ideology trumped evidence.* Portsmouth, NH: Heinemann.

Bernhardt, E. B. (2000). Second-language reading as a case study of reading scholarship in the 20th century. In M. Kamil, P. Mosenthal, P. D. Pearson, & R. Barr (Eds.). *Handbook of reading research: Vol. 3* (pp. 791–811). Mahwah, NJ: Erlbaum.

Bruner, J. (1960). *The process of education.* Cambridge, MA: Harvard University Press.

Cohen, D. K., & Barnes, C. A. (1993). Conclusion: A new pedagogy for policy? In D. K. Cohen, M. W. McLaughlin, & J. E. Talbert (Eds.), *Teaching for understanding: Challenges for policy and practice* (pp. 240–75). San Francisco: Jossey-Bass.

Coles, G. (2002). *Great unmentionables: What national reading reports and reading legislation don't tell you.* Portsmouth, NH: Heinemann.

Collier, V. P. (1987). Age and rate of acquisition of second language for academic purposes. *TESOL Quarterly, 21*(4), 617–41.

Collier V. P. (1992). A synthesis of studies examining long-term language minority student data on academic achievement. *Bilingual Research Journal, 16*(1-2), 187–212.

Collier, V. P. (1995). Promoting academic success for ESL students: Understanding second language acquisition for school. Jersey City, NJ: New Jersey Teachers of English to Speakers of Other Language—Bilingual Educators.

Commission on Reading of the National Council of Teachers of English. (2004a). *A call to action: What we know about adolescent literacy and ways to support teachers in meeting students' needs.* Retrieved June 18, 2008, from http://www.ncte.org/about/policy/guidelines/118622.htm

Commission on Reading of the National Council of Teachers of English. (2004b). *On reading, learning to read, and effective reading instruction: An overview of what we know and how we know it.* Retrieved March 2008, from http://www.ncte.org/about/over/positions/category/read/118620.htm

Cummins, J. (1981). The role of primary language development in preventing educational success for language minority students. In California State Department of Education, Office of Bilingual Bicultural Education (Ed.), *Schooling and language minority students: A theo-*

retical framework (pp. 3–49). Los Angeles: California State University, Evaluation, Dissemination and Assessment Center.

Cummins, J. (1996). *Negotiating identities: Education for empowerment in a diverse society.* Ontario, CA: California Association for Bilingual Education.

Darling-Hammond, L. (1991). The implications of testing policy for quality and equity. *Phi Delta Kappan, 73*(3), 220–25.

Eisner, E. (1991). What really counts in schools. *Educational Leadership, 48*(3), 10–11, 14–17.

Falk, B. (1998). Testing the way children learn: Principles for valid literacy assessments. *Language Arts, 76*(1), 57–66.

Fix, M., & Passel, J. S. (2003, January). *U.S. immigration: Trends and implications for schools.* Paper presented at the National Association for Bilingual Education's NCLB Implementation, New Orleans, LA.

Fosnot, C. T. (1989). *Enquiring teachers, enquiring learners: A constructivist approach for teaching.* New York: Teachers College Press.

Freeman, D. E., & Freeman, Y. S. (2000). *Teaching reading in multilingual classrooms.* Portsmouth, NH: Heinemann.

Freeman, Y. S., & Freeman, D. E. (1998). *ESL/EEF teaching: Principles for success.* Portsmouth, NH: Heinemann.

Fu, D. (1995). *My trouble is my English: Asian students and the American dream.* Portsmouth, NH: Boynton/Cook.

Fu, D. (2003). *An island of English: Teaching ESL in Chinatown.* Portsmouth, NH: Heinemann.

Fu, D. (2007). Teaching writing to English language learners. In T. Newkirk & R. Kent (Eds.), *Teaching the neglected "r": Rethinking writing instruction in secondary classrooms* (pp. 225–42). Portsmouth, NH: Heinemann.

Fu, D. (in press). Teaching ESL writing at the secondary level. In T. Newkirk & R, Kent (Eds.) *21st century writing: New directions for secondary classrooms.* Portsmouth, NH: Heinemann.

Fu, D., & Matoush, M. (2006). Writing development and biliteracy. In P. K. Matsuda, C. Ortmeier-Hooper, and X. You (Eds.). *The poli-*

tics of second language writing: In search of the promised land (pp. 5–29). West Lafayette, IN: Parlor Press.

Garan, E. (2002). *Resisting reading mandates: How to triumph with the truth.* Portsmouth, NH: Heinemann.

Garcia, G. E. (2000). Bilingual children's reading. In M. Kamil, P. Mosenthal, P. D. Pearson, & R. Barr. (Eds.) *Handbook of reading research: Vol. 3* (pp. 813–34). Mahwah, NJ: Erlbaum.

Gay, G. (2000). *Culturally responsive teaching: Theory, research, and practice.* New York: Teachers College Press.

Gebhard, M. (2002/2003). Getting past "See Spot Run." *Educational Leadership, 60*(4), 35–39.

Gee, J. (1990). *Social linguistics and literacies: Ideology and discourses.* London: Falmer Press.

Gutierrez, K., Baquedano-Lopez, P., & Asato, J. (2001). "English for the children": The new literacy of the old work order, language policy, and educational reform. *Bilingual Research Journal, 24*(1 & 2), 87–112.

Hudelson, S., Poynor, L., & Wolfe, P. (2003). Teaching bilingual and ESL children and adolescents. In J. Flood, D. Lapp, J. R. Squire & J. M. Jensen (Eds.) *Handbook of research on teaching the English language arts* (2nd ed, pp. 421–34). Mahwah, NJ: Erlbaum.

Krashen, S. (1992). *Fundamentals of language education.* Torrance, CA: Laredo.

Krashen, S. (1993). *The power of reading: Insights from research.* Englewood, CO: Libraries Unlimited.

Krashen, S. (1996). *Under attack: The case against bilingual education.* Culver City, CA: Language Education Associates.

Ladson-Billings, G. (1994). *The dreamkeepers: Successful teachers of African American children.* San Francisco: Jossey-Bass.

Macedo, D. (1999/2000). The illiteracy of English-only literacy. *Educational Leadership, 57*(4), 62–67.

Martinez, S. (2006). Explaining patterns of disengagement of Mexican American adolescents in high school. Unpublished doctoral dissertation, University of Chicago.

Nieto, S. (2002/2003). Profoundly multicultural questions. *Educational Leadership*, 60(4), 6–10.

Piaget, J. (1970). *The science of education and the psychology of the child* (D. Coltman, Trans.). New York: Penguin.

Rose, M. (1989). *Lives on the boundary*. New York: Penguin Book.

Rosenblatt, L. (1976). *Literature as exploration* (3rd ed.). New York: Noble and Noble.

Ruiz-de-Velasco, J., & Fix, M. (2000). *Overlooked & underserved immigrant students in U.S. secondary schools*. Washington, DC: Urban Institute.

Schatler, S. (1997). Assets to reading instruction: Second language learners in our classrooms. *Ohio Reading Teacher*, 31(7), 7–10.

Sumida, A. Y., and Meyer, M. A. (2006). T^4 = Teaching to the fourth power: Transformative inquiry and the stirring of cultural waters. *Language Arts*, 83(5), 437–49.

Thomas, W. P., & Collier, V. P. (2003). *What we know about effective instructional approaches for language minority learners*. Arlington, VA: Educational Research Service.

Tse, L. (2001). *Why don't they learn English? Separating fact from fallacy in the U.S. language debate*. New York: Teachers College Press.

Valenzuela, A. (1999). *Subtractive schooling: U.S.-Mexican youth and the politics of caring*. Albany: State University of New York Press.

Vygotsky, L. (1978). *Mind in society: The development of higher psychological processes*. Cambridge, MA: Harvard University Press.

Wells, C. G., & Chang-Wells, G. L. (1992). *Constructing knowledge together: Classrooms as centers of inquiry and literacy*. Portsmouth, NH: Heinemann.

Wiggins, G. (1993). *Assessing student performance: Exploring the purpose and limits of testing*. San Francisco: Jossey-Bass.

Wright, W. W. (2006). A catch-22 for language learners. *Educational Leadership*, 64(3), 22–27.

CHAPTER NINE

Reaching and Teaching Thoughtful Literacy to Readers Who Struggle: Instruction That Increases Motivation and Achievement

MICHAEL L. SHAW

St. Thomas Aquinas College

In the midst of a heat wave last summer, I bought two new air conditioners to replace ancient, ineffective units that made lots of noise but did little to cool our living room and bedroom. I expected that all I'd have to do was to slide the old units out and slide the new units in. Wow, was I naïve! The first thing I noticed when I opened the carton was a *Manual of Instructions* for installing the unit. Instant panic! Can you imagine a PhD in language, literacy, and learning panicking at the requirement to read a short text that is intended to help people install a new air conditioner? Yet this daunting task caused me to panic. You see, in spite of all my professional success, I have been classified by my wife and friends as mechanically disabled (MD). Give me a mechanical problem to solve—like installing an air conditioner or fixing a leaky pipe—and I panic when I have to read the instruction manual. I begin to sweat and shake. I shut down.

So that day I used every reading strategy I knew to comprehend difficult text. I slowed down my reading. I read aloud to hear what the manual said to do. I looked at the diagrams and read the captions. I tried doing exactly what I thought the manual was telling me to do. Some of it worked, but I just knew that some things I was doing were wrong. In the end I called a friend who is a skilled handyman. He earns his living working in a machine shop and has an extensive background reading instruction manuals. He easily read the manual and installed the first air conditioner while I observed. I noted how he interpreted the instructions and applied the information. I told him that I wanted to install the second air conditioner, and asked him to monitor my performance. I slowly reread the instructions, sometimes reading out loud, and applied what I thought to be the appropriate installation steps based in my comprehension of the text. I continually looked to my friend for affirmation and guidance—which he generously provided as my *teacher*. Again, there were some steps that I correctly applied, but there were still other steps where I needed my friend's guidance. At the end, I was able to successfully install the air conditioner; but I was still a long way from being able to *independently* read an instruction manual to be able to achieve reading goals that center on mechanical applications. I would still need a lot more explicit demonstrations and guided practice to build the knowledge base that would empower me to be a confident, successful instruction-manual reader.

My entire experience affirmed the comment Yetta Goodman made to me (personal communication, 2002) when she said, "We are all struggling readers when we have to read texts that are removed from our experience." It also affirmed the critical importance of having a knowledgeable teacher as a mentor.

Consider what would happen to me if I had to read instruction manuals every day, without the support of a knowledgeable, skillful, caring teacher. Pretty soon the constant frustration would lead me to either shut down or act out.

Also, consider that I did not need to be able to read the instruction manual because I had a friend to help me install the air conditioners. Not being able to read this manual did not affect my life, my happiness, or my self-esteem. Sadly, the same cannot be said for our students, who are required to read the books and other texts we provide every day in school. They experience on a daily basis the constant frustration that leads them to shut down or act out. And, sadly, their failed reading experiences have a major impact on their lives, happiness, and self-esteem.

Read the following statements of students enrolled in our reading clinic. They echo the feelings of countless numbers of students who struggle with reading and writing:

All my friends are reading chapter books and I have to read these stupid baby books.

I'm just dumb.

I hate to read.

It's not simply that these students find reading and writing hard; it's that the day-in and day-out frustrations transform children and adolescents from the passionate, enthusiastic, motivated learners they once were in kindergarten and first grade into disempowered, defeated, unmotivated learners who believe that they are fated to a world of failure. In a few short years of school, many struggling readers and writers experience the devastating *Cycle of Failure* (see Figure 9.1) that creates a downward spiral, which in many cases paralyzes them from taking active steps to achieve reading success, and which will ultimately lead to dropping out and a life of closed opportunities.

The first and most important step in reversing this cycle is to begin to build the *Cycle of Success* (see Figure 9.2) used by successful readers because experiencing success motivates engagement (Cambourne, 1995), builds empowerment, and creates a commitment to achieve more success. As motivation increases, comprehension also increases (Guthrie & Davis, 2003). This then leads to a commitment to read more, which, in turn, continues to significantly increase reading achievement (Anderson, Wilson, & Fielding, 1988; Allington & McGill-Franzen, 1989).

This chapter focuses on what we know about teaching readers who struggle, how we know it, and on instruction that makes an impact on motivation and achievement. It builds on our extensive research base that establishes what we know about the teaching of reading; and it makes a strong case that we must teach *thoughtful literacy* to all readers, including readers who struggle, in order to make an impact on closing the achievement gap and helping *all* students achieve reading success. This chapter argues that teaching readers who struggle does not mean teaching differently from the way we teach all readers, but requires multiple adaptations to respond to the specific educational needs of students who are experiencing reading difficulties.

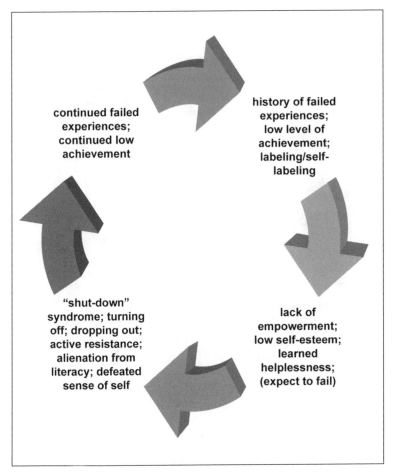

FIGURE **9.1.** *Cycle of Failure.*

Research Base: What We Know and How We Know It for Teaching Thoughtful Reading to Readers Who Struggle: Keys for Breaking the Cycle of Failure and Building the Cycle of Success

While there are many conceptualizations of what it means to read (Braunger & Lewis, 2006), there is a consensus that reading is the active process of constructing meaning based on the reader's

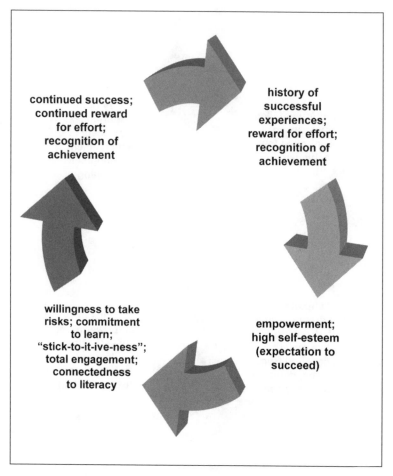

FIGURE 9.2. *Cycle of Success.*

prior knowledge and experience, information suggested in the text, and the context of the reading experience (International Reading Association, 1998). In addition, there is widespread consensus that reading is a complex, purposeful process that draws upon the multiple sources of information acquired by the reader through life experiences and print experiences. As stated by the Commission on Reading (2004), "Reading is a complex and purposeful sociocultural, cognitive, and linguistic process in which readers simultaneously use their knowledge of spoken and written language, their knowledge of the topic of the text, and their knowledge of their culture to construct meaning with text" (p. 1).

Thus, reading depends on bringing meaning *to* text in order to construct meaning *from* text. This is the essence of comprehending printed text, which is the objective of all reading. In other words, it doesn't matter if we have great sight-word knowledge and vocabulary, have fabulous decoding skills, and can read fluently *if* all those essential preconditions do not work together to achieve the overarching goal of reading, which is comprehending what we read and being able to respond to the text with thoughts, ideas, and feelings.

Many researchers, including Gaskins (1998), Primeaux (2000), and Allington (2006), have identified the need to rethink the skills/drill approach that traditionally has been used to teach readers who struggle. These researchers emphasize that it is important to provide authentic instruction that explicitly and systematically teaches skills and strategies used by successful readers. As Gaskins noted in her directorship of the Benchmark School for readers who struggle, recognized by the U.S. Department of Education as a school of excellence, "Quality instruction at Benchmark means meeting students where they are with respect to affect, motivation, and cognition; explicitly teaching them strategies for taking charge of tasks, situations, and personal styles; and scaffolding the successful completion of academic tasks" (p. 536). The Benchmark School uses the *gradual release of responsibility* model (Pearson & Gallagher, 1983) that immerses students in systematic, authentic reading experiences through daily lessons that include a continuum of teacher support and scaffolding to guide students into independence through read-alouds, think-alouds, shared reading, guided reading, and independent reading. We have learned that instruction for readers who struggle should not be a different type of instruction than that provided for all students, but we need to be more systematic and explicit through multiple demonstrations; and we need to provide more intense opportunities for guided and independent practice to reinforce skills and strategies. Table 9.1 identifies the knowledge, skills, and strategies that successful readers know and use, and that we need to teach readers who struggle.

What Successful Readers Know	What to Teach Struggling Readers for Success	Effective Methods
Reading is the process of constructing meaning from text.	To focus on constructing meaning from every text they read.	◆ Use story map. ◆ Set purpose for reading. ◆ Focus on identifying author's message. ◆ Focus on making personal connections.
Reading is a purposeful activity to accomplish goals.	To determine purpose every time they read.	◆ Set purpose for reading. ◆ Focus on identifying author's message.
Reading is rewarding. We get a pay-off from reading and it brings us joy.	To choose books that help them experience success and enjoyment.	◆ Create independent reading program, including book clubs and literature discussions. ◆ Teach students how to make wise choices for independent reading so they can comprehend and enjoy the reading experience (e.g., five-finger rule).
The reading experience consists of before-reading, during-reading, and after-reading thoughts and actions that enable the construction of meaning.	To understand and apply what good readers do before reading, during reading, and after reading.	◆ Explicitly teach before-reading, during-reading, and after-reading strategies by thinking aloud and demonstrating. ◆ Have students reflect on every reading experience.
Reading is an active, transactional process that centers on thinking and self-monitoring for meaning.	To self-monitor for meaning while reading.	◆ Model self-monitoring for meaning, including rereading. ◆ Explicitly teach students to integrate three curing systems to read for meaning: Does it make sense? Does it sound right? Does it look right?
Readers think about the big ideas in texts that relate to their own lives and the world.	To think about what the author wanted to communicate that relates to one's own life and the world.	◆ Focus on author's intended message. ◆ Reread the ending of a text, where author most often emphasizes the message. ◆ Note for young children that animal stories are often intended to teach human lessons (fables, fairy tales, folk tales).
Good writers leave the reader with more questions than answers.	To question the author: *I wonder* . . .	◆ Demonstrate generating questions, and demonstrate potential answers.
Comprehension depends on fluent, expressive reading with attention to punctuation.	To read fluently and expressively with attention to punctuation.	◆ Model fluent reading. ◆ Communicate how fluent reading enables readers to read for meaning. *continued on next page*

TABLE 9.1 What Successful Readers Know: What to Teach Struggling Readers for Success, Effective Methods

Table 9.1 continued

Reading centers on the application of a repertoire of strategies that enable the construction of meaning.	A repertoire of before-reading, during-reading, and after-reading strategies that help them problem solve in order to read for meaning.	◆ Explicitly introduce before-reading, during-reading, and after-reading strategies. ◆ Demonstrate strategy use through read-aloud/think-aloud lessons. ◆ Explain how before-reading, during-reading, and after-reading strategies support reading for meaning.
Reading is contextual. We create an environment that supports reading.	To create the environment that allows them to focus on their reading.	◆ Create risk-free environment that supports all readers.
Reading depends on prior knowledge of content and concepts.	To activate their prior knowledge before reading, and to fill in gaps in their knowledge base.	◆ Create before-reading strategies that activate prior knowledge (e.g., K-W-L, semantic mapping).
Reading depends on an extensive vocabulary and sight-word knowledge.	Strategies to expand vocabulary and increase sight-word knowledge.	◆ Introduce essential vocabulary words. ◆ Teach sight-word identification at all levels. ◆ Teach strategies for figuring out new vocabulary words in context (e.g., blank out/cover over unknown word and substitute known word that makes sense).
Reading depends on knowledge of our alphabetic system.	Phonemic awareness and decoding strategies.	◆ Teach phonemic awareness, phonics, decoding skills within authentic reading contexts. ◆ Create activities that enable students to apply phonemic awareness and phonics skills in activities that include authentic reading and writing activities. ◆ Create socially interactive activities to support learning.
Reading depends on prior knowledge of text structures and organization.	To have reading experiences in a wide variety of genres with a wide variety of text structures and organization.	◆ Focus on importance of text structures and organization, including nonfiction scavenger hunt that requires students to locate specific text elements (Robb, 2003).
Reading is personal, social, and cultural. We construct meaning on the basis of our life experiences.	To interact with others, and to understand and value multiple perspectives.	◆ Create think-pair-share experiences. ◆ Create literature discussion groups. ◆ Create socially interactive learning centers.
We read a lot!	To read a lot!	◆ Provide many opportunities for independent reading, including literature discussion groups. ◆ Create school-home connections to encourage independent reading.

What Do Thoughtful Readers Know? What Do We Need to Teach Readers Who Struggle?

Reading Is a Purposeful Process

Thoughtful readers implicitly know that we do not read to pronounce words on a page or to get to the final period. We read to achieve personal, social, emotional, cultural, and professional goals that we could not achieve without reading.

▶ **Think back to everything you read today. What did you read and why did you read it? What goals were you achieving?**
The New York State Learning Standards for the English Language Arts (1996) identify four overarching purposes for reading:

- ◆ Reading for information and understanding

- ◆ Reading for literary response and expression

- ◆ Reading for critical analysis and evaluation

- ◆ Reading for social interaction

While all reading involves the integration of two or more of these purposes, I believe these four purposes encompass virtually all reasons for reading. I can't think of a purpose for all of my own reading that does not fit within these four. Can you?

Readers who struggle often think that the purpose of reading is to pronounce all the words on a page. They have not internalized the understanding that reading is meaningful activity to achieve goals, answer questions, and enrich their lives. We must focus on helping readers who struggle establish purpose for every reading experience.

Reading Is a Strategic Purpose Composed of Three Phases: Before Reading, During Reading, and After Reading

Thoughtful readers do not simply pick up printed text and begin reading. We implicitly use strategies that will help us achieve our goals. Often we don't even realize that we are using these strategies: we just instinctively do what we do as a *habit of mind* because the strategies have enabled us to be successful, thoughtful readers. As noted by Pressley (1998), "Exceptionally skilled reading is very active reading, from before reading begins to after it is concluded. Much of the activity can be described as strategic responses articulated with prior knowledge related to the topic of the reading" (p. 5). Similarly, Keene and Zimmerman (1997) note, "Many of the studies that examined the thinking of proficient readers pointed to only seven or eight thinking strategies used by proficient readers. . . . Researchers suggested that teachers focus instructional time and creative energy on helping students gradually learn to use these strategies as they read a variety of texts at all grade levels" (p. 21).

▶ Think about the strategies you use when reading a text. What strategies do you use before reading the text to prepare your mind for constructing meaning? What strategies do you use during reading to support comprehension? What strategies do you use after you reach the last period to make sure that your reading made an impact on your life?

Thoughtful readers implicitly apply before-reading, during-reading, and after-reading strategies because they understand that the overarching purpose of reading is to process print in order to make an impact on their lives. Successful readers implicitly know that this is the purpose of reading, and successfully apply these strategies to accomplish this goal. Many of our readers who struggle do not implicitly know these strategies or the purpose of reading. They mistakenly believe that their more successful peers magically understand what they are reading, without realizing that they can achieve the same success if they use before-reading, during-reading, and after-reading strategies. We need to *explicitly* teach the strategies needed for thoughtful comprehension through think-alouds, demonstrations, and modeling in every reading lesson we teach.

Table 9.2 summarizes the essential before-reading, during-reading, and after-reading strategies we need to teach readers who struggle. Before-reading strategies are used to establish the knowledge base we need to connect to the text; to form an expectation about the story, information, or ideas we think will be developed as we read; and to establish our purpose for reading. During-reading strategies are used to make sure we *stop and think* about the information and ideas being communicated through the text, and to self-monitor for understanding. After-reading strategies are used to personally respond to the text by thinking about the *big* ideas in the text, such as the themes and life lessons the author was communicating; by making connections; and by extending the text through discussion, writing, art, music, drama, and research to learn more.

Successful readers implicitly use all these strategies. We need to systematically and explicitly teach readers who struggle, to help them take ownership of this repertoire of strategies that lead to reading success.

TABLE 9.2. Essential Reading Strategies

Explicitly focus on these essential strategies in every reading lesson until students have internalized them and can apply them automatically and instinctively.

Before Reading	During Reading	After Reading
◆ Activate prior knowledge ◆ Sample text ◆ Predict ◆ Form purpose for reading	◆ Stop-and-think to summarize and predict ◆ Figure out unknown words to support understanding ◆ Use sensory images (visualize, hear dialogue, feel, smell, taste) ◆ Make personal connections: identify with characters and/ or events ◆ Think about important messages ◆ Read all the text on the pages ◆ Recognize that an author's *big* idea is often at the end of the text	◆ Retell/summarize ◆ Identify author's intended message(s), themes, big ideas ◆ Make connections to self, the world, other experiences ◆ Generate questions: "I wonder . . ." ◆ Extend reading through writing, oral discussion, art, drama, research, technology

Reading Is a Social and Cultural Process

Thoughtful readers know that they bring vast *funds of knowledge* (Moll, 1994) to every reading experience: knowledge that was developed through a history of social and cultural experiences. They draw upon their knowledge of the world and their knowledge of print to construct meaning. They actively use their *schema*, or mental model of the world, to make sense of printed text and create interpretations of text based upon their prior knowledge (Rumelhart, 1980).

▶ **Think about the articles you read in today's newspaper. How does your history of experience impact on your interpretation of world events? How does reading these articles connect you to other people and to the world?**

Readers who struggle often do not realize that they have reading experiences and knowledge of print that they can apply to new reading experiences. Examples include knowledge and experience with story structure, using known words to figure out new words, and connecting stories to prior knowledge. Instead, they approach every reading experience as if they are a blank slate stepping into the unknown. We need to guide students to tap into the knowledge bases they already bring to reading by using K-W-L charts, semantic webs, and quick-writes to tap into prior knowledge; engaging them in pre-reading discussions that focus on essential information that will be presented in the text; and reinforcing print knowledge and skills that they should use when they read. Our readers who struggle do not recognize that they bring a strong knowledge base to reading. They do not apply what they know to make connections to text. We need to show them that they bring a solid knowledge base to reading that they can use to comprehend printed text.

Reading Is a Metacognitive Process

Thoughtful readers know that reading centers on reflecting about the skills and strategies they must use to comprehend printed text. *Metacognition* refers to one's knowledge concerning one's own cognitive processes and products (Flavell, 1976). Readers who

According to fifth graders, good readers . . .

- read between the lines
- understand the message the author is sending
- write down notes
- read with expression
- make connections
- look for important parts
- use sticky notes to mark things worth discussing
- can summarize what they have read
- read many different genres
- are aware of why literary techniques are used
- recommend good books to people
- discuss books
- self-question
- create pictures in minds
- read over well-written parts
- look up words they don't understand
- make inferences
- make predictions
- love to read

Stacy then added . . .
  - recognize fact and fiction
  - recognize multiple perspectives
  - share ("Look what I found," "Listen to this," "You've got to read this")
  - read for meaning
  - take risks
  - predict . . . and then confirm or revise

Stacy concluded the class chart with this quote from Keene and Zimmerman's (1997) book *Mosaic of Thought*: "We read . . . to make meaning of our lives and to connect to those who have come before us and those who share the planet with us. We read to do our jobs, to learn, to explore, to adventure, to bring order to chaos, to open new vistas, to better understand the world around us, and to develop compassion for the human condition. Great writing leaves us with more questions than answers" (p. 217).

FIGURE **9.3.** *Stacy's fifth graders reflect on their reading strategies.*

struggle need to be guided to think about the skills and strategies they are using to construct meaning from text. Stacy, a fifth-grade teacher and reading specialist, knows the importance of teaching all her students to be metacognitively strategic readers. Figure 9.3 shows the chart her students created that identify the strategies they use when reading. The year after Stacy completed this chart with her fifth graders, she moved to first grade. While there

Student #1
Read with icspreshin. Paos at pereid. Look at the end sound. Look at the picher. Make prdisons. Acs quweshtins. Read the blrb.

Student #2
Readrs pos at the end of a peareaed. Readrs pount to the words. Readrs make prdicrshins. Readrs make sagestions for the arthr. Readrs sand oout words. Readrs look at the pichrs.

Student #3
Poze at pereeits. If you don't know a word cevr it up and read the rest. I strt to srech it out. Readers uooze exrprechin. If you cent read a book put it back/ you can look at the pichrs. Read's tace ther time.

Figure 9.4. *Stacy's first graders reflect on their reading strategies.*

are obvious developmental differences between first and fifth grade that impact on text selection and strategy priorities, Stacy knew that it was important for all her first graders to become metacognitively aware of the strategies they use to achieve reading success.

Figure 9.4 shows three personal reflections on reading by Stacy's first-grade students (spelling presented exactly as written). Notice that her students are gaining control of their reading. They are learning the strategies thoughtful readers use to construct meaning from text. Stacy knows that her readers who struggle will need extra support to achieve reading success, but she also knows that the reading goals are the same for *all* readers.

Summary of the Reading Base

Thoughtful readers know that reading is purposeful activity. They implicitly apply a variety of before-reading, during-reading, and after-reading strategies to construct deep meaning of text that uses the literal information in the text to think about the bigger meanings the author intends to communicate. And they use their funds of knowledge to build connections between what they know and what they are going to read. This is what we need to teach readers who struggle. We must guide them to set purposes for reading, so they know *why* they are reading. We must explicitly teach before-reading strategies that serve to focus readers' attention on the text to be read, activate their prior knowledge, and help them form expectations about what they might learn from the text. We must explicitly teach during-reading strategies that serve to focus readers' attention on making sure they are reading for meaning—by emphasizing stop-and-think strategies to summarize, make connections, predict, think about important ideas, and solve print problems such as figuring out unfamiliar words. We must focus on after-reading strategies that use the information communicated in the text to think about *big* ideas that make an impact on their lives, and encourage them to express personal response through discussion, writing, art, research, or other creative responses. We must teach students to draw upon their funds of knowledge so they can build on what they already know to make connections to new information and ideas.

Successful readers implicitly do all of the above without thinking about it. We have internalized a metaunderstanding for achieving reading success that enables us to be enriched by our reading experience. Sadly, many readers who struggle have not internalized this metaunderstanding, and have not learned to internalize the repertoire of strategies required to get the payoff from reading. Thus, to reach and teach readers who struggle, we must focus on explicit, systematic strategy instruction: continually modeling our own thinking; providing multiple opportunities for guided practice; and, using the gradual release of responsibility model, moving students to independent application that demonstrates that they have internalized the reading process used by thoughtful readers and can implicitly apply it when the teacher is no longer present. Teaching this process is our yearlong commitment. Our year-end payoff is the celebration of our students' motivation to read, and their increased achievement.

Chatarina, a fourth-grade teacher, puts these principles into action to help all her students, including her students who struggle, achieve reading success. She immerses her students in a variety of reading experiences every day that teach them to be thoughtful readers. She co-created the strategy chart below with her students (see Table 9.3) to emphasize that successful readers do not simply apply strategies: they understand *why* they apply them, how strategies build on their funds of knowledge, and how they support reading success.

TABLE 9.3. Strategies Used by Thoughtful Readers

Before Reading	
Strategy Used	**Because . . .**
◆ Read title and author; look at front cover.	◆ Title and cover may stimulate interest and serve as a motivator to read. If reader has read books by the same author, it may (or may not) set a purpose for reading.
◆ Read back cover and inside flap; take a picture walk.	◆ Reader gets information about the text, author, and topic, which may activate schema.
◆ Try out the text.	◆ Thoughtful readers make sure the text is not too difficult to read.
◆ Activate prior knowledge.	◆ What readers bring to the text strongly affects their comprehension.
◆ Make predictions.	◆ This gives the reader a purpose for reading to check if predictions come true.
◆ Ask questions.	◆ This gives the reader a purpose for reading to find answers.
◆ For expository text: look at pictures; read captions, titles, subtitles, bolded words, charts, diagrams; check vocabulary.	◆ These strategies activate readers' schema, increase prior knowledge, and build awareness of text features and structures to increase comprehension.
During Reading	
◆ Stop and think about what they are reading.	◆ This helps to monitor their understanding.
◆ Make pictures in their minds.	◆ This brings the text to life.
◆ Reread.	◆ This clears up confusion and helps readers remember important details and facts.
◆ Make predictions.	◆ This sets a purpose for continued reading and makes the readers adjust comprehension.
◆ Look at pictures and graphs.	◆ This helps in understanding confusing parts.
	continued on next page

Table 9.3 continued

◆ Ask questions.	◆ This clarifies confusion and sets a purpose for continued reading.
◆ Make connections to personal life, other books or movies, or life in general.	◆ This makes books come alive and activates the readers' schema.
◆ For expository text: stop and retell in their own words in their mind, to someone else, or on paper.	◆ This is a way to check if the reader understands the content and can recall facts.
◆ Take notes and use graphic organizers.	◆ This helps the reader organize thoughts and facts.
After Reading	
◆ Think about what they read.	◆ Readers find out if they understood what they read, if they liked it, how it connects to their lives, and if they have unanswered questions.
◆ Retell.	◆ This is a way to check if the reader understands the text and can recall facts.
◆ Look back/reread.	◆ The reader wants to clarify confusing parts or enjoy and share favorite parts.
◆ Think about why the author wrote the text.	◆ This helps the reader understand the main idea, lesson, or message.
◆ React through discussions, writings, or drawings.	◆ Sharing makes reading more enjoyable, points out different views, clarifies concepts, and enables readers to make more connections to other books, movies, their lives, or the world.

To make an impact on readers who struggle, we need to focus on systematic, explicit instruction of these essential before-reading, during-reading, and after-reading strategies used by successful readers.

We also need to focus on developing the knowledge base in phonemic awareness, phonics, automatic sight-word knowledge, fluency, and vocabulary (National Institutes of Health, 2000).

Meaningful approaches to developing phonemic awareness and phonics knowledge include daily writing, developing word patterns, making words (Cunningham, 2005), and have-a-go spelling where students are challenged to spell unfamiliar words by using their knowledge of letter sounds. Meaningful approaches to increasing automatic sight-word knowledge include word walls, reader's theater, repeated readings, and writing. Meaningful approaches to developing fluency include shared readings, peer reading, and reader's theater. Meaningful approaches to increasing vocabulary include teaching strategies that use context, creating vocabulary charts, and using new vocabulary in oral discussion and writing.

The Role of the Teacher

We are the most important factor in making a difference in the literacy lives of our students who struggle with reading. It is our knowledge, understanding, and performance skill that will break the Cycle of Failure and build the Cycle of Success. The International Reading Association (2000) noted in its position statement that "every child deserves excellent reading teachers because teachers make a difference in children's reading achievement and motivation to read" (p. 1). Similarly, Darling-Hammond's (2000) research concluded that "the effects of well-prepared teachers on student achievement can be stronger than the influences of student background factors such as poverty, language background, and minority status" (p. 37).

We all must envision ourselves as *literacy mentors* who are teaching literacy apprentices. Consider that all your excellent teachers served as your mentors. Now, examine more closely the roles of a mentor. What does it mean to be a mentor?

First, a mentor must motivate and inspire apprentices. How do we do this? We must share our passion for reading. We must be a cheerleader for reading. We must celebrate students when they are reading. We must make reading the center of the learning universe.

Second, a mentor must be a role model for successful reading. This means that we must share our reading lives with our students, including the reading strategies we use to achieve reading success.

Third, as mentors we must respect and build on the funds of knowledge that our students bring to the literacy learning process. All students, including students who struggle with reading, bring rich family and community experiences to school that establish a strong knowledge base for learning. We must build bridges to the family and community lives of our students so that we can create links to reading. Thus, we must use texts that relate to student lives. We must encourage students to make personal connections between texts and their own experiences. We must empower students to teach us things they know and understand that we might not have experienced.

Fourth, as mentors we must challenge our students who struggle with reading to learn and achieve more than they think they know and can do. But our challenges must be *achievable* challenges that always lead to successful learning experiences. Thus, we must understand how to use assessment to determine each student's current level of knowledge, understanding, and performance skill in order to plan instruction that teaches within each student's *zone of proximal development* (ZPD) (Vygotsky, 1978) where we provide sufficient support to successfully scaffold learning (Bruner, 1983) in order to move students from a level of dependence to a level of greater independence. These achievable challenges center on the teacher making informed, thoughtful decisions regarding text choice, instructional focus, and literacy extension responses.

Fifth, as mentors we must systematically and explicitly teach, demonstrate, and model every skill and strategy we want students to learn. We tend to think of the phrase *systematic, explicit instruction* as applying to phonics instruction (National Institutes of Health, 2000), but students who struggle with reading need to experience systematic, explicit instruction in all areas of reading: instruction that clearly explains and demonstrates applications of all the skills and strategies used by thoughtful readers. We must continually model our own uses of these skills and strategies so that students can develop the schema that gives them the mental model they need to be able to apply these skills and

To motivate and inspire

To be a role model

To respect and build on the funds of knowledge learners bring to the
literacy learning process

To challenge with achievable challenges

To systematically and explicitly teach, demonstrate, and model

To guide and support

To provide opportunity for meaningful practice

To care and encourage

To advise and answer questions

To continually assess what the learner knows and what the learner needs
to know

To respond to the learner's individuality by building on strengths in order
to overcome weaknesses

To respond and provide feedback through honest, open dialogue

To accept approximations as part of the process of learning

To move learners toward independence

To celebrate effort and achievement—the payoff

FIGURE 9.5. *What does it mean to be a literacy mentor?*

strategies in their own reading (Rumelart, 1980). Figure 9.5 identifies the essential roles of a literacy mentor.

We need to understand the similarities and differences between teaching successful readers and readers who struggle. Table
9.4 highlights the emphasis for all readers, as well as the special
needs of readers who struggle. Note that the focus for readers
who struggle is no different from the focus for all readers; more
intensive instruction and very careful decision making are needed
to build both affective and cognitive success.

Conclusion

Reaching and teaching students who struggle requires a comprehensive, multifaceted approach. As Gaskins (1998) notes, reaching and teaching readers who struggle involves a lot more than

TABLE 9.4. Similarities and Differences between Teaching All Readers and Teaching Struggling Readers

Emphasis for All Readers	Special Needs of Readers Who Struggle
Goals: Success, empowerment, achievement, enjoyment High standards and expectations, and achievable challenges Principles that guide instruction; building effective habits of mind Creating a supportive learning environment Using assessment to guide instruction and texts Immersing learners in purposeful engagements with literacy across the curriculum throughout the day; large blocks of time in authentic reading and writing through a comprehensive, balanced literacy program Building school/home connections and encouraging extensive reading outside school Thoughtful discussions around texts; the best reading instruction flows on a sea of rich discussion Thoughtful reading/writing connections; writing to deepen understanding Ownership and independence	Needs: Building motivation, self-esteem, confidence, empowerment, ownership, sense of success; affirming the reading experience through coaching, cheerleading, and successful text experiences that drive interest to engage More explicit instruction and demonstrations of what good readers do More immediate payoffs for effort through affirming human response More authentic practice; repeated reading More careful text choices for guided reading to ensure success More explicit and purposeful guiding to scaffold for success; supplying essential support to ensure achievement (predicting, power tracking; stop-and-think, self-monitoring for meaning) Adaptation of difficult texts and assignments; providing choice More explicit, embedded word study linked to assessed needs emerging from text reading More small-group guided reading and shared reading instruction More 1:1 reading conferences that link careful assessment (*kidwatching*) with specific feedback, discussion, and reflection ("What did you do that good readers do?" "What do you need to practice?") More opportunities to respond to texts through oral discussion and writing More opportunities for original writing

direct instruction. The following summarizes the research and identifies the essential steps to make a difference in the literacy lives of our readers who struggle.

Helping Our Struggling Readers Requires a Comprehensive, Multifaceted Approach

◆ Careful assessment to identify level of performance, and to determine what the student knows and what the teacher needs to teach

◆ Commitment to differentiated instruction that provides appropriate texts, instruction, and assignments that enable *all* students to engage and achieve success

◆ Focus on high-standards achievement for all students; while we adapt texts and instruction to meet the needs of different learners, high standards remain the same; all students must be guided to be thoughtful comprehenders of text who can use the information suggested in the text to identify big ideas and important messages, and can make personal connections to their lives, other texts, and the world

◆ Articulation with support personnel to make sure that everyone is working on a common approach to instruction in common texts

◆ Proactive outreach to parents to involve them in a partnership for the education of their children.

◆ Thoughtful decision making that engages struggling readers in every aspect of the learning process because the texts, instruction, and assignments enable total involvement and the opportunity to experience success

◆ Commitment to creating a classroom community of learners where all students feel valued, where all perspectives and voices are respected, and where all students work together to learn

---

Successful readers bring a wealth of implicit knowledge and understanding to every reading experience. They know that reading centers on constructing meaning from text. They know that they are reading for a purpose. They know that they have important funds of knowledge to build on to make connections to what they read. They know that they have a repertoire of skills and strategies to use in order to achieve their reading goals. Successful readers implicitly do all of the above without thinking about it. They have internalized a metaunderstanding of all the factors that thoughtful readers have integrated to achieve reading success. Sadly, many readers who struggle have not internalized this metaunderstanding, and may not have internalized the repertoire of strategies required to get the *big* ideas from text and read for thoughtful literacy. Thus, our entire focus for reaching and teaching readers who struggle must be on explicit, systematic instruction that teaches them the metaunderstanding applied by their more successful peers. We can do this through a process that uses the gradual release of responsibility model to provide multiple opportunities of demonstration and modeling, guided application, and independent practice. Teaching this process requires a commitment to high standards for all students; ongoing assessment to guide instruction and monitor progress; flexible grouping; differentiated instruction; and most important, ensuring that every reading experience for a reader who struggles leads to success rather than reinforces failure. The process isn't easy, but the payoff is the celebration of our students' motivation to read, and their increased achievement.

References

Allington, R. L. (2006). *What really matters for struggling readers: Designing research-based programs.* (2nd ed.). Boston: Pearson/ Allyn and Bacon.

Allington, R. L., & McGill-Franzen, A. (1989). Different programs, indifferent instruction. In D. Lipsky & A. Gartner (Eds.), *Beyond separate education: Quality education for all* (pp. 75–98). Baltimore, MD: Brookes.

Anderson, R. C., Wilson, P., & Fielding, L. (1988). Growth in reading and how children spend their time outside of school. *Reading Research Quarterly, 23*(3), 285–303.

Braunger, J., & Lewis, J. (2006). *Building a knowledge base in reading* (2nd ed.). Newark, DE: International Reading Association; Urbana, IL: National Council of Teachers of English.

Bruner, J. (1983). *Child's talk: Learning to use language.* New York: Norton.

Cambourne, B. (1995). Toward an educationally relevant theory of literacy learning: Twenty years of inquiry. *Reading Teacher, 49*(3), 182–90.

Commission on Reading of the National Council of Teachers of English. (2004). *On reading, learning to read, and effective reading instruction: An overview of what we know and how we know it.* Urbana, IL: National Council of Teachers of English.

Cunningham, P. M. (2005). *Phonics they use: Words for reading and writing* (4th ed.). Boston: Pearson/Allyn & Bacon.

Darling-Hammond, L. (2000). How teacher education matters. *Journal of Teacher Education, 51*(3), 166–73.

Flavell, J. H. (1976). Metacognitive aspects of problem solving. In L. B. Resnick (Ed.), *The nature of intelligence* (pp. 231–35). Hillsdale, NJ: Erlbaum.

Gaskins, I. W. (1998). There's more to teaching at-risk and delayed readers than good reading instruction. *Reading Teacher, 51*(7), 534–47.

Guthrie, J. T., & Davis, M. H. (2003). Motivating struggling readers in middle school through an engagement model of classroom practice. *Reading & Writing Quarterly, 19*(1), 59–85.

International Reading Association. (1998). *Standards for reading professionals.* Newark, DE: International Reading Association.

International Reading Association. (2000). *Excellent reading teachers: A position statement of the International Reading Association.* Newark, DE: International Reading Association.

Keene, E. O., & Zimmerman, S. (1997). *Mosaic of thought: Teaching comprehension in a reader's workshop.* Portsmouth, NH: Heinemann.

Moll, L. (1994). Literacy research in community and classrooms: A sociocultural approach. In R. B. Ruddell, M. R. Ruddell, & H. Singer (Eds.), *Theoretical models and processes of reading* (4th ed., pp. 179–207). Newark, DE: International Reading Association.

National Institutes of Health. National Institute of Child Health and Human Development. (NICHD). (2000). *Report of the National Reading Panel. Teaching children to read.* (NIH Publication No. 00-4769). Washington, DC: Government Printing Office.

New York State Department of Education. (1996). *Learning standards for English language arts* (Rev. ed.). Albany, NY: Department of Education. Retrieved July 3, 2008, from http://www.emsc.nysed.gov/ciai/ela/pub/elalearn.pdf

Pearson, P. D., & Gallagher, M. C. (1983). The instruction of reading comprehension. *Contemporary Educational Psychology, 8*(3). 317–44.

Pressley, M. (1998). *Reading instruction that works: The case for balanced teaching.* New York: Guilford Press.

Primeaux, J. (2000). Shifting perspectives on struggling readers. *Language Arts, 77*(6), 537–42.

Robb, L. (2003). *Teaching reading in social studies, science, and math: Practical ways to weave comprehension strategies into your content area teaching.* New York: Scholastic.

Rumelhart, D. E. (1980). Schemata: The building blocks of cognition. In R. J. Sopiro, B. C. Bruce, & F. Brewer (Eds.), *Theoretical issues in reading comprehension: Perspectives from cognitive psychology, linguistics, artificial intelligence, and education* (pp. 38–58). Hillsdale, NJ: Erlbaum.

Vygotsky, L.S. (1978). *Mind in society: The development of higher psychological processes.* Cambridge, MA: Harvard University Press.

III

WHERE DO THE COMMISSION ON READING DOCUMENTS TAKE US?

CHAPTER TEN

What We Know about Reading Curricula and Best Practices: The Decision-Making Matrix

PENNY SILVERS
DePaul University

MARGARET YATSEVITCH PHINNEY
University of Wisconsin–River Falls

R esearch has shown that it isn't the program or the materials that support learning, it's the teacher's ability to effectively assess students' growth needs, to select materials that will support growth, and to creatively and effectively teach to those needs (Allington & Johnston, 2000, 2002; Bond & Dykstra, 1967; Darling-Hammond, 1999; Dykstra, 1968; Graves & Dykstra, 1997; Langer, 2002; Pressley, Allington, Wharton-McDonald, Block, & Morrow, 2001; Taylor, Pearson, Clark, & Walpole, 1999). Good teachers are astute observers of process and knowledgeable decision makers, as well as skilled practitioners. The tool we describe here allows teachers and other school personnel to apply their knowledge about reading and language arts, and to use their ability to make informed decisions about students' needs. It is a systematic way to include the *real* experts in the quest for measurable results and annual yearly progress (AYP). It allows a school to move away from "teacher-proof" programs and materials, and to put local decision making about good practice in the hands of local decision makers.

The key word in the title of this chapter is *decision*: "a conclusion or resolution made after consideration" (*Oxford American Dictionary*, 2005). In support of teachers as decision makers, one of the projects of the Commission on Reading of the National Council of Teachers of English (NCTE) was to create a tool that could be useful to the decision makers in a particular school, district, or state as they choose programs and materials that will meet their self-established goals for reading instruction. The aim of this matrix tool is to provide an initial checklist of possible features and components that teams of decision makers might want to consider when selecting a reading program.

Members of the Commission on Reading are selected by NCTE. They are chosen for their expertise, knowledge, and experience in teaching and researching about reading and literacy-related issues. The majority of the members are currently teaching children and/or university students, or are providing professional development for practicing teachers. Two consecutive subcommittees of the Commission on Reading worked for nearly three years to develop the tool we are presenting here. (The complete *Features of Literacy Programs: A Decision-Making Matrix* can be found in Appendix C and is downloadable from the NCTE website, allowing for customization according to local needs.) During this time, the features listed in the checklist went through multiple revisions, as a bevy of reading experts examined the kinds of components and elements found in a wide variety of research studies, reading programs, and reading approaches. Additionally, classroom teachers and curriculum specialists have field-tested the *Decision-Making Matrix* in their schools and districts to assess its relevance and usefulness in making curricular decisions about literacy.

The features listed in the matrix reflect the theoretical and philosophical perspectives of many of the research studies that are referenced in the NCTE guideline *On Reading, Learning to Read, and Effective Reading Instruction* (see Appendix A). It is also important to note that while these features are grounded in research, whether the features are *desirable* depends on the belief systems of the decision makers using the matrix; the particular instructional needs of the student population for which reading materials are being selected; and local, state, and federal mandates. The Commission on Reading wanted the decision makers who will be using the matrix to have a way to express their beliefs about reading and language arts. This matrix provides a unique opportunity for discussion about the participants' current understanding of literacy practices, and provides a vehicle for bringing their beliefs and issues to the surface to be discussed, examined, and ultimately formed into a shared belief system about literacy.

Bringing the Matrix to Life: Getting Started by Talking and Inquiring

The *Decision-Making Matrix* is a dynamic document that has the power to transform its users and help create a community of thinkers, learners, and knowledgeable literacy educators. Before looking over the matrix features and beginning a collaborative discussion, participants are asked to complete two statements about reading. These two statements invite the participants to write a brief explanation of *what they believe reading is* and *what they feel reading instruction should be.* These are critical statements and must be the starting point for using the matrix. It is assumed that when the curriculum committee or program selection group convenes, these statements will open the discussion and generate much insight into personal philosophies, understandings, and beliefs about reading and reading instruction. What usually emerges from these two statements is a lively conversation about each participant's views of reading. Through talk, it will become clear that each person brings a unique perspective to the group with a slightly (or greatly) different view of what reading is—and how to teach it.

Matrix users tell us that they learn so much about colleagues from these collaborative conversations. This shared dialogue will lead to greater success in decision making, as beliefs are expressed, questions are asked, research begins to inform, and participants come to a shared understanding of good reading practices. When this occurs, the reading programs being considered become tools to support what is valued by the participants, rather than controlling and driving the curriculum. It is our hope that as the matrix is used, the participants' shared beliefs and collective knowledge of reading will help guide them through the selection process. In this way, program choices will be made based on the identified strengths and weaknesses of the program being evaluated, rather than on promises made by the publishers to entice a district to adopt their program. Through informed decision making, the matrix can help support the emergence of a shared belief system about literacy that can positively impact the quality of reading instruction in a school or district, and can assist in the selection of materials that support what the group believes to be the best literacy practices. This shared belief system is reinforced when participants talk about the final question: "How close is the match between the program and your definition of reading, and what do you believe reading instruction should be?" (Commission on Reading, 2005, p. 7).

Using the Matrix: An Overview

After the personal reflection is completed and beliefs and understandings have been discussed, the participants focus on questions associated with the categories framed in the matrix, such as materials, instruction, approaches to teaching reading, assessment, and professional development. The Commission has categorized the features into the following sections:

Media/Tools

Materials

Participant Structures

Instructional Approaches

Comprehension

Word Recognition and Word Study

Reading and Writing Connection

Student Role

Assessment

Professional Resources and Development

We will discuss each section individually. Within each category are more specific associated features. At the bottom of each list are additional spaces for users to add features that they feel are important. To the right of each feature are five columns. Column #1 offers a value from 1 to 4 for each feature established by the Commission based on its support of reading as a meaning-making process (see Comprehension below for elaboration). The Commission indicated the numerical rating of each feature, according to the members' collective beliefs and knowledge about reading. They wanted these ratings to be used as a guide if the local users wished. However, the Commission also wanted users to feel free to indicate their own rating values for each feature without being unduly influenced by the Commission's ratings. Column #2 provides space to value each feature according to local decision makers' beliefs about reading and the local instructional needs. Some users prefer to white-out the Commission's numerical rating column and establish local values from the start, and that's fine. Of greatest importance are the discussions that ensue in the process of establishing these values. These discussions are a critical component of the decision-making process and have the potential to clarify the local understandings and purposes underlying the choices that are made.

The remaining three columns in the matrix are titled *Degree of Presence* and are labeled H (high), M (medium), and L (low). These allow for a qualitative evaluation of the degree to which a particular feature is emphasized in the program or materials being considered. For example, if reader's and writer's workshops are considered very important by the users, they would look through the program materials expecting to see a high degree of presence. They would put a check mark in the H box if they found it to be highly present in the program. However, if these workshops were not highly present, they would indicate either M or L.

After going through the features in the matrix, and closely examining the program materials to indicate degree of presence, the users would then tally (or note in some way) those features that coincided with their numerical ratings, and those features that were in disagreement with their ratings. So if reading and writing workshops were valued with a rating of 4 by the local users and found to have a high degree of presence, that would be noted as a positive. If users found a low degree of presence, this would indicate that a feature valued by the local users was minimally (or not) available to them in this particular program. By the end of the matrix, there will be a clear indication of the strengths and weaknesses of the program being evaluated, based on what the local users value. Upon analysis, missing instructional components can then be supplemented at the local level, or the program can be eliminated as not meeting the district curricular needs.

The matrix shows visually whether a program is a good match for the district or school. Often, users are amazed at how little connection there is between a program being evaluated and the curricular needs of the district. They find that even though a program may have been highly recommended and publicized, it lacks components valued by the local users. On the other hand, they may find that with just a few additions, a program may be a good match for their needs.

Decision makers are encouraged to adjust the matrix in any way that serves their purposes. For example, a school may only need materials to support one particular aspect of reading instruction, such as the Reading and Writing Connection. The decision makers would then focus solely on those features in the matrix and not analyze any of the other features. However, all the categories and features are worth reviewing at some point to discuss local needs, assess what is working or what needs to be improved, or simply start conversations about good literacy instruction. The matrix reflects the most current thinking and research in reading and literacy instruction, so using it provides not only meaningful data about programs, but also encouragement for good, research-supported literacy practices.

Exploring the Matrix Features

Following are brief descriptions and rationales for each category of features in the matrix.

Media/Tools

Books

Authentic connected texts, complete and unabridged

Predictable texts

Decodable texts

Abridged texts

Skills-based texts

Leveled texts

Nonfiction texts

Classroom libraries

Controlled vocabulary

Original illustrations

Publisher-substituted illustrations

Videotapes

Internet

Computer software

Audiotapes

School-to-home connections

Suggestions for extended readings

Recall-level worksheets

Books, of course, are the primary tool for teaching reading, and publishers offer us myriad choices. In the trade book market alone, thousands of new titles are offered every year in addition to new versions of old titles. We live in a Golden Age of children's literature, in which some of the most thoughtful writers and most talented artists are presenting us with sensitive and beautiful material that we, in turn, may use to inspire our students. Yet even excellent children's literature can go out of print almost as fast as it appears, so keeping up with—and taking advantage of—the good offerings becomes a full-time task in itself. (A passionate, well-informed media specialist in a school is a true blessing!) It is for this reason that we feel every teacher-in-training should take a course dedicated solely to the study of children's literature. That course should include practice and discussion related to assessing the *quality* of the literature encountered. Later, when we assess anthologies of children's literature for use in teaching reading, we will understand why it is so important that stories be unabridged and contain all the original illustrations. We understand that a good fiction or nonfiction picture book is an intentional and skillful choreographing of text and illustrations. To change either is to unnecessarily diminish the quality inherent in the original.

Materials written specifically for teaching beginning reading can be a mixed bag. Some have good-quality illustrations, and the content not only captures interest but is predictable and well designed for scaffolding readers as they learn to take cues from the graphophonic system. Other materials use highly controlled vocabulary designed to follow an arbitrary sequence of phonics rules and patterns. The results can sound so contrived and artificial that comprehension is virtually impossible. Illustrations are often without character or artistic quality. With the availability of such a rich body of literature, we want to spend our money on books with lively, interesting words and content rather than "Matt can pat a tan cat on a flat mat," and on compelling or stunning illustrations with a recognizable style.

With respect to tools, as teachers we are increasingly urged to bring our students into the computer age. In fact, we often find ourselves being brought in *by* our students. They come to kindergarten having watched thousands of hours of television and played hundreds of hours of video games. We may sometimes find ourselves competing with these intense interests as we try to encourage our students—even at the college level—to engage with books and in discussions of ideas. Commercial interests, of course, are deeply tuned in to the marketplace and what sells. They have developed a variety of tools targeting reading teachers: interactive video games, audiotapes, smart boards, instructional films, computer software such as PowerPoint and Excel, electronic and online course organizational programs such as Blackboard and Desire2Learn (D2L), email, and online home-to-school communications systems.

Many of these tools are extremely useful, and constant refinements make them more so on a monthly basis. All of them cost money, some many thousands of dollars. The hardware alone takes huge chunks out of our precious funds. Before selections are made, careful study of an item's usefulness is necessary to ensure that money isn't being taken away from hiring good teachers and buying good books. Research shows that having access to books and time to read are critical factors in literacy development (Block & Mangieri, 2002; Braunger & Lewis, 2006; Elley, 1992; International Reading Association, 1999).

Materials Represent

Authentic multicultural perspectives (text and illustrations)

Accurate, current information

Wide range of purposes

High literary quality

Range of authors

Multiple disciplines

Multiple genres

Content likely to engage and interest readers

Content that is age and developmentally appropriate

Content that is of interest to both genders

Conceptual or thematic structures

This list allows us to look at the *orientation* of the materials with respect to a variety of factors. The members of the Commission on Reading feel that materials should represent a range of exposures for learners. A wide variety of genres, disciplines, and authors present many points of view, writing styles, and ways of transmitting information and ideas. Authentic multicultural perspectives help students learn about, understand, and appreciate the many ways humans have come to organize themselves in a global world. Exposure to well-researched and up-to-date information provides students with the grounding they will need as they pass from grade to grade and into the workplace. Students stay involved when the materials are highly engaging and motivating. If reading material is developmentally and experientially appropriate, students will feel successful and come back for more. They will begin to understand that reading and writing are processes that give them more satisfaction and enjoyment than the effort it takes to construct meaning. Structures that promote a thematic or conceptual approach provide a framework for making associations between the new and the known. Students learn to think broadly, deeply, and critically—a goal in raising future participants in a democratic society.

Participant Structures/Groupings

Whole class

Small groups

Individual (instructional and independent)

Flexible groups (interest, ability)

Pull-out instruction

Fixed-ability groups

Research shows that students learn in different ways (International Reading Association, 1999). That tells us that any approach to teaching should include a variety of arrangements to accommodate the diversity of learning styles and preferences present in any instructional setting. Whether out of shyness, fear, or interaction style, some students are just not comfortable contributing in a large-group setting. Such individuals will be disenfranchised if the only participant structure available is a whole-class organization. Others may be "performers" by nature and shine best when they have a large audience, but their imaginations do not thrive when they must work alone. To ensure that every voice can be heard, it is necessary to regularly provide opportunities for whole-class, small-group, and individual work.

The Commission members feel that flexible grouping is preferable to fixed-ability groups. Research shows that children who are placed in ability groups not only tend to stay in those groups permanently, but they actually fall further behind their peers as time goes by (Braunger & Lewis, 2006). Similarly, given the social nature of learning to read (Applebee, Langer, Nystrand & Gamoran, 2003; Pressley, 2002; Vygotsky, 1978), the Commission members feel that pull-out instruction should be kept to a minimum, and that students should be kept with their peers as much as possible. This requires that curriculum planning allow for differentiated instruction within the instructional structures of the classroom.

Instructional Approaches

Scripted, sequenced, teacher-directed

Student-generated topics and questions

Strategies and skills taught in isolation

Strategies and skills embedded in meaningful text

Scaffolded instruction toward independence

Discussion

Role play

Projects

Extensive independent reading (SSR, free-choice reading)

Student choice of instructional texts

Literature study

Guided reading

Shared reading

Partner reading

Language is used for making meaning—meaning to transmit to others, and meaning to develop understanding of and for oneself. We also know that children learn from the concrete to the abstract (Piaget & Inhelder, 1969). The *concrete* of language is its wholeness, its meaningfulness. The *abstract* of language is its parts: the smaller the parts—such as individual sounds in spoken language, or individual letters in written language—the more abstract it is, and the harder it is to understand. To learn letters and words separately from authentic meaning-making purposes is like learning about carburetors without knowing what an engine is. They are meaningless exercises. The instructional implication is that skills and strategies must be taught in the context of real reading activities rather than in isolation. They are understood as they fit into the process of meaning making. And since meaning comes out of personal interests and experiences, provision for student input into the curriculum should be a part of the program rather than a completely teacher- or program-directed sequence.

Our goal in teaching reading should be to work toward our own obsolescence, to scaffold children's learning so that they take over the reading process for themselves. Free-choice reading of self-chosen texts and literature studies interspersed with frequent opportunities for discussion are the best methods for promoting independence. Focus on particular growth areas needed to promote or refine reading efficiency is carried out through judicious use of role-play activities, projects, and shared and guided reading sessions.

Comprehension

Development of higher-level thinking and critical literacy

Emphasis on meaning making with connected text, including focus on using fiction and nonfiction text structures and features

Emphasis on application of skills in isolated text excerpts

Multiple perspectives, themes, and interpretations

Independence in learning/self-directed

Development of cognitive strategies (predicting, questioning, confirming, summarizing, inferring)

Development of metacognitive strategies

Support of risk taking

Development of multiple cueing systems

Opportunities for comprehension work

before reading

during reading

after reading

Intertextuality

Development of schema

connections to current knowledge

development of new knowledge

Reading is defined as "a complex, purposeful, social and cognitive process in which readers simultaneously use their knowledge of spoken and written language, their knowledge of the topic of the text, and their knowledge of their culture *to construct meaning* [italics ours]. Effective reading instruction is grounded in a professional knowledge of *how readers make sense of print* [italics ours] and how students learn" (Commission on Reading, 2004, p. 1). Cambourne (1988) suggested that reading is comprehension. Without a purposeful focus on meaning making, reading is no more than the calling of sounds associated with letters. Therefore, in its valuation of the components of reading (Assessment Column #1 of the matrix), the Commission has judged each feature or component in view of its support of meaning making as a "complex, purposeful, social and cognitive process" (Commission on Reading, 2005, p. 1).

Subfeatures are listed to reflect the complexity of the comprehension process and the multiple influences that affect reading overall. Given the centrality of comprehension, the Commission has valued nearly all the features as "essential." Only the feature "Emphasis on application of skills in isolated text excerpts" is rated as not important to effective literacy instruction.

Word Recognition and Word Study

Phonemic awareness in isolation

Phonemic awareness in context

Phonological awareness

Phonics in isolation

Phonics in context

Alphabetic principle

Sight words

Reading fluency with comprehension

Reading fluency without comprehension

Miscues as a window into cue and strategy utilization

Decoding of pseudo words

Word families

Experiential base for vocabulary

Etymological focus for vocabulary

Vocabulary lists

Vocabulary from text

Vocabulary building with roots and affixes

Word lists

Concept-driven vocabulary instruction

To use print as a cueing system for making meaning, literacy learners must develop an understanding of the alphabetic principle: language consists of a system of symbols representing units of meaning in particular contexts. Proficient, fluent readers who comprehend well are able to recognize most words automatically, on sight. Using the meaningful context of the text combined with their background (experiential) knowledge of the relevant topic vocabulary and some knowledge of word families, roots, and affixes, they can quickly decode virtually all texts they encounter.

In keeping with the definition of reading as a meaning-making process, studying how print works is best done in the context of authentic reading activities. Programs that advocate extensive time on word study in isolation from real reading for real purposes are not as effective as those that focus on how individual words function in support of the meaning-making process. Studying the smallest parts of language (individual sounds, individual letter-sound relationships, blending of nonsense syllables) in lists or through worksheet exercises takes time away from understanding how those symbol units function in the process of making meaning.

Reading and Writing Connections

Constructed spelling as approximation

Spelling as a window into phonics knowledge

Response to text in students' own words

Response to text as fill-in-the-blanks

Reading and writing integrated (for example, text as a source for student writing opportunities)

Essay form

Multiple-choice responses to reading

Discussions about individual and social uses of literacy

Reading and writing are mutually supporting processes (DeFord, 1981; Smith, 1994; Tierney & Shanahan, 1991). In the course of using the alphabet for personal writing, literacy learners learn how the alphabetic principle operates not only in the process of using it to make meaning from authors' work, but by representing their own meanings through writing. By writing rough drafts, journal entries, and non-published material using constructed spelling, literacy learners must *think* about how language sounds and how those sounds are represented symbolically. When they have tried to approximate the spelling of an unfamiliar word on their own, using whatever knowledge they have acquired about phonics at that point in their development, they are more likely to notice that word and how it is spelled when they encounter it during reading. The notion of "authorship" is reinforced when learners have opportunities to *become* authors themselves. By trying out a variety of genres for authentic purposes, they develop an understanding of the purposes for which different kinds of writing are used and how those writing forms are organized

(Duke & Pearson, 2002). Thus, over time the processes of reading and writing support each other; the learner's own literacy engagements become self-instructional activities.

For example, through writer's workshop, students study the craft of writing, analyze favorite authors, write in various genres, conference, revise, publish, and become proficient communicators and language users. They are encouraged to ask and answer their own inquiry questions during units of study, and they collaborate with peers, using language to explore new ideas. Through technology, students can use word processing to write, illustrate, research, email, and communicate in different ways.

With many and varied opportunities to write, read, share, and collaborate with others, students are learning not only to be fluent, proficient readers and writers. They are learning about the way language works—about the power embedded within words and texts. They are using words for particular purposes; analyzing what they are reading for implicit meaning, beliefs and assumptions; and thinking from a critical literacy perspective as meaning is inferred through reading or constructed through writing (Comber, 2001; Vasquez, Egawa, Harste, & Thompson, 2004).

Student Role

Choice of reading selections

Choice of reading extension activities

Documenting and assessing reading growth via self-reflection, portfolio development, process journals, and so on

Completion of reading logs

Problem-solving and resourcefulness encouraged

Increased independence and responsibility

Social interaction around literacy

Inquiry into own and others' literacy processes and practices

Risk taking in reading and writing encouraged

Choice is an important factor in literacy development. Time engaged in reading freely leads to proficiency (Elley, 1992; Krashen, 1996, 2004); learners will read more when they are motivated by their own interests and can engage in post-reading activities that connect to those interests. When readers are interested, they will often tackle reading material and projects that are challenging beyond their independent reading level. For example, children take on the Harry Potter series even though parts of it may be quite difficult for them in terms of their vocabulary development and knowledge of some decoding and syntactic skills. They become risk takers if they are not punished or proclaimed failures when they undertake reading and writing tasks that may cause them to make mistakes. Conversely, if they are perpetually required to read material that is not of interest to them and is also at their frustration level, they begin to see reading as a painful and irrelevant experience, and they reject engagement whenever possible (Smith, 1988).

Provision for social interaction is vitally important. It is through active, meaningful discourse that oral language is learned. Reading and writing are language processes; and sharing interests, insights, and perspectives on what we read leads to broader and deeper comprehension of reading material. With choices and sufficient time to discuss ideas and engage in meaningful literacy experiences, students will learn about language and how to use it effectively in pursuit of answers to their inquiries across the curriculum and out into the world.

Assessment

Formal, standardized

Unit tests

Classroom based, ongoing (running record, miscue analysis, retelling, anecdotal observations, student reading histories, records of reading)

Multiple-choice comprehension tests

Student directed

Written reactions and responses to texts

Portfolios

Lists of learners' reading experiences

The Commission on Reading's matrix states, "All instruction is based on a careful observation of learners' reading to determine appropriate instruction" (2005, p. 1). Harste, Woodward, and Burke (1984) talked about the learner as informant, an outcome of their research involving the close, systematic, and rigorous observation of readers and writers in action. Similarly, the Goodmans talked about *kidwatching* to indicate that the students, themselves, are our curricular and learning informants (Owocki, G. & Goodman, Y., 2002). When we observe students' learning processes, so much more is revealed than if we only grade their finished products and papers. Student progress is often most visible through observing *process* rather than product alone.

Assessment should be multifaceted and multimodal. All too often, reading programs reduce assessment to scores on unit tests, standardized measures, or levels on reading inventories. We believe that assessment is a powerful tool for students to become partners in their own learning along with their teacher. Informal indicators of learning processes can provide rich data for assessment, and should be a visible and valued part of any literacy program.

For example, to assess comprehension, provision should be made to observe participation in various kinds of discussions— paired, small group, and large group. A thorough retelling associated with miscue analysis or running records is an important assessment component (Goodman, Watson, & Burke, 1987, 2005). Written responses and projects, content transformations, dramatic enactments, and artistic interpretations also provide insight into a student's comprehension of a particular text. For assessment of meaning-making strategies, a program should include information about, and materials for, analyzing a student's miscues in the context of reading connected, meaningful texts (Goodman, 1973). Knowledge gained from such assessments should be shared with the students so that they can participate in their own goal setting for becoming more strategic readers (Goodman & Marek, 1996).

Finally, but perhaps most important, teachers must be aware of their students' levels of engagement in reading. Portfolios of representative literacy-related activities, records of books read independently, observations of absorption during free reading periods, and level of enthusiasm during discussions serve to inform the teacher's knowledge of students' motivation, attitudes, and commitment to reading. Much can be learned about what a student knows and how she approaches literacy tasks when we spend time in focused observation of her strategies for making meaning, followed by systematic analysis of the observation data.

Professional Resources and Development

Scripts for implementation of program

Data on student outcomes

Support for teacher research (for example, teacher inquiry topics and findings)

Support for meeting needs of individual students (resources, instructional approaches)

Resources and professional development experiences to build teacher knowledge about learning and literacy

Research and theory base of the program provided

Support for teacher as instructional decision maker

Provision for parent education, support, and involvement

The last section of the matrix addresses support systems for teachers. The position of the Commission is that teachers need to keep abreast of developing theory and research in the field. Good teachers are good thinkers. They are willing to broaden and deepen their knowledge bases and learn new strategies and perspectives. Programs should support and scaffold teachers' ongoing development. A program under consideration should provide avenues and resources for doing so. For example, a program that provides Internet access to regularly updated research sites that are well organized, easily negotiated, and written in understandable language would be a benefit to thinking teachers. A program that provides for choices—so that teachers may select materials, approaches, and schedules that allow them to meet the needs of their particular students—supports thoughtful teacher decision making. Scripted and highly sequenced programs do not allow teachers to customize for their students, and are not considered worthwhile by the Commission.

Using the Matrix: Some Final Thoughts

The *Decision-Making Matrix* can be used in various ways for different purposes. If the goal is a total reading program adoption, all the sections and features of the matrix should be used to examine the program materials. Sometimes individuals or small groups of users can each take sections of the matrix to evaluate their program, and then report back to the whole committee. Participants can also use the program evaluation experience as an opportunity to crystallize the group's understanding of literacy practices, and bring in some of the research listed at the end of the matrix for study and discussion. Occasionally, unfamiliar words used within sections cause some discomfort for the users. When there is uncertainty about a technical term or learning process, we suggest digging into some of the research, and talking about the technical words together to figure out their meaning. This can become a strong learning opportunity for the whole group, as participants discuss and clarify their own beliefs and expand their understanding of literacy practices. We want to remind users that there are no right or wrong answers or solutions.

Some users feel the matrix is suited more to elementary level programs than secondary. They also feel there is an emphasis on early literacy development because of the section Word Recognition and Word Study. While these features are very important to consider for primary grades, they can generate meaningful conversations among all grade levels. However, if the users feel these features are not important for their consideration, the section can be skipped, and users can focus on the features they feel to be most important.

Many middle school and secondary teachers have different scheduling configurations for language arts instruction. Some have block scheduling, which provides a way to combine reading with grammar, writing, and other language arts content. Others teach reading separately from language arts. Regardless of the format, we hope that all teachers involved in literacy (including subject area teachers if possible) will be able to participate in the literacy discussions that impact programs or the selection of materials.

The term *reading programs* does not apply exclusively to a comprehensive basal reading series. It can also refer to language arts curricula, materials, content and subject area reading selections, and learning outcomes. Although teachers of grades 6 through 12 do not necessarily have reading programs, they do select reading materials and literature to meet their curricular expectations. A discussion of the matrix features can be of great help in shaping literacy instruction, selecting materials, guiding approaches to teaching and learning, and choosing literature that meets the needs of the district or school and its students.

Conclusion

In this chapter we have presented the *Decision-Making Matrix*, developed by the Commission on Reading, as a decision-making tool for literacy instruction. The entire document is in Appendix C of this book, and we hope you will look carefully at the matrix as you read about its features and how to use it. We have tried to anticipate your questions based on our own use of the matrix and on feedback from those who have already used it. However, we recognize that any ideas, issues, or conflicts will ultimately be resolved by the local teachers, coordinators, and administrators who are responsible for making curricular choices.

We believe this document can be a powerful vehicle for exploring beliefs about reading, generating productive conversations about literacy and learning, and building a shared knowledge base and pedagogical framework that is aligned with current best practices in language arts instruction. Most of all, we know it can provide a way to honor students' own literacies, individual needs, interests, and inquiries through the thoughtful curricular and instructional literacy decisions made by informed professional educators.

References

Allington, R. L., & Johnston, P. H. (2000). *What do we know about effective fourth-grade teachers and their classrooms?* (CELA Research Report No. 13010). Albany: National Research Center on English Learning and Achievement, State University of New York.

Allington, R. L., & Johnston, P. H. (Eds.). (2002). *Reading to learn: Lessons from exemplary fourth-grade classrooms.* New York: Guilford Press.

Applebee, A. N., Langer, J. A., Nystrand, M., & Gamoran, A. (2003). Discussion-based approaches to developing understanding: Classroom instruction and student performance in middle and high school English. *American Educational Research Journal, 40*(3), 685–730.

Block, C. C., & Mangieri, J. N. (2002). Recreational reading: 20 years later. *Reading Teacher, 55*(6), 572–80.

Bond, G. L., & Dykstra, R. (1967). The cooperative research program in first-grade reading instruction. *Reading Research Quarterly, 32* (4), 348–427.

Braunger, J., & Lewis, J. P. (2006). *Building a knowledge base in reading* (2nd ed.). Newark, DE: International Reading Association; Urbana, IL: National Council of Teachers of English.

Cambourne, B. (1988). *The whole story: Natural learning and the acquisition of literacy in the classroom.* Auckland, NZ: Ashton Scholastic.

Comber, B. (2001). Critical literacy: Power and pleasure with language in the early years. *Australian Journal of Language and Literacy, 23*(pt. 3), 168–81.

Commission on Reading of the National Council of Teachers of English. (2004). *On reading, learning to read, and effective reading instruction: An overview of what we know and how we know it.* Retrieved June 16, 2008, from http://www.ncte.org/about/policy/guidelines/118620.htm

Commission on Reading of the National Council of Teachers of English. (2005). *Features of literacy programs: A decision-making matrix.* Retrieved June 16, 2008, from http://www.ncte.org/library/files/About_NCTE/Overview/ReadingMatrixFinal.pdf

Darling-Hammond, L. (1999). *Reshaping teaching policy, preparation, and practice: Influences of the National Board for Professional Teaching Standards* (ED 432570). United States Department of Education, Office of Research and Improvement. Washington, DC: American Association of Colleges of Teacher Education.

DeFord, D. E. (1981). Literacy: reading, writing, and other essentials. *Language Arts, 58*(6), 652–58.

Duke, N. K., & Pearson, P. D. (2002). Effective practices for developing reading comprehension. In A. E. Farstrup & S. J. Samuels (Eds.), *What research has to say about reading instruction* (3rd ed., pp. 205–42). Newark, DE: International Reading Association.

Dykstra, R. (1968). Summary of the second-grade phase of the Cooperative Research Program in primary reading instruction. *Reading Research Quarterly, 4*(1), 49–70.

Elly, W. B. (1992). *How in the world do students read? IEA study of reading literacy.* The Netherlands: International Association for the Evaluation of Educational Achievement. (ERIC document Reproduction Service No. ED360613)

Goodman, K. (Ed.). (1973). *Miscue analysis: Applications to reading.* Urbana, IL: ERIC Clearinghouse on Reading and Communication Skills.

Goodman, Y., & Marek, A. M. (1996). *Retrospective miscue analysis: Revaluing readers and reading.* Katonah, NY: Richard C. Owen.

Goodman, Y., Watson, D. J., & Burke, C. L. (1987). *Reading miscue inventory: Alternative procedures.* New York: Richard C. Owen.

Goodman, Y., Watson, D. J., & Burke, C. L. (2005). *Reading miscue inventory: Alternative procedures* (2nd ed.). Katonah, NY: Richard C. Owen.

Graves, M. F., & Dykstra, R. (1997). Contextualizing the first-grade studies: What is the best way to teach children to read? *Reading Research Quarterly, 32*(4), 342–44.

Harste, J. C., Woodward, V. A., & Burke, C. L. (1984). *Language stories and literacy lessons.* Portsmouth, NH: Heinemann.

International Reading Association (IRA). (1999). *Using multiple methods of beginning reading instruction: A position statement of the International Reading Association.* Newark, DE: International Reading Association. Retrieved January 14, 2007, from http://www.reading.org/resources/issues/positions_multiple_methods.html

Krashen, S. D. (1996). *Every person a reader: An alternative to the California Task Force Report on Reading.* Culver City, CA: Language Education Associates.

Krashen, S. D. (2004). *The power of reading: Insights from the research* (2nd ed.). Westport, CT: Libraries Unlimited.

Langer, J. A. (2002). *Effective literacy instruction: Building successful reading and writing programs.* Urbana, IL: National Council of Teachers of English.

Owocki, G., & Goodman, Y. (2002). *Kidwatching: Documenting children's literacy development.* Portsmouth, NH: Heinemann.

Oxford American Dictionary (2005). New York: Oxford University Press.

Piaget, J., Inhelder, B. (1969). *The psychology of the child* (H. Weaver, Trans). New York: Basic Books.

Pressley, M. (2002). Metacognition and self-regulated comprehension. In A. E. Farstrup & S. J. Samuels (Eds.), *What research has to say about reading instruction* (3rd ed., pp. 291–309). Newark, DE: International Reading Association.

Pressley, M., Allington, R. L., Wharton-McDonald, R., Block, C. C., & Morrow, L. M. (2001). *Learning to read: Lessons from exemplary first-grade classrooms.* New York: Guilford Press.

Smith, F. (1988). *Joining the literacy club: Further essays into education.* Portsmouth, NH: Heinemann.

Smith, F. (1994). *Writing and the writer* (2nd ed.). Hillsdale, NJ: Erlbaum.

Taylor, B. M., Pearson, P. D., Clark, K. F., & Walpole, S. (1999). *Beating the odds in teaching all children to read* (CIERA Report No. 2-006). Ann Arbor: Center for the Improvement of Early Reading Achievement, University of Michigan.

Tierney, R. J., & Shanahan, T. (1991). Research on the reading-writing relationship: Interactions, transactions, and outcomes. In R. Barr, M. L. Kamil, P. B. Mosenthal, & P. D. Pearson (Eds.) *Handbook of reading research: Vol. 2* (pp. 246–80). New York: Longman.

Vasquez, V., Egawa, K., Harste, J., Thompson, R. (Eds.) (2004). *Literacy as social practice*. Urbana, IL: National Council of Teachers of English.

Vygotsky, L. S. (1978). *Mind in society: The development of higher psychological processes*. Cambridge, MA: Harvard University Press.

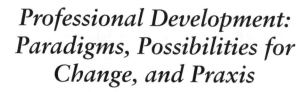

CHAPTER ELEVEN

Professional Development: Paradigms, Possibilities for Change, and Praxis

BRENDA R. HAWKINS
Jamestown Education Foundation
Jamestown, Rhode Island

A s our nation's population continues to grow and become increasingly diverse, schools must change to meet the needs and demands of an increasingly multicultural, multilingual, and global society. The challenges to be faced in the future will not be met by individuals who learn skills designed for the past in schools today. Teachers of children who will be adults during a fast-paced era characterized by continual change must help their students develop the ability and desire to learn independently, quickly, and selectively. The process of professional development is an important concern in education because teachers will not develop the necessary skills to meet these needs as a result of being trained to follow a new set of directions found in the latest edition of a program manual. Traditional, top-down training models of professional development may result in compliance but will not effect significant change in teaching, nor significant school improvement. Innovative ways of interpreting the process of teaching and learning within the context of schooling must be considered (Giroux, 1988; Hargreaves, 1994; Moll, 1990; Weiss, 1995).

Despite the general acknowledgment that schools need to change, popular approaches to instruction remain largely the same, as do curricular theories that inform them (Routman, 1996). Language and literacy learning are central to development across all areas of curriculum and provide the focus for much discussion and debate. However, commercial reading programs, which have not changed their essential form and function since they became popular in the 1920s, are in place in most schools (Crawford, 1995; Goodman, Shannon, Freeman & Murphy, 1988; Shannon & Goodman, 1994). Value for these programs has been reinforced by the standards movement, government policies, and laws, such as the No Child Left Behind (NCLB) Act, which impose uniform literacy curricula and assessments on children. A transmission orientation to teaching and learning underlies this form of instruction for children, as well as for their teachers, and remains unquestioned (Miller & Seller, 1985).

The rationale frequently named for buying commercial reading programs is that teachers are not capable of teaching students to read without the common grade-level texts and their accompanying manuals and materials (Smith, 1986). This rationale of unqualified teachers leads to a focus on the topic of professional growth and development. Within programmatic systems of teaching and learning, professional development is represented as the training of technicians to implement programs. Rather than improve their ability to facilitate literacy development, this training deskills teachers and disconnects them from their work (Shannon, 1989; Smith, 1986; Witherell & Noddings, 1991). The work of teachers must evolve to meet continually increasing demands and to reflect what is currently known about literacy learning. This will not result from simply training them periodically to implement new programs. Teachers' growth must be supported in ways that will help them meet new challenges creatively. Therefore, we need to reconsider popular instructional practices in relation to processes of the growth and development of teachers, as well as in relation to the education of children in schools (Sergiovanni & Starratt, 1993).

Literacy educators must understand the development of reading, writing, and language; the learning processes of their students; and how to select and use materials that will support each child's unique literacy growth. Unfortunately, too many teachers do not have the freedom or the flexibility to control their teaching or their own professional development with regard to literacy education. Most teachers are compelled to follow the instructional path that is laid out for them. Implementation of reading programs passes for literacy education, and the training of teachers to implement those programs passes for professional development. Teachers who must implement reading programs are tied to materials and to instructional approaches detailed for them in the accompanying manuals. These programs, described as comprehensive, provide stories and lessons arranged in a predetermined sequence. All children will read the same stories and will be paced through the same exercises, sometimes in a lockstep fashion and sometimes at variant rates of speed, for the purpose of passing the same test. The teachers, then, are teaching programs rather than teaching children to become literate. Interpretations of teaching, learning, and literacy within the boundaries of programmed instruction are narrow, and professional development is commonly offered to teachers in the same one-size-fits-all manner in which literacy lessons are offered to children in schools. A reading series consultant may explain a new manual, or an "expert" may train teachers to implement the newest top-down reform mandated by individuals who do not spend their time in classrooms and do not know the learners. As a result, programmed instruction continues to dominate literacy education, and much of what happens in schools in the name of literacy learning is meaningless to the learners. Within this prescribed context for learning, the diverse needs of students will not be met, and they will not be prepared to face a constantly changing and unknown future.

The purpose of this chapter is to discuss possibilities for professional growth of literacy teachers in relation to various approaches to professional development, with reference to metatheories of curriculum and instruction, and with consideration given to andragogical models of adult education. Sergiovanni and Starratt (1993) offered the categories of inservice training, staff development, and renewal as a framework for discussing teacher growth. Metatheories of curriculum and instruction that overarch theories of teaching and learning are identified as *transmission*, *transaction*, and *transformation* (Miller & Seller, 1985). *Andragogy* is a view of adult learning that distinguishes the education of adults as separate from the education of children, or pedagogy (Knowles, 1990). Predominant models of adult education are based on adult characteristics, adult life situations, and changes in consciousness (Merriam & Caffarella, 1991). Inservice training, a top-down approach, is located within a transmission orientation to teaching and learning. Staff development, a negotiated approach, is located within a transactional orientation to education. Andragogy and models of adult education based on adult characteristics and life situations overlap transactional and transformational orientations (Knowles, 1980, 1990; Merriam & Caffarella, 1991). Renewal, a self-directed process compatible with models of adult education based on change in consciousness, represents transformational learning (Miller & Seller, 1985; Sergiovanni & Starratt, 1993).

Approaches to Professional Development

As they discussed the professional development approaches of inservice, staff development, and renewal, Sergiovanni and Starratt (1993) suggested that professional development in the renewal category should be prioritized, while inservice work should be minimal, even though the opposite practice is in place. "All three have a role to play, but the full range of growth opportunities for teachers . . . are available only when renewal is emphasized and supported by staff development as needed. In contrast, in-service programming should play a very limited role. This ordering of the three is in direct contrast to that which now dominates current practice" (p. 265).

Inservice programs are represented by training. The emphasis is on the technical aspects of teaching, and teachers are viewed as having "limited capacity or will to figure out things for themselves" (Sergiovanni & Starratt, 1993, p. 266). Teachers are considered laborers or technicians working at a job (Giroux, 1988; Shannon, 1989). Training programs are developed and implemented in a highly directive, controlling fashion. Teachers are usually required to participate in training programs and must then follow specific directions in their teaching. As learners, teachers are not given responsibility for their own learning, and their unique needs are not considered.

The inservice approach to teacher development focuses on improving knowledge and skills that are mandated and imposed upon teachers. Teachers are treated as people who need to be trained, rather than as individuals who can and should develop themselves. When teachers are given no control over the adoption of new skills and programs, it shows that they are not respected as professionals, and their ability to make classroom judgments is questioned (Hargreaves & Fullan, 1992). Adult learners are viewed as passive and compliant recipients of the knowledge and skills determined for them by individuals who have power over their lives (Merriam & Caffarella, 1991). Education is task oriented, activities are carefully sequenced, and learning is evaluated in relation to previously defined and observable outcomes. Unfortunately, although imposed training programs may be the simplest form of professional development for administrators to implement, they may actually have the effect of inhibiting, rather than fostering, the learning of adults (Brookfield, 1990).

Staff development is a process of problem solving and inquiry-based learning. The process is characterized by experiences that focus on needs that teachers participate in identifying. The teacher is considered to be a professional and a reflective problem solver. Supervisors are supportive in their roles, and responsibility for determining learning experiences for teachers is shared (Sergiovanni & Starratt, 1993). This approach views teacher development as self-understanding, and recognizes the importance of personal development along with professional development. Value is demonstrated for teachers as individuals, as active learners, and as participants in determining their own learning experiences (Hargreaves & Fullan, 1992).

Models of adult education compatible with the staff development approach to professional growth (Sergiovanni & Starratt, 1993) are based on adult characteristics and life situations. Characteristics of adult learners emphasize the power individuals have in determining what they will learn. Adults are self-directing, intrinsically motivated learners who participate in negotiating their own learning experiences. Adult learning is informed by life experiences, focused on relevant problem solving, and related to personal needs (Merriam & Caffarella, 1991).

Renewal is a continual growth process that occurs through reflection and reconsideration of personal needs and goals. Professional development is not separated from personal fulfillment.

Rather, it encompasses development of the personal self. Teachers are valued as learners, and teaching is viewed as an avocation. As learners, teachers have the responsibility to name their needs and to identify the experiences that will meet those needs (Sergiovanni & Starratt, 1993). Within this frame, teaching is considered a way of life: teachers engage in rethinking educational practices, and they rely upon intellectual (Giroux, 1988) as well as personal practical knowledge (Connelly & Clandinin, 1985) to inform their work.

Professional development as a renewal process encourages critical reflection, voluntary and creative collaboration, and risk taking within a supportive environment. Trust, respect, time, and money are provided for teachers who are endowed with the authority to control the context of their teaching and their learning. Resource allocations are determined by teachers, and the popular and unfortunate habit of spending funds on experts and trainers is avoided (Hargreaves & Fullan, 1992). Within the category of professional development as renewal, adults are viewed as self-motivated, autonomous, and reflective learners who seek to improve their work and their lives (Merriam & Caffarella, 1991).

Metatheories of Curriculum and Instruction

Transmission, transaction, and transformation are the three metatheories that overlap and inform professional development and literacy education practices. This multiple theoretical overlap is the source of much confusion, particularly in relation to literacy education, because the same term is often applied to instructional practices that are dissimilar. Analysis of theoretical orientation is missing from practical discussions of schooling, and too many educators are not even aware that there are multiple, competing theories of teaching and learning. This lack of awareness contributes to the confusion (Hawkins, 2001).

Educational approaches informed by transmission theories of curriculum and instruction treat learners as passive recipients of knowledge. Skills, facts, and values are named by central authorities, then passed out in a uniform, predetermined sequence.

This form of education, which has been predominant in American schools for many years, is frequently irrelevant to the lives of students and teachers, who must march lock-step through the program paces.

A transmission orientation to curriculum emphasizes traditional approaches to teaching that focus on mastery of basic skills and textbook learning. This is known as "banking education" because knowledge is seen as being deposited into passive learners, just as money is deposited into a bank account (Freire, 1990). Teachers are restricted to a technical role. They are expected to teach the same predetermined stories and skills to all students, regardless of individual student differences. This prevents teachers from developing the ability to support literacy learners in individualized and meaningful ways. It also prevents students from learning that literacy is a source of pleasure and a powerful political tool. Many exemplary literacy teachers, who are viewed as role models for others, do not support this approach to instruction. Unfortunately, in frequent cases, even the best teachers are confined to this form of development and practice by institutional constraints imposed upon them by school, district, and government authorities (Hawkins, 2001).

The transactional position is founded on the work of John Dewey (1938), who believed that the aim of education is represented by growth, and that problem solving and inquiry should be the emphasized learning processes (Miller & Seller, 1985). He felt that schools should operate as communities and facilitate student participation in a democratic society (Miller & Seller, 1985, p. 64). Vygotsky (1978, 1986) described learning as a social transactional process that occurs in what he has identified as the *zone of proximal development* (*ZPD*) (1978). Learners internalize concepts through active participation and with the support of language use as a tool for learning. In this learning process, a bridge is built between the known and the unknown.

Educators who locate themselves within this paradigm view education as a dynamic process in which students interact with teachers, learning environments, and each other as they continue to grow. The process of teaching and learning is negotiated (Hancock & Hill, 1988) and social, as well as psychological, aspects of education are considered (Miller & Seller, 1985). Educational practices informed by transactional theories of curriculum are developmentally appropriate and enable teachers to personalize their instruction. A transactional orientation to education encompasses learner-centered instruction. Teachers and students may work together to learn about topics that have been predetermined for them by programmatic criteria, or they may work together to investigate areas of personal interest, and to seek answers to their own questions (Weaver, Chaston, & Peterson, 1993).

Transformative education challenges the status quo and encompasses a social change agenda that has been influenced by the work of Paulo Freire, Jonathan Kozol, Henry Giroux, and Michael Apple (Miller & Seller 1985; Stanley, 1992). Transformational curriculum emphasizes the interconnectedness of all phenomena, the uniqueness of individuals, and sociopolitical concerns (Miller & Seller, 1985). Within this paradigm, learning is *change* (Files, 1992). Learning is also understood as a process of reflection and action, or praxis, which leads to transformation (Brookfield, 1990; Freire, 1990).

Transformative educators believe that the school should fit the child, rather than expecting the child to conform to school regimentation. Students are prepared for active participation in a democratic society, to address issues of social justice, and to use literacy as a powerful tool to effect social change. Critical literacy educators find themselves working within this realm (Edelsky, Altwerger, & Flores, 1991; Shannon, 1990). They are working for change (Weiler, 1988) and for the common good (Daloz, 2000) by developing projects of possibility (Simon, 1992). They ask questions about what is *not* written, examine social relations of control and oppression, and teach students to use literacy in powerful ways.

Adult Learning

Knowles (1980) popularized the concept of andragogy, in contrast to pedagogy, which values adult experiences and needs, and views adult learners as autonomous, self-motivated, and self-directed. Two key principles of adult learning are that (1) knowledge is actively constructed by the learner, not passively received from the environment, and (2) learning is an interactive process of interpretation, integration, and transformation of one's experiential world.

Adult motivation for learning is internal, and learners are responsible for their own growth. Autonomous adults plan their own learning experiences. Life experiences are the triggers for problem-centered learning, which is reflected upon, monitored, and manifested in some form of action (Merriam & Caffarella, 1991, p. 41). Adult learning is voluntary, collaborative, and respectful. Facilitation of adult learning is a nurturing process of critical reflection and praxis. Critical reflection "helps students to realize that dominant values, 'commonsense' wisdoms, generally accepted standards, and prevailing social or political arrangements are cultural constructs . . . which can be dismantled or reframed by human agency" (Brookfield, 1990, p. 23). Praxis—reflection plus action—is the process of combining theory and practice. Praxis leads to transformation (Freire, 1990, p. 119).

When attempting to support development in adulthood, it's important to remember that adults determine their own learning needs and that they are in control of their own learning (Brookfield, 1990; Galbraith, 1990; Knowles, 1980; Mezirow, 1985). "No concept is more central to what adult education is all about than self-directed learning. . . . By definition, the self-directed learner diagnoses his or her own learning needs and formulates his or her own learning goals" (Mezirow, 1985, p. 17).

Characteristics of Adult Learning

◆ Adults are self-directed and autonomous; they choose what to learn.

◆ Adults plan their own learning experiences.

◆ Motivation for learning is internal rather than external.

◆ Life experiences serve as the content or as triggers to learning.

◆ Learning is problem centered rather than subject centered.

◆ Adults reflect on learning and monitor changes taking place.

◆ Learning is manifested in action or some form of expression (Merriam & Caffarella, 1991).

Considering Conditions for Change

Sarason (1995) stated that an understanding of the culture of schools is essential for anyone wishing to facilitate educational change. He made four generalizations pertaining to school culture that identify forces of oppression and resistance in relationships between teachers and those who control their work. First, change is initiated at the highest level of administration; rarely does it begin with teachers. Second, resistance against required change subverts innovation. Third, teachers are controlled in a top-down fashion; they lack power to control the conditions of their work, and they are not respected by the public or by administrators who have formal authority over them. Lastly, those who analyze the effectiveness of education and conduct research on teaching do not involve teachers in the process, and commonly serve only to criticize them for work that they have no authority to control.

Given the school context described, and despite the billions of dollars being spent on change initiatives, there is little reason to expect that any significant change will be effected in schools. The failure of change initiatives is related to the identified conditions under which teachers must work, and to the failure of innovators to realize that what they think is "far less important than what teachers think" (Sarason, 1995, p. 74). The change process could be effectively facilitated through the empowerment of teachers. Empowered teachers have opportunities to make choices, they are autonomous, and they are given responsibility to control the conditions of their work and their learning. Teachers who are empowered as learners and decision makers will work for change rather than resist it (Short & Greer, 1993, p. 165).

Possibilities for Change in Professional Development

The old training model of professional development is commonly accepted, even though it is incompatible with what is known about adult learning and growth. The National Staff Development Council names standards for teachers' professional development, and there is no expectation that adult learners identify their own needs and determine experiences that will help them reach their goals. These standards are evolving toward a staff development approach, yet they continue to represent a training model for teachers (Zepeda, 1999).

Staff development offers a negotiated process for teacher growth and is a better option than training. Many who write about professional development of teachers consider the concepts of training and staff development. However, they do not suggest the option of empowering teachers to control the conditions of their own learning, and do not mention the concept of renewal (Daresh & Playko, 1995; Jones, 1993; Loucks-Horsley, et al., 1987; Zepeda, 1999). This omission limits the possibilities for teachers' growth and for school improvement.

Renewal is the best approach for professional development of teachers (Sergiovanni & Starratt, 1993). Teachers must be viewed as intellectuals rather than as technicians, and must be empowered with the responsibility to control their own learning. Collegial networks, collaborative efforts, and the development of professional identities are important for teachers as their focus changes from technical to intellectual work (Giroux, 1988; Little, 1993; Miller & Seller, 1985; Short & Greer, 1993).

Although it is more complicated than implementing a one-size-fits-all program, administrators can facilitate teachers' growth in ways that support authentic, personally meaningful learning. Administrators can be role models who read and discuss professional literature, take risks, support collaboration and innovation, and demonstrate value for learning in a collegial manner. Teachers need to be respected and trusted with the responsibility to control their own learning and the conditions for learning in classrooms (Weaver, 1992).

Within a transformational paradigm, informed by theories of adult education, an administrator could lead change by creating conditions that support ongoing improvement and free teachers from oppression. The administrator could be an empowering mentor who supports independence, advocates constant growth, and understands the work of education as praxis (Brookfield, 1990; Freire, 1990; Miller & Seller, 1985).

Renewal as Praxis

Empowered teachers are self-motivated to improve their teaching. Their personal desire to improve their teaching ability motivates them to search for knowledge. As adult learners, these teachers are motivated by internal rather than external factors; their learning is problem centered, and it is connected to real-life needs, not imaginary or hypothetical situations. They continually ask their own questions, search for information, and share their knowledge. Personally rewarding professional development experiences influence pedagogy and improve literacy instruction, while restoring enthusiasm for teaching. For these empowered teachers, their learning informs their teaching, and they reflect upon the impact of new ideas or techniques (Merriam & Caffarella, 1991). Their work is praxis and leads to transformation (Brookfield, 1990; Freire, 1990).

The search for knowledge is an ongoing process of renewal. Empowered teachers are active, contributing members of adult learning communities. Collectively, they read professional literature, belong to study groups, observe other teachers, conduct their own research, discuss their learning with colleagues, participate actively in professional organizations, and take courses. Mentors influence their work, and they also learn through teaching. In addition to working with children, they may serve as mentors to student teachers, teach graduate courses, make presentations at workshops and conferences, and write for publication (Hawkins, 2001).

Reading

An important condition for teachers' continual growth is that teachers must read. Journals received with professional memberships, books on topics of interest, and texts for graduate courses are worthwhile resources. Teachers can search for answers to their questions and look for role models in professional literature. Reading is an important source of support to teachers. They can read about the work of other educators who share their concerns. Feelings of isolation are replaced with comfort when teachers find classrooms and schools that serve as models. Nancie

Atwell (1998), Carol Avery (1993), Lucy Calkins (1994), Mary Cowhy (2006), Shelley Harwayne (1999), Pat McLure (Newkirk, 1992), and multiple others who find the time to share their own stories, are beloved mentors to many teachers.

Study Groups and Informal Support Groups

Ongoing study groups are helpful. Teachers thrive when they are able to discuss their work informally, share information, encourage each other, and collaboratively influence and inspire one another. Supportive communities, where teachers are free to suggest topics and respond with ideas, enable them to grow together as professionals. This is why TAWL (Teachers Applying Whole Language) groups have been so important to teachers for decades (Newman, 1990).

Unfortunately, the popularization of study groups has led some administrators and professional development providers, operating within a transmission paradigm, to develop training tools for study groups. Rather than participate in a self-motivated, collaborative search for knowledge, teachers in some schools are assigned to study groups where they are held to questions, time limits, and topics determined for them and provided in the form of lesson plans named *protocols*. These protocols appear in formats that clearly direct and limit teacher participation. "Protocols for engaging in discussion," developed by the National School Reform Faculty, the Annenberg Institute, and the Coalition of Essential Schools, exist in multiple forms, including a "connections protocol," a "tuning protocol," and a "standards protocol" (Sweeney, 2003). These protocols do more to prevent discussion than to facilitate the process.

Observation, Collaboration, and Teacher-Research

Opportunities to visit other classrooms and schools in order to learn about new approaches to instruction are helpful. However, these experiences must be collaborative in order to be valuable. The opportunity to discuss lessons within a supportive group of colleagues is also important to the learning process.

Teacher-researchers feel that the research process is important to their professional growth and to their work with children. Many teachers believe that teachers must be researchers. They ask questions based on the needs of students, then read about the topic, and experiment with methods and materials to learn how to best support students' growth. Teacher-researchers are usually able to show parents and administrators a broader range of students' development than would otherwise be visible.

Sharing Information

Excellent teachers are thoughtful about their teaching and their learning. They reflect on their practice, their reading, and their interactions with other professionals; and they keep the needs of their students as their focus. As part of the process of reflection, these teachers share their knowledge, their practices, and their questions with a public audience, and they seek feedback. They demonstrate lessons, make presentations at conferences, teach courses, and write for publication. They often agree that writing clarifies thought and language, and that when they are observed and receive feedback from peers, the process sharpens their skill and helps them improve.

Participation in Professional Organizations

Active involvement in professional organizations is important for teacher development. Teachers should be encouraged and enabled to participate in local, regional, national, and international conferences and workshops. Too many teachers are actually prevented from attending professional organization conferences and meetings. Additionally, they should be rewarded if they become members of executive boards, conference planning committees, and editorial boards.

Graduate Studies and Mentor Relationships

Many teachers turn to graduate school and mentors to meet their intellectual and professional social needs. Regular conversations with interested educators, and with reference to shared reading or experience, are stimulating and important when common interest, rather than forced participation, is the motivation for involvement. Returning to school to learn more about areas of special interest is a path that also leads to stronger formal authority. Mentors are respectful and can show teachers how to take control of their own learning and teaching. They are supportive and encouraging role models who help aspiring leaders through collaboration and can bring them into collegial networks.

Conclusion

Professional development of literacy teachers will improve when it is informed by theories of adult learning that are compatible with the concept of andragogy, and when the renewal process is prioritized (Hawkins, 2001). The andragogical process involves providing support to learners as they set their own goals, plan their own learning experiences, and monitor their own growth. Clark (1992) advocated self-directed professional development, and stated that

> research on teacher thinking supports the position that teachers are more active than passive, more ready to learn than resistant, more wise and knowledgeable than deficient, and more diverse and unique than they are homogeneous. This is a flattering and optimistic picture, and it is not true of all teachers in all situations. But it is true often enough to be taken seriously, as a point of departure for asking "What can we do to make professional development programmes work for professional teachers?" The answer is deceptively simple: we must give the responsibility for professional development to teachers themselves. (p. 76)

Teachers who are respected and supported as professional decision makers, and who control their own learning and teaching, will make a positive difference. Krause (1992) noted that the best education instills in students "a passion for learning that will stay with them for the rest of their lives," and that this can only be accomplished "by teachers who themselves are passionate about learning" (p. 229). In order to demonstrate flexibility and value for lifelong learning, teachers must have the support and freedom to pursue their own learning goals. The responsibility for adult growth belongs to individual learners (Merriam & Caffarella, 1991).

Schools can become learning communities where teachers work with their students to envision and strive toward the creation of a better world through the development of projects of possibility (Freire, 1990; Simon, 1992). Instead of teaching skills and programs, literate adults can mentor students into the "literacy club" and help them learn to use literacy in powerful ways to gain and maintain control of their lives (Smith, 1988a). Teachers can be supported as professional adults who are aware of their own needs and capable of directing their own learning (Hawkins, 2001). Students and teachers can collaborate to ask and search for answers to meaningful questions, to develop innovative approaches to literacy education, and to share their experiences with others. Classrooms and schools can become supportive democratic communities where autonomous learners of all ages develop caring relationships, critical perspectives, and strong voices, as they collaborate to envision and create a more just society and a better world for future generations.

References

Apple, M. W. (1982). *Education and power*. Boston: Routledge & Kegan Paul.

Apple, M. W. (1996). *Cultural politics and education*. New York: Teachers College Press.

Atwell, N. (1987). *In the middle: Writing, reading, and learning with adolescents*. Portsmouth, NH: Heinemann.

Atwell, N. (Ed.). (1990). *Coming to know: Writing to learn in the intermediate grades*. Portsmouth, NH: Heinemann.

Atwell, N. (1998). *In the middle: New understandings about writing, reading, and learning* (2nd ed.). Portsmouth, NH: Boynton/Cook.

Avery, C. (1993). *And with a light touch: Learning about reading, writing, and teaching with first graders*. Portsmouth, NH: Heinemann.

Brookfield, S. D. (1990). *The skillful teacher: On technique, trust, and responsiveness in the classroom.* San Francisco, CA: Jossey-Bass.

Brooks, J. G., & Brooks, M. G. (1999). *In search of understanding: The case for constructivist classrooms.* Alexandria, VA: Association for Supervision and Curriculum Development.

Calkins, L. M. (1983). *Lessons from a child.* Exeter, NH: Heinemann.

Calkins, L. M. (with Harwayne, S.). (1991). *Living between the lines.* Portsmouth, NH: Heinemann.

Calkins, L. M. (1994). *The art of teaching writing.* Portsmouth, NH: Heinemann.

Clark, C. M. (1992). Teachers as designers in self-directed professional development. In A. Hargreaves & M. G. Fullan (Eds.), *Understanding teacher development* (pp. 75–84). New York: Teachers College Press.

Connelly, F. M., & Clandinin, D. J. (1985). Personal practical knowledge and the modes of knowing: Relevance for teaching and learning. In Elliot Eisner (Ed.), *Learning and teaching the ways of knowing* (pp.174–98). Chicago: University of Chicago Press.

Cowhy, M. (2006). *Black ants and Buddhists: Thinking critically and teaching differently in the primary grades.* Portland, ME: Stenhouse.

Crawford, P. (1995). *Reading bound: A deconstruction of the basal teachers' manual.* Unpublished doctoral dissertation, Pennsylvania State University, University Park.

Daloz, L. (2000). Transformative learning for the common good. In J. Mezirow (Ed.), *Learning as transformation: Critical perspectives on a theory in progress* (pp. 103–23). San Francisco: Jossey-Bass.

Daresh, J. C., & Playko, M. A. (1995). *Supervision as a proactive process: Concepts and cases* (2nd ed.). Prospect Heights, IL: Waveland Press.

Dewey, J. (1938). *Experience and education.* New York: Macmillan.

Edelsky, C., Altwerger, B., & Flores, B. (1991). *Whole language: What's the difference?* Portsmouth, NH: Heinemann.

Emery, D. J. (1998). *Teacher and principal attitudes toward study groups as a professional development model.* Unpublished doctoral dissertation, University of Houston.

Files, J. S. (with Wills, P. S.) (1992). Learning from teachers how to support their growth. In C. Weaver & L. Henke (Eds.), *Supporting whole language: Stories of teacher and institutional change* (pp. 43–65). Portsmouth, NH: Heinemann.

Fletcher, R. (1991). *Walking trees: Teaching teachers in the New York City schools.* Portsmouth, NH: Heinemann.

Freire, P. (1985). *The politics of education: Culture, power, and liberation.* South Hadley, MA: Bergin & Garvey.

Freire, P. (1990). *Pedagogy of the oppressed.* New York: Continuum.

Freire, P., & Faundez, A. (1989). *Learning to question: A pedagogy of liberation.* New York: Continuum.

Freire, P., & Macedo, D. (1987). *Literacy: Reading the word and the world.* South Hadley, MA: Bergin & Garvey.

Galbraith, M. W. (Ed.) (1990). *Adult learning methods.* Malabar, FL: R. E. Krieger.

Giroux, H. (1988). *Teachers as intellectuals: Toward a critical pedagogy of learning.* Granby, MA: Bergin & Garvey.

Giroux, H. (1997). *Pedagogy and the politics of hope.* Boulder, CO: Westview Press.

Glickman, C. (Ed.). (1992). *Supervision in transition: The 1992 ASCD yearbook.* Alexandria, VA: Association for Supervision and Curriculum Development.

Glickman, C. (1998). *Revolutionizing America's schools.* San Francisco: Jossey-Bass.

Goodman, K., Shannon, P., Freeman, Y., & Murphy S. (1988). *Report card on basal readers.* Katonah, NY: Richard C. Owen.

Hancock, J., & Hill, S. (Eds.). (1988). *Literature-based reading programs at work.* Portsmouth, NH: Heinemann.

Hargreaves, A. (1994). *Changing teachers, changing times: Teachers' work and culture in the postmodern age.* New York: Teachers College Press.

Hargreaves, A., & Fullan, M. G. (Eds.). (1992). *Understanding teacher development.* New York: Teachers College Press.

Harwayne, S. (1999). *Going public: Priorities and practice at the Manhattan New School.* Portsmouth, NH: Heinemann.

Hawkins, B. (2001). *Reflections of teachers who lead in literacy education: Learning, teaching, pedagogy, and professional development.* Unpublished doctoral dissertation, Pennsylvania State University, University Park.

John-Steiner, V. (1997). *Notebooks of the mind: Explorations of thinking* (Rev. ed.). New York: Oxford University Press.

Jones, E. (Ed.). (1993). *Growing teachers: Partnerships in staff development.* Washington, DC: National Association for the Education of Young Children.

Knowles, M. S. (1980). The modern practice of adult education: From pedagogy to andragogy (Rev. ed.). Englewood Cliffs, NJ: Cambridge.

Knowles, M. S. (1990). *The adult learner: A neglected species* (4th ed.). Houston: Gulf.

Kouzes, J. M., & Posner, B. Z. (1987). *The leadership challenge: How to get extraordinary things done in organizations.* San Francisco: Jossey-Bass.

Kozol, J. (1967). *Death at an early age.* Boston: Houghton Mifflin.

Kozol, J. (1991). *Savage inequalities: Children in America's schools.* New York: Crown.

Krause, P. (1992). Should a superintendent advocate one set of educational beliefs? In C. Weaver & L. Henke (Eds.), *Supporting whole language: Stories of teacher and institutional change* (pp. 225–45). Portsmouth, NH: Heinemann.

Lieberman, A., & Miller, L. (1999). *Teachers: Transforming their world and their work.* Alexandria, VA: Association for Supervision and Curriculum Development.

Little, J. W. (1993). Teachers' professional development in a climate of educational reform. *Educational Evaluation and Policy Analysis, 15*(2), 129–52.

Loucks-Horsley, S., Harding, C., Arbuckle, M., Murray, L., Dubea, C., & Williams, M. (1987). *Continuing to learn: A guidebook for teacher development.* Andover, MA: Regional Laboratory for Educational Improvement of the Northeast and Islands.

McQuillan, J. (1998). *The literacy crisis: False claims, real solutions.* Portsmouth, NH: Heinemann.

Merriam, S. B., & Caffarella, R. S. (1991). *Learning in adulthood.* San Francisco: Jossey-Bass.

Merriam, S. B., & Cunningham, P. M. (Eds.). (1989). *Handbook of adult and continuing education.* San Francisco: Jossey-Bass.

Mezirow, J. (1985). A critical theory of self-directed learning. *New Directions for Continuing Education, 25,* 17–30.

Miller, J., & Seller, W. (1985). *Curriculum, perspectives and practice.* New York: Longman.

Moll, L. (1990). Social and instructional issues in educating "disadvantaged" students. In United States Department of Education, *Better schooling for the children of poverty: Alternatives to conventional wisdom: Vol 2. Commissioned Papers and Literature Review.* Washington, DC: USDE Office of Planning, Budget, and Evaluation.

Newkirk, T. (with McLure, P.) (1992). *Listening in: Children talk about books (and other things).* Portsmouth, NH: Heinemann.

Newkirk, T., & Atwell, N. (Eds.). (1988). *Understanding writing: Ways of observing, learning, and teaching* (2nd ed.). Portsmouth, NH: Heinemann.

Newman, J. M. (Ed.). (1990). *Finding our own way: Teachers exploring their assumptions.* Portsmouth, NH: Heinemann.

Noddings, N. (1992). *The challenge to care in schools: An alternative approach to education.* New York: Teachers College Press.

Routman, R. (1988). *Transitions: From literature to literacy.* Portsmouth, NH: Heinemann.

Routman, R. (1991). *Invitations: Changing as teachers and learners K–12.* Portsmouth, NH: Heinemann.

Routman, R. (1996). *Literacy at the crossroads: Crucial talk about reading, writing, and other teaching dilemmas.* Portsmouth, NH: Heinemann.

Sarason, S. B. (1995). *School change: The personal development of a point of view.* New York: Teachers College Press.

Sergiovanni, T. J. (1994). *Building community in schools.* San Francisco: Jossey-Bass.

Sergiovanni, T. J. (1996). *Leadership for the schoolhouse: How is it different? Why is it important?* San Francisco: Jossey-Bass.

Sergiovanni, T. J., & Starratt, R. J. (1993). *Supervision: A redefinition* (5th ed.). New York: McGraw-Hill.

Shannon, P. (1989). *Broken promises: Reading instruction in twentieth-century America*. Granby, MA: Bergin & Garvey.

Shannon, P. (1990). *The struggle to continue: Progressive reading instruction in the United States*. Portsmouth, NH: Heinemann.

Shannon, P. (Ed.). (1992). *Becoming political: Readings and writings in the politics of literacy education*. Portsmouth, NH: Heinemann.

Shannon, P., & Goodman, K. (Eds.). (1994). *Basal readers: A second look*. Katonah, NY: Richard C. Owen.

Short, P. M., & Greer, J. T. (1993). Restructuring schools through empowerment. In J. Murphy & P. Hallinger (Eds.), *Restructuring schooling: Learning from ongoing efforts*. Newbury Park, CA: Corwin Press.

Simon, R. I. (1992). *Teaching against the grain: Texts for a pedagogy of possibility*. New York: Bergin & Garvey.

Smith, F. (1983). *Essays into literacy*. Exeter, NH: Heinemann.

Smith, F. (1985). *Reading without nonsense* (2nd ed.). New York: Teachers College Press.

Smith, F. (1986). *Insult to intelligence: The bureaucratic invasion of our classrooms*. Portsmouth, NH: Heinemann.

Smith, F. (1988a). *Joining the literacy club: Further essays into education*. Portsmouth, NH: Heinemann.

Smith, F. (1988b). *Understanding reading* (4th ed.). Hillsdale, NJ: Lawrence Erlbaum.

Smith, F. (1998). *The book of learning and forgetting*. New York: Teachers College Press.

Stanley, W. B. (1992). *Curriculum for utopia: Social reconstructionism and critical pedagogy in the postmodern era*. Albany, NY: State University of New York Press.

Sweeney, D. (2003). *Learning along the way: Professional development by and for teachers*. Portland, ME: Stenhouse.

Vygotsky, L. (1978). *Mind in society: The development of higher psychological processes*. Cambridge, MA: Harvard University Press.

Vygotsky, L. (1986). *Thought and language.* Cambridge, MA: MIT Press.

Weaver, C. (1992). A whole language belief system and its implications for teacher and institutional change. In C. Weaver & L. Henke (Eds.), *Supporting whole language: Stories of teacher and institutional change* (pp. 3–23). Portsmouth, NH: Heinemann.

Weaver, C. (Ed.). (1998). *Reconsidering a balanced approach to reading.* Urbana, IL: National Council of Teachers of English.

Weaver, C., Chaston, J., & Peterson, S. (1993). *Theme exploration: A voyage of discovery.* Portsmouth, NH: Heinemann.

Weaver, C., & Henke, L. (Eds.). (1992). *Supporting whole language: Stories of teacher and institutional change.* Portsmouth, NH: Heinemann.

Weiler, K. (1988). *Women teaching for change: Gender, class & power.* South Hadley, MA: Bergin & Garvey.

Weiss, C. (1995). The four "I's" of school reform: How interests, ideology, information, and institution affect teachers and principals. *Harvard Educational Review, 65*(4), 571–92.

Witherell, C., & Noddings, N. (Eds.). (1991). *Stories lives tell: Narrative and dialogue in education.* New York: Teachers College Press.

Wolk, S. (1998). *A democratic classroom.* Portsmouth, NH: Heinemann.

Zepeda, S. J. (1999). *Staff development: Practices that promote leadership in learning communities.* Larchmont, NY: Eye on Education.

CHAPTER TWELVE

Real Stories, Real Successes: Maintaining Best Practices While Coping with the Restrictions of No Child Left Behind

LAURA ROBB

It's lunch hour. The head of literacy of a northeastern city, where the majority of students are African American and Latino American, and I debrief the morning training session I have just completed. We discuss the importance of finding funds for class-room libraries and for units of study that include a range of reading levels to meet the instructional needs of all students in each class (Robb, L., 2002, 2006; Tomlinson, 1999). Money is tight. And government funds for diverse reading materials aren't an option.

"Let me tell you our experience with government funding," says the literacy leader. I'm listening carefully, knowing that I will soon be writing this chapter.

"When our district applied for a $525,000 Reading First Grant, the governor's office sent a message stating that unless we purchased the Voyager program (one of the programs on the government's approved list) we would not receive funding. I explained that Voyager was inappropriate for the cultural backgrounds of the students we serve. I also pointed out that choosing one program for all children wouldn't work because each class reflects a range of unique student needs and challenges as well as multiple reading levels. It took months of haggling and negotiating for our district to receive funding so that we could choose materials that would improve literacy among children in our schools."

As I travel around the country and work with teachers in urban and rural school districts, I hear similar stories about government pressures to purchase an "approved" program. The practices of the Reading First initiative are riddled with corruption (International Reading Association, 2006a) such as the experience of the literacy coach I described above. Two practices, in particular, demand attention: (1) the Department of Education developed an application package that obscured requirements of the No Child Left Behind (NCLB) law; and (2) the Department of Education intervened to influence a state's selection of a reading program. Such corrupt practices send the message that education should not be in the hands of politicians who are unfamiliar with the needs of students throughout this country.

Some federally approved reading programs, such as Success for All, are rigidly scripted to ensure that all students receive the same lesson. However, the research of Marie Clay, other literacy educators, and the Commission on Reading in its report *On Reading, Learning to Read, and Effective Reading Instruction*, clearly shows that since children enter school with different literacy experiences and prior knowledge, they do not all receive and process lessons in the same way (Allington, 2001, 2002, 2006; Brown, R., Pressley, M., Van Meter, P., & Schuder, T., 1996; Clay, 1993; Commission on Reading, 2004b).

The Success for All program used in Baltimore, Maryland, showed that students made gains through second grade. However, by the time these students entered sixth grade, they were reading the equivalent of three to four years below grade level (Pogrow, 2006). One size doesn't fit all children. Moreover, skill-and-drill on phonics in the lower grades doesn't create students who can think, analyze, and interpret information. It does create what educators call "word callers," students like fifth grader Jake (pseudonym) who could read every word of a *Washington Post* news article correctly. But Jake couldn't retell anything he had read.

The statistics are in for NCLB and Reading First. I've cited the results in the Baltimore schools—results that clearly show thousands of children have been left behind because of the inflexibility and shortcomings of the NCLB legislation. "Many left behind," states an article in the December 2006/January 2007 issue of the International Reading Association's (IRA) *Reading Today*. "Only eight states can claim even moderate success over the past 15 years at boosting the percentage of their poor or minority students who are at or above proficient in reading, math, and science" (2006c, p. 7).

Studies in 2005 by the National Assessment of Educational Progress (NAEP) comparing the results of state reading tests to the NAEP reveal a wide gap between these two. State scores were 30 to 50 percent lower than NAEP scores. NAEP invites learners to infer, connect, and problem solve, and students struggle with these inferential skills. This gap suggests that many states have lowered their standards on state tests so that more students will pass and fewer schools will fail under the federal NCLB Act (Azzam, Perkins-Gough, & Thiers, 2006). An equally important NAEP statistic for reading tests of fourth and eighth graders indicates that the achievement gaps in reading from 1992 to 2005 between white and Hispanic and white and African American students show no measurable gains. To put this information into perspective, and to understand why it's imperative that we call for a drastic overhaul of NCLB, it's helpful to review the basic tenets of the NCLB Act. In the section that follows, I present a year-by-year overview of the high points of the legislation so you can understand why so many respected educators are calling for change.

An Overview of No Child Left Behind Legislation

In 2002 President George W. Bush signed the NCLB legislation into law, and public school accountability started with 2001–2002 test scores. The 2002–2003 school year received a list of four requirements based on the NCLB law:

◆ Reading and math tests must be given annually in each of three grade spans (3–5; 6–9; 10–12).

◆ All newly hired teachers and teaching assistants must meet the NCLB set of standards.

- Title I schools that for two consecutive years were designated "in need of improvement" must offer students the option of transferring to high-performing schools.

- A Title I school designated "in need of improvement" for three consecutive years must offer extra services to low-performing students.

In 2004, Margaret Spellings, the nation's secretary of education, promised greater flexibility for implementing the results of NCLB testing. The year 2005 saw several state challenges to the NCLB testing program, and some states received permission to develop modified tests for students in disadvantaged subgroups such as special education and English Language Learners (ELLs). The NCLB law also states these requirements:

- All teachers will be "highly qualified" by June 30, 2006.

- Science tests will be administered annually in each of these grade spans: 3–5; 6–9; 10–12.

- By the end of the 2013–2014 school year, every student in the United States will be proficient in reading and math.

Driven by NCLB legislation, school districts around the nation have been teaching to the tests with the hope of making Adequate Yearly Progress (AYP) and the 2014 benchmark. It's important to understand the parameters of AYP in order to follow why this element of the NCLB Act frustrates educators throughout the nation. AYP represents the annual academic performance targets in reading and math that school districts and the state must reach to be on track for reaching the NCLB 2014 target of 100 percent proficiency for all students. So even though a subgroup such as special education students in a school might improve, the school may still fail to make AYP. Indeed, rather than applaud the special education students' progress, federal officials may deliver a bitter message of failure for the entire school: that is, a school that fails to pass the AYP goal for the one subgroup may still be designated "failing."

Schools Change Curriculum in an Effort to Meet AYP and NCLB Requirements

In their article in *Phi Delta Kappan*, "The Goals of Education," Rothstein and Jacobsen (2006) point out that the NCLB era of accountability has low-performing, high-poverty schools focusing more and more on basic academic skills by eliminating or cutting back on music, art, social studies, and physical education (Jennings & Rentner, 2006; Rothstein & Jacobsen, 2006). Moreover, we are not preparing students to be productive and contributing citizens of a democracy when we remove history, civics, cultural geography, and developing students' ability to problem solve, think inferentially, and analyze data. The lack of recess and physical education affects students' concentration and learning, and contributes to our national childhood obesity problem. Even Ben Franklin understood that commonsense fact when in 1749 he "proposed that Pennsylvania establish a public school that should place as much emphasis on physical as on intellectual fitness because 'exercise invigorates the soul as well as the body'" (Rothstein & Jacobsen, p. 267).

Fed up with the NCLB law that fails to address the wide range of challenges facing our nation's schools as it forces schools to adopt one-size-fits-all approved programs and one accountability system, some states have begun to ask for test exemptions for special populations. When the Department of Education turns down requested exemptions for ELL, special education, and learning-disabled students, states have adopted policies that Popham calls "NCLB Pap Ploys" (2005, p. 788). These ploys include schools putting all their energy into teaching those children who can pass the tests; maintaining the reading and math levels of students who will pass the test; and ignoring the struggling learners who won't pass with one year's support. Many states also adjust the number of students in a subgroup so that they aren't included in AYP. When an inflexible federal law pushes states into a corner, then states will find ways to get around the law. In the scramble to get federal approval under NCLB, the very children who need support don't receive it, leaving them to fall even further behind (Kozol, 2005; Popham, 2005; Stiggins, 2005).

Until changes that benefit children and teachers are enacted by Congress, school districts will respond in multiple ways. Some will refuse federal funding; others will accept funds and work around the legislation; and still others will continue their best-practice teaching because their test scores make the cutoff. These are all positive responses to flawed legislation. As you read on, you'll discover how one school system and two schools decided to put their students first, and worked to reach every learner in their schools.

Schools That Accept Reading First Funding and Work Around It

School districts all over the country have accepted Reading First dollars and purchased one of the government-approved programs. When I consent to work with such a school district, I do not coach teachers in their language arts block. Because the block is taken up with the delivery requirements of the one-size-fits-all scripted program being used, it's pointless for me to try to differentiate reading instruction. What I do suggest is that teachers bring in best practices and materials at diverse reading levels, and teach reading in the science and social studies curricula. An interesting side note to teaching reading by meeting students at their instructional levels comes from Pogrow's article in *Phi Delta Kappan*. When Pogrow wrote to the U.S. Department of Education proposing his approach to teaching basic skills to low-performing schools, he received this response: he "had not submitted scientific evidence that teaching students where they are at is better than teaching them where they are not" (Pogrow, 2006, p. 226).

Like Pogrow, I feel this is a mindless approach that defies logic, common sense, and decades of thoughtful ethnographic observation of students engaged in learning. It's also the rationale that permits the Department of Education to push one-size-fits-all programs. The research of Tomlinson (1999), Allington (2001), Ambruster, Lehr, and Osborn (2001), and Brown et al. (1996) demonstrates that successful teaching begins with meeting children where they are and nudging them forward.

In a Virginia school that wishes to remain anonymous, I recently supported a fifth-grade teacher who had twenty-four students: 29 percent African American, 47 percent Hispanic, and 24 percent European American. Students' reading levels ranged from early first grade to tenth grade. The next closest reading level to tenth grade was seventh grade. The teacher and I gathered more than forty books about the ocean—books that reflected the instructional reading range in the class. Read-alouds became the common text for students as they watched me model think-alouds, demonstrating how I applied Questioning the Author (QtA) (Beck & McKeown, 2006); composed journal responses; and took notes. Students improved their reading, vocabulary, thinking, and note-taking skills because their teacher and I did not focus on phonics and skill-and-drill worksheets, but instead gave them texts they could *read* and learning experiences that were authentic and accessible to each child. The Commission on Reading document titled *A Call to Action: What We Know about Adolescent Literacy and Ways to Support Teachers in Meeting Students' Needs* (2004a) supported our instructional decisions. ELLs reading at a first- and second-grade level worked closely with me, or with their teacher, so we could support their reading and enlarge their speaking, thinking, and writing vocabularies. While some schools make such accommodations, there are also school systems that have not applied for Reading First funds because they believe that best practices, differentiated reading instruction, and balanced literacy have served their students well.

Staunton City Schools, Staunton, Virginia

I have coached teachers and facilitated workshops and professional study groups for Staunton City Schools for several years. With an enrollment of 2,761 students spread over one high school, one middle school, and four elementary schools, 40 percent of Staunton's students are economically disadvantaged, 16 percent are disabled, and 28 percent are African American, Hispanic, and Asian American. Sarah Armstrong, assistant superintendent of instruction, along with the superintendent and resource leaders, made the decision not to apply for Reading First money when the possibility became available. I emailed Sarah and her director of literacy, Larry Barber, and invited them to respond to questions that I posed. As you continue to read, you'll learn why Staunton City Schools chose to continue differentiating instruction with literature-based materials in all subjects. My questions are in italics; the responses include the name of the responder.

Can you explain your reasons for not applying for Reading First money?

Sarah Armstrong: I was at a University of Virginia [UVA] partnership meeting and listened to a presentation by Mary Abouzeid about the Reading First Grant that UVA would be administering. About twenty school divisions in Virginia had representatives there to hear the presentation. I was attentive to the kinds of intervention that were being endorsed as part of these funds. It was very clear that a Texas model was being promoted, and that all participants would need to adhere to that model. I was familiar with the Open Court phonics approach and did not believe that it was consistent with the diagnostic approach that we used in Staunton. I believed that the one school that was eligible for Reading First should be consistent with the division approach and so did not apply for the funds.

What kinds of support did you put in place to support reading at the primary and elementary level without Reading First dollars?

Larry Barber: Staunton City Schools developed a comprehensive, balanced literacy curriculum in 2002–2003 to guide instruction for our students. The curriculum focuses on the key components of read-alouds, shared reading, guided reading, writer's workshop and word study. Each component of the curriculum is explained in detail, with the major focus of teaching students reading, spelling, and writing *strategies* that will enable each student to access content material at all levels. We have spent the past three years implementing a writer's workshop model for all our classrooms. Students spend forty-five to sixty minutes daily in writer's workshop. All focus lessons are based on good-quality literature. We have extensive schoolbook rooms filled with leveled fiction and nonfiction literature to support the student regardless of his or her reading level.

How do staff development and the ongoing training of teachers support your efforts?
Larry Barber: Professional study and continual training of staff is the way to develop a group of teachers who can make a difference in children's lives [Allington, 2002; Darling-Hammond & Berry, 2006; Weaver, 2006]. Staunton City Schools has an aggressive staff development program that trains teachers in all aspects of the balanced literacy curriculum. We offer courses in the summer at local universities and during the school year to support our literacy effort. We have a full-time literacy coordinator who meets with classroom teachers to support their efforts in reading, word study, and writing. She models different strategies the teacher can use in teaching any component of the literacy curriculum. Our students are placed in leveled materials throughout the day. We have a major emphasis on differentiation in our classrooms. We have a strong Title I reading program in each elementary school, and these teachers offer reading expertise to classroom teachers as well as working with groups of students daily. Our philosophy is that research-based quality instruction and methodology is far superior to any "prepackaged" rote program.

When did you hire differentiation specialists? Why did you do this? What kind of background did these specialists have? Did you do any training?
Sarah Armstrong: After reading the question you may wonder, *What is a "differentiation specialist" and how can that person help my child?* At times, teachers are at a loss as to how to provide instruction that is appropriate for all students in the classroom, and they find themselves teaching to the middle. When teachers *differentiate instruction*, they use students' daily assessments to design lessons for a diverse

classroom, taking into account the different reading levels, experiences, and interests of students. Differentiation specialists, like literacy coaches, are experts at designing lesson plans to meet the needs of diverse learners and can share with classroom teachers some of the best ways to help all students learn.

A major role of the differentiation specialist (DS) is to consult regularly with classroom teachers regarding content and activities that will encourage all students as readers, writers, and thinkers. We know it is not appropriate to lecture children or to attempt to cover material needed for review by putting workbooks in front of them, hoping that students will absorb the information they need for a test or assessment. Students need to be actively engaged as learners; they need to have new information presented in ways that can hook to things they already know to help them make connections to new learning. Therefore, to support quality instruction, the DS might agree to model strategies for the teacher, co-teach a lesson, or work with a specific group. Interactions between the DS and a teacher will vary from week to week, as they work to improve students' learning and teaching practices.

Staunton City Schools has been on the cutting edge of instructional improvement with this program, which has existed since the 2000–2001 school year. I believe that all principals and teachers would tell you now that they couldn't do the important job of teaching diverse learners without the support of differentiation specialists.

There is a third kind of school that I mentioned when I presented the three kinds of school I'd discuss. In this school, state test scores are high enough for a school *not* to adopt a grade-level basal anthology, and instead continue with instructional practices that meet the reading levels of all students in their schools. However, many of the schools whose students score high still don't make AYP because of one or two subgroups lagging, such as learning disabled students or students who can't speak or read English because they are new to the United States.

Johnson Williams Middle School, Clarke County, Virginia

I interviewed Evan Robb, principal of Johnson Williams Middle School in rural Berryville, Virginia, where about 15 percent of the 450 students receive free or reduced lunch.

Why does your faculty use a literature-based curriculum instead of basal anthologies?
Evan Robb: My staff has never worried about keeping a literature-based curriculum because since its inception, state test results indicate that students' instructional needs have been met. My hunch is that if performance were low, then the central office, staff, and I would have concerns as to the program's instructional worth. My concern about a literature-based program is that its success is connected with teachers' skills. If turnover at a school is high, a significant amount of effort should be given to ongoing professional development to maintain the integrity of a literature-based program. What makes a literature-based program work at my school is the combination of good literature at students' instructional levels, sharing of strategies and materials among teachers, and continual professional development to keep everyone abreast of best practices.

My focus on staff development for using literature in all subjects is a long-term approach based on the premise that as teachers improve their instructional knowledge, it results in increasing their confidence in using a literature-based approach as long as it's coupled with solid evidence of student growth. Also, I have moved staff away from using the same books year in and year out. We focus on themes and choose books that are thematically consistent, but offer choice based on student reading level.

Why do you think students improved without funds from the government and government-sponsored programs?
Evan Robb: The source of funds is not a factor. How funds are used is the key. A federal- or state-funded program that wears blinders regarding the most effective approaches to creating literate learners is of no use, so the funds would

have no value. There is an aspect of "selling your soul" when you accept funds that are tied to a specific pedagogy. In our school division, the task of the many committed educators is to be relentless about the most effective ways to help a child read and write and "do math." If it is not doable in a government-sponsored program, then the moral high ground is to refuse the funds.

Would you make the same decision today? Why?
Evan Robb: I still would refuse participation in Reading First were it made available today. We have tried to have a consistent and engaging literacy program involving writing workshops, shared and guided reading, word study using words in context and not isolated patterns, and real literature. The cultivation of thinking is paramount. Reading First appeared to be caught up in the technical aspect of what had to be taught as opposed to the more authentic pursuit of how children learn. Our goal is to build learners, not pursue programs.

Does you school receive NCLB money? Do you have the freedom to spend it if you take it?
Evan Robb: We do not receive specific money for funding NCLB. I believe money will go to schools only if they are not meeting federal standards. In essence NCLB is an unfunded mandate for many schools in this country.

At your school, you and teachers use nine-week assessments instead of final exams. Can you explain why?
Evan Robb: Traditionally, teachers give final exams to help them establish a grade for a subject. Rarely do teachers use students' performance on an exam to guide instruction. After the exam, the curriculum moves forward even if there are students who did not understand important concepts. Nine-week assessments are crafted by teams of teachers who carefully analyze the results to plan interventions for students, to reteach material, and to insure, as much as possible, that students understand key concepts in a subject before moving on.

What exactly are nine-week assessments and how are they created?

Evan Robb: I have written extensively about nine-week assessments in my book *The Principal's Leadership Source Book: Practices, Tools, and Strategies for Building a Thriving School Community* [2007]. I will give a summary of these assessments and what each one contains. If the mission in education and your school is for all students to learn, then changing traditional exams can support that mission. One way to do that is by using nine-week diagnostic assessments. Even if you sense that your teachers will embrace this change, I urge you to have open discussions with key instructional players such as literacy coaches, curriculum developers, and team leaders or department chairs. I never recommend making decisions based on presumptions. These conversations may take time, but they're an excellent opportunity to get a sense of your school's pulse.

The nine-week assessment initiative is beneficial as long as your school has mapped and aligned curricula to state standards, at least in subjects where testing occurs. Without alignment, your assessments might not provide data that reflect a knowledge of the state curriculum. Nine-week assessments are carefully developed diagnostic tests given at the same time by teachers who teach the same subject. Teachers collaborate to develop these assessments, which reflect the curriculum that's been covered and contain approximately fifty questions. Teachers pay particular attention to test construction: how long the test is, the type of questions, and how each question relates to a specific state standard. The nine-week assessment should have questions similar to those on your state test; this is critical, for it helps students become test-wise. [The appendix at the end of this chapter includes the instructional decisions made by the team of teachers, but written up by the English teacher.] However, for these types of assessments to support your population and state requirements, teachers must collaborate to create, grade, and interpret them. This is why members of a department collaborate to construct their test and administer the same test to students. Moreover, all students receive the same study guide, one designed by subject department members, so they can review the same material prior to the nine-week assessment. Collaborating to design the study guides is a way to insure that students review the same material. Reviewing in class provides another constant, for assigning this as homework can result in some students studying more than others. Teachers in a subject decide on the number of review periods they will set aside, for if one teacher reviews heavily and another doesn't, then the data are invalid.

The second and third nine-week assessment tests contain five to eight cumulative review questions that come from the previous test. This helps teachers know which students need additional support and who has absorbed the materials. After students take the nine-week assessment tests, teachers of the same subject collaborate to analyze data: they're looking for strengths and weaknesses regarding content. Teachers also look at which types of questions students had difficulty answering—inferential, cause and effect, factual, sequence, and so on. I can use this data to ask questions and to challenge teachers to find ways to reteach students who don't demonstrate recall and understanding of the content.

Teachers and I also use the data to predict student performance on the state test. Ultimately, if the correlation between the two is high, we probably have a good test. If not, the assessment and benchmarks may need adjusting for the next year.

What kinds of gains have you seen after implementing nine-week assessments?
Evan Robb: After instituting nine-week assessments, we have seen a 10 percent gain in standardized reading, writing, and math scores. Most likely this is because the assessment allows us to collectively pinpoint deficiencies and act on them in a thoughtful manner. In addition, teachers study students' performance on a weekly basis and use data collected to adjust instruction and meet students' needs. These formative assessments can pinpoint areas of specific weakness and open the door for conversations among teachers—often resulting in more sharing and supporting each other.

The assessments can and do make a difference. Moreover, using assessments to inform and improve instruction and plan interventions enables our school to do well on standardized tests. Doing well on mandated tests, in turn, gives us the freedom to choose learning materials for our students and continue using a literature-based program.

These real stories and successes that I've shared demonstrate the need for changes in NCLB. In the next section I offer suggestions for change that educators and researchers throughout the country support.

Suggestions for Change

Education initiatives like NCLB should serve all populations in a nation. Ideally, they should empower teachers to grow as professionals, and they should include ways to meet the needs of children who can't meet a benchmark such as the 2014 goal of NCLB. Here are some changes that could improve education in this country.

- Provide funding for ongoing professional study to insure that the quality of teaching remains high.

- Create realistic goals for children—goals that recognize that every child does not learn in the same way, and that children arrive at school with diverse literacy backgrounds, life experiences, and levels of ability. The goal should be to help all children reach their potential.

- Return to a curriculum that includes the arts and social studies, and that strives to create literate, thinking citizens.

- Include frequent formative assessments to determine whether children have made progress.

- Remove all punitive aspects of the law, and provide real help with funding that considers a school's culture and population.

- Fund the improvement of the schools where children learn, so our nation's children come to schools that are not in disrepair, overcrowded, and crawling with rats and roaches.

- Fund school and community libraries.

♦ Recognize that all children cannot meet a rigid deadline. Think of the range in ages of young children who learn to walk and speak at different times. Should we punish their parents for these variations from the average?

Before I close and leave you with questions to ponder, I want to share the results of a recent poll conducted by the Association for Supervision and Curriculum Development (ASCD) that asked this question: How has NCLB positively affected your school district? According to the poll, 60 to 65 percent of respondents agreed that this law has had no positive effect; and 3.91 percent noted that the law had not narrowed the achievement gap nor provided more financial resources (2006).

Closing Thoughts and Lingering Questions

Three prominent and respected education associations have called for changes in NCLB before Congress renews the Act: NCTE, IRA, and ASCD.

At the IRA conference in Chicago in 2005, an internationally known and highly regarded panel of educators spoke out against specific rigidities in the NCLB law. P. D. Pearson, professor and dean, University of California–Berkeley, questioned NCLB's adequately yearly progress goal this way: "Is it better to do our damnedest trying to reach a goal we know we will never achieve, or should we set more realistic, more achievable goals that appear to sell some kids short?" When he opened the panel discussion, S. J. Samuels, professor of educational psychology, University of Minnesota, echoed the feelings and anxieties of principals and teachers throughout the nation when he stated that the NCLB goal of having all children, including special education, learning disabled, and ELLs, at the proficient level by 2014 is unrealistic. Samuels also pointed out that countries consistently scoring at the top of international reading assessments have never had 100 percent of their students at proficient levels (International Reading Association, 2006c). Obviously, the NAEP scores and the scores based on assessments of the Thomas B. Fordham Institute (2006) point to the fact that students will not reach this unreasonable goal of NCLB. Moreover, to me, such a goal indicates our federal government's and Department of Education's lack of knowledge about how children learn, and lack of knowledge of the benefits of ongoing classroom assessment to measure children's progress and to plan instruction and interventions that meet each child's needs (Black & William, 1998; Stiggins, 2005).

The questions that follow do cast a negative light on NCLB and Reading First. It's always been interesting to me that the Republican Party, which stands for less government interference, has chosen, along with many Democrats, to take over education in this country—a right that should belong to states and local communities (Jennings & Rentner, 2006). These are questions that educational organizations such as NCTE and IRA need to continue to raise and answer:

- ◆ What motivates the Department of Education to push certain reading programs?

- ◆ Why doesn't the Department of Education understand that all children don't learn at the same rate, and that the prior knowledge children bring to school differs widely?

- ◆ Why does the Department of Education insist that students who can't read and write, and who barely speak English, take state-mandated tests?

- ◆ What has motivated the federal government to be so rigid about AYP?

- ◆ Does the federal government have an agenda regarding public schools that the people of this nation are not aware of?

- ◆ Why is it that the federal government isn't adequately funding NCLB, yet demands that states meet the Act's standards without adequate funding?

- ◆ Why do high-performing schools have all the flexibility in avoiding aspects of NCLB, and low-performing schools receive the bulk of the punishments?

- ◆ What's happening to good students who do poorly on the tests?

- ◆ Why isn't there adequate funding for ongoing professional study, especially when research shows that teachers make a difference in children's learning?

Appendix

Nine-Week Assessments at Johnson Williams Middle School

Here is an example of the narrative that Katy Schain, English teacher at Johnson Williams Middle School, creates for students who require her support.

Katy will set up tutorials to support Amy. Some of these will be teacher and study tutorials, while others will place Amy in a small group of students with similar needs.

Background Information

Amy is an eighth-grade student; I have carefully monitored her this year. Amy is bilingual with a strong verbal understanding of English; she is on a monitored status with ESL. Amy did not pass her fifth-grade Virginia Standards Test on Writing by ten points.

Amy's difficulties lie in the nuances of the English language. She has trouble with complex sentences and vocabulary; with support she can overcome these obstacles.

On the sixth-grade Writing Pretest Assessment, Amy scored a 390; passing is 400. Amy's areas of weaknesses included standards that call for the student to select specific vocabulary and information; organize and understand the central idea of writing; revise writing for word choice and sentence fluency; and recognize and correct number and tense agreement issues. Again, this shows Amy's weaknesses to be partially based on her understanding of the English language.

After each specific standards unit studied, an assessment is given; students have an opportunity to correct the items they miss. Initially, Amy gets about 60 percent of the questions correct; when she reviews the errors, she ends up with 90 to 95 percent of the answers correct. She usually chooses the "trick" answer rather than the correct one. She has improved with word choice, understanding the central idea, and revising. Subject-verb agreement in tense and number remains an issue.

References

Allington, R. L. (2001). *What really matters for struggling readers: De-signing research-based programs.* New York: Longman.

Allington, R. L. (2002). What I've learned about effective reading in-struction from a decade of studying exemplary elementary school teachers. *Phi Delta Kappan, 83*(10), 740–47.

Allington, R. L. (2006). Fluency: Still waiting after all these years. In S. J. Samuels & A. E. Farstrup (Eds.), *What research has to say about fluency instruction*. Newark: DE: International Reading Association.

Ambruster, B. B., Lehr, F., & Osborn, J. M. (Eds.). (2001). *Put reading first: The research building blocks for teaching children to read*. Washington, DC: National Institute for Literacy.

Association for Supervision and Curriculum Development. A firsthand look at NCLB: Responses by e-mail to our questions: How is NCLB affecting you? *Educational Leadership, 64*(3), 48–52.

Azzam, A., Perkins-Gough, D., & Thiers, N. (2006). Special report: The impact of NCLB. *Educational Leadership, 64*(3), 94–96.

Beck, I. L., & McKeown, M. G. (2006). *Improving comprehension with questioning the author*. New York: Scholastic.

Black, P. & William, D. (1998). Inside the black box: Raising standards through classroom assessment. *Phi Delta Kappan, 80*(2), 139–48.

Brown, R., Pressley, M., Van Meter, P., & Schuder, T. (1996). A quasi-experimental validation of transactional strategies instruction with low-achieving second-grade readers. *Journal of Educational Psychology, 88*(1), 18–37.

Clay, M. (1993). Marie Clay responds. *Reading in Virginia, 18*, 1–3.

Commission on Reading of the National Council of Teachers of English. (2004a). *A call to action: What we know about adolescent literacy and ways to support teachers in meeting students' needs*. Retrieved June 16, 2008, from http://www.ncte.org/about/policy/guidelines/118622.htm

Commission on Reading of the National Council of Teachers of English. (2004b). *On reading, learning to read, and effective reading instruction*. Retrieved June 16, 2008,from http://www.ncte.org/about/over/positions/category/read/118620.htm

Darling-Hammond, L., & Berry, B. (2006). Highly qualified teachers for all. *Educational Leadership, 64*(3), 14–20.

Herman, J. L., & Baker, E. L. (2006). Making benchmark testing work. *Educational Leadership, 63*(3), 48–54.

International Reading Association (IRA). (2006a). IRA responds to report on Reading First. *Reading Today, 24*(2), 1.

International Reading Association (IRA). (2006b). Hot topic: NCLB. *Reading Today, 23*(6), 20.

International Reading Association (IRA). (2006c). Many left behind. *Reading Today, 24*(3), 7.

Jennings, J., & Rentner, D. S. (2006). Ten big effects of the No Child Left Behind Act on public schools. *Phi Delta Kappan, 88*(2), 110–13.

Kozol, J. (2005). *The shame of the nation: The restoration of apartheid schooling in America.* New York: Crown.

National Council of Teachers of English. (2006). Suggestions for NCLB Reform. *Tennessean.* www.tennessean.com.

Pogrow, S. (2006). Restructuring high-poverty elementary schools for success: A description of the hi-perform school design. *Phi Delta Kappan, 88*(3), 223–29.

Popham, W. J. (2005). How to use PAP to make AYP under NCLB. *Phi Delta Kappan, 86*(10), 787–91.

Robb, E. (2007). *The principal's leadership source book: Practices, tools, and strategies for building a thriving school community.* New York: Scholastic.

Robb, L. (2002). Multiple texts: Multiple opportunities for teaching and learning. *Voices from the Middle, 9*(4), 28–32.

Robb, L. (2006). *Teaching reading: A complete resource for grades 4 and up.* New York: Scholastic.

Rothstein, R., & Jacobsen, R. (2006). The goals of education. *Phi Delta Kappan, 88*(4), 264–72.

Stiggins, R. (2005). From formative assessment to assessment for learning: A path to success in standards-based schools. *Phi Delta Kappan, 87*(4), 324–28.

Thomas B. Fordham Institute (2006). *The Fordham report 2006: How well are states educating our neediest children?* Retrieved June 16, 2008, http://www.edexcellence.net/detail/news.cfm?news_id=363

Tomlinson, C.A. (1999). *The differentiated classroom: Responding to the needs of all learners.* Alexandria, VA: Association for Supervision and Curriculum Development.

Weaver, T. (2006). A positive agenda for ESEA. *Educational Leadership, 64*(3), 32–36.

————————IV————————

APPENDIXES: THE THREE COMMISSION ON READING DOCUMENTS

APPENDIX A

On Reading, Learning to Read, and Effective Reading Instruction: An Overview of What We Know and How We Know It

by the Commission on Reading of the National Council of Teachers of English

There is an ongoing debate about reading. What is it? How is it learned? How is it most effectively taught? The Commission on Reading of the National Council of Teachers of English has compiled the following overview of what the profession knows about reading, learning to read, and effective reading instruction and referenced some of the large body of research that has given rise to this view. It then outlines policies that promote learning to read.

Reading and the Reading Process

Reading is a complex and purposeful sociocultural, cognitive, and linguistic process in which readers simultaneously use their knowledge of spoken and written language, their knowledge of the topic of the text, and their knowledge of their culture to construct meaning with text.[1] Each of these types of knowledge impacts the sense that readers construct through print. Readers easily comprehend text with familiar language but are less successful at comprehending text with unfamiliar language.[2] Readers easily comprehend text on familiar topics but are less successful at comprehending texts on unfamiliar topics.[3] At the same time, the interpretations readers construct with texts as well as the types of texts they read are influenced by their life experiences.[4]

Reprinted from http://www.ncte.org/about/over/positions/category/read/118620.htm.

The sociocultural, cognitive, and linguistic systems readers use to make sense of print are largely intuitive. For example, few are aware that they use their life experiences to interpret text, and that as life experiences differ from reader to reader and from community to community so, too, do interpretations of a given text. Similarly, few are aware that when they are reading about statistics they understand the phrase *all the figures on the right-hand side of the table* means numerals in rows and columns, but when they are reading about crafts they understand the same phrase means figurines on a piece of furniture;[5] nevertheless, they do.

The systems readers use to make sense of print are interrelated and partially redundant. For instance, in the sentence *There are some books on the table*, the words *some* and *are* and the letter *s* in *books* signal that there is more than one book. This redundancy permits readers to sample print, using only what they need to construct meaning effectively and efficiently.[6] Readers also use these interrelated systems to make predictions concerning what the print says, to confirm or disconfirm their predictions, and to connect these meanings to form a coherent understanding of the text.

Readers read for different purposes. Sometimes they read for pleasure. Sometimes they read for information. Their reason for reading impacts the way they read. They may skim or read carefully depending on why they are reading. Throughout this process, readers monitor the meaning they are constructing. When the text does not meet their purposes they may switch to another text. Readers expect what they are reading to make sense. They use a repertoire of strategies, such as rethinking, re-reading, or reading on to clarify ideas, to make sure they understand what they read in order to accomplish their purposes.

Writers also contribute to how well readers are able to read a text. The writer's language and knowledge of the topic as well as skill in using written language influence the reader's ability to construct meaning. The degree to which readers and writers share the same understanding of the language and the topic of the text influence how well they communicate with each other.

Learning to Read

Learning to read is a lifelong process. People begin developing knowledge that they will use to read during their earliest interactions with families and communities. In their preschool years, children learn to understand and use spoken language and learn about their world through meaningful interactions with others.

Children also learn about written language as more experienced readers provide meaningful demonstrations of reading and writing.[7] Some of the earliest demonstrations they receive include reading environmental print (such as the word *stop* on a stop sign), making and using grocery lists, writing and reading notes, and reading and discussing children's stories and letters from friends.

Through these demonstrations by others, children learn the pleasures and purposes of print. They also learn to read and write their names and the names of family members. In addition, they learn vocabulary typical of written language, such as how different types of texts such as grocery lists, personal letters, and fairy tales are structured. They also learn basic concepts of print such as the message of print in books continues across pages. The more children interact with spoken and written language, the better readers they become.[8]

As children learn to read continuous text, they use their intuitive knowledge of spoken language and their knowledge of the topic to figure out print words in text.[9] For example, if a more experienced reader reads *Catch me, catch me, if you can* to young children while pointing to the print, children use their memory of what was read to them to help them figure out which words in the sentence represent *catch* and *me*.

As children learn to read new text independently, they continue using their intuitive knowledge of spoken language, their growing knowledge of written language, and their knowledge of the topic of the text to construct meaning. Consequently, beginning readers read words in the context of a story with familiar language on a familiar topic better than they read words out of context, as in lists or on flash cards.[10] For example, a beginning reader may read *horse* as *house* when encountering it in a list but read it correctly in a story about cowboys. Beginning readers also comprehend stories with familiar language better than stories with unfamiliar language such as unfamiliar "book" language[11] or contrived language such as the language in decodable texts.[12]

At the same time, as children learn to read more and more words in context, they use their developing knowledge of patterns of letter-sound correspondences in familiar words to figure out how to pronounce unfamiliar words.[13] For example, children who have learned to read *small* and *smile* and *cart* and *part* can figure out that *sm-* is pronounced /sm/ and *-art* is pronounced /art/ and then figure out how to pronounce *smart*.

The more children read, the better readers they become.[14] Children read more when they have access to engaging, age-appropriate books, magazines, newspapers, computers, and other reading materials. They read more on topics that interest them than on topics that do not interest them.

Reading supports writing development[15] and writing supports reading development.[16] For example, through reading readers learn the power of a strong introduction and eventually use such knowledge as they write their own pieces. Conversely, writing develops awareness of the structures of language, the organization of text, and spelling patterns, which in turn contributes to reading proficiency.

Learning to read in one language accelerates learning to read in other languages.[17] When readers learn to read text written in a language they understand, they transfer an intuitive understanding of what reading is and how to read when reading in other languages.

Children vary in the experiences they bring to learning to read, including different cultures, background knowledge, oral and written languages, experiences with print,[18] and access to print.[19] Nevertheless, all readers use their life experiences, their knowledge of the topic, and their knowledge of oral and written language to make sense of print and all learners benefit from instruction that helps them make sense of print.[20]

Readers continue to grow in their ability to make sense of an increasing variety of texts on an increasing variety of topics throughout their lives as they learn more spoken and written language, acquire more knowledge on an ever-expanding variety of topics, and have more and more life experiences.

Effective Reading Instruction

Effective reading instruction helps learners make sense of written language.[21] It builds on what learners know at any given time to help them learn more. Effective instruction is grounded in a professional knowledge of how we read and how we learn to read. It is best provided by knowledgeable, caring teachers who organize instruction to meet the varying needs of all their students.[22]

Teachers provide effective reading instruction when they:

♦ Expect all students to achieve.[23]

♦ Know their students as individuals, including their interests, their attitudes about reading, and their school, home, and community experiences.

♦ Carefully observe each student's reading in multiple contexts in order to provide appropriate instruction and monitor progress.

- Create a risk-free environment that supports social interaction, open discussion of ideas, and multiple perspectives.

- Teach students about reading within the context of authentic reading using texts with authentic language.

- Read to students daily using a variety of text types, including various types of fiction and nonfiction and multicultural literature, on a variety of topics to build their students' familiarity with written language and their background knowledge on a variety of topics.

- Use a variety of instructional groupings, including whole group, small group, and individual instruction, to provide multiple learning experiences.[24]

- Use multiple instructional methods such as shared reading,[25] guided reading, and literature discussion circles as appropriate for their students.

- Focus on the ideas represented by written language rather than the words on the page.[26]

- Build background knowledge of topics and language that enables students to understand what they read.[27]

- Teach before-, during-, and after-reading strategies for constructing meaning of written language, including demonstrations and think-alouds.

- Encourage students to use effective reading strategies such as self-monitoring for meaning and self-correcting when meaning breaks down.[28]

- Provide specific feedback to students to support their reading development.

- Provide opportunities for inquiry and language study, including vocabulary, word and text structures, and spelling patterns, that emerge from authentic reading experiences.[29]

- Provide regular opportunities for students to respond to reading through discussion, writing, art, drama, storytelling, music, and other creative expressions.

- Provide daily opportunities for students to read books of their own choice in school.[30]

- Provide daily opportunities for students to write on topics of their own choice in school.[31]

◆ Provide regular opportunities for students to work together to learn through reading and writing.

◆ Build partnerships with families to read and write regularly at home.[32]

◆ Provide regular opportunities for students to engage in a variety of authentic literacy experiences in social studies, science, math, and other curricula areas.[33]

◆ Provide regular opportunities for students to reflect on their learning.[34]

◆ Provide ongoing support to students who need additional instruction.

◆ Gradually release instructional responsibility to support independent reading.[35]

◆ Reflect on their students' progress and their own teaching practices in order to make changes that meet the needs of students.

Policies That Promote Learning to Read

Schools, school districts, and governmental and non-governmental agencies promote reading achievement when they:

◆ Respect teachers as professionals, value their knowledge of the students and community they serve, and encourage them to develop and adjust lessons according to the instructional needs of their students.

◆ Establish and maintain an instructional materials selection policy through which educators with knowledge of the reading process, how readers learn to read, and effective literacy instruction guide the selection of reading instructional materials, including trade books and technological resources, for the schools for which they are responsible. Those involved in the process should have no commercial interests in the outcome of the process.

◆ Provide learners with a wide variety of engaging, age-appropriate reading materials, free of stereotypes and compatible with community values, to read for pleasure and information.

◆ Provide learners with a rich curriculum in social studies, science, math, fine arts, and other subject matters so they can comprehend reading materials on an ever-expanding variety of topics.

- ◆ Provide learners who have not yet learned to read in any language with beginning reading instruction in a language in which they are competent.

- ◆ Provide teachers with a wide variety of reading materials with authentic language, free of stereotypes and compatible with community values, to use for instruction.

- ◆ Provide opportunities for teachers, parents, educational leaders, and the public to continue growing in their understanding of how we read, how we learn to read, and effective reading instruction.

Research Cited

The Reading Process

1. Kucer, S. B. (2005). *Dimensions of literacy: A conceptual base for the teaching of reading and writing* (2nd ed.). Mahwah, NJ: Erlbaum.

2. Ruddell, R. B. (1965). The effect of oral and written patterns of language structure on reading comprehension. *The Reading Teacher, 18*, 270–275.

   Tatham, S. (1970). Reading comprehension of materials written with select oral language patterns: A study at grades two and four. *Reading Research Quarterly, 5*, 402–426.

3. Bransford, J. D., & Johnson, M. K. (1972). Contextual prerequisites for understanding: Some investigations of comprehension and recall. *Journal of Verbal Learning and Verbal Behavior, 11*, 711–726.

   Chiesi, H. L., Spilich, G. J., & Voss, J. F. (1979). Acquisition of domain-related information in relation to high and low domain knowledge. *Journal of Verbal Learning and Verbal Behavior, 18*, 257–273.

   Lipson, M. Y. (1983). The influence of religious affiliation on children's memory for text information. *Reading Research Quarterly, 18*, 448–457.

   Pearson, D., Hansen, J., & Gordon, C. (1979). The effect of background knowledge on young children's comprehension of explicit and implicit information. *Journal of Reading Behavior, 11*, 201–209.

Spillich, G. J., Vesonder, G. T., Chiesi, H. L., & Voss, J. F. (1979). Text processing in domain-related information for individuals with high and low domain knowledge. *Journal of Verbal Learning and Verbal Behavior, 18*, 275–290.

Taylor, B. (1979). Good and poor readers' recall of familiar and unfamiliar text. *Journal of Reading Behavior, 11*, 375–388.

4. Bloome, D., & Green, J. (1985). Looking at reading instruction: Sociolinguistic and ethnographic approaches. In C. N. Hedley & A. N. Barratta (Eds.), *Contexts of reading* (pp. 167–184). Norwood, NJ: Ablex.

5. Rumelhart, D. E. (1985). Toward an interactive model of reading. In H. Singer & R. B. Ruddell (Eds.), *Theoretical models and processes of reading* (3rd ed., pp.720–750). Newark, DE: International Reading Association.

6. Goodman, K. (1996). *On reading.* Portsmouth, NH: Heinemann.

Kucer, S., & Tuten, J. (2003). Revisiting and rethinking the reading process. *Language Arts, 80*, 284–290.

Smith, F. (2004). *Understanding reading* (6th ed.). Mahwah, NJ: Erlbaum.

Learning to Read

7. Ferreiro, E., & Teberosky, A. (1982). *Literacy before schooling.* Portsmouth, NH: Heinemann.

Goodman, Y. (1986). Children coming to know literacy. In W. Teale & E. Sulzby (Eds.), *Emergent literacy.* Norwood, NJ: Ablex.

Heath, S. B. (1983). *Ways with words.* New York: Cambridge University Press.

Wells, G. (1986). *The meaning makers.* Portsmouth, NH: Heinemann.

8. Feitelson, D., & Goldstein, Z. (1986). Patterns of book ownership and reading to young children in Israeli school-oriented and nonschool-oriented families. *The Reading Teacher, 39*, 924–930.

Feitelson, D., Kita, B., & Goldstein, Z. (1986). Effects of listening to series stories on first graders' comprehension and use of language. *Research in the Teaching of English, 20*, 339–356.

Heath, S. B. (1983). *Ways with words.* New York: Cambridge University Press.

Wells, G. (1986). *The meaning makers.* Portsmouth, NH: Heinemann.

9. Ferreiro, E., & Teberosky, A. (1982). *Literacy before schooling.* Portsmouth, NH: Heinemann.

   Manning, M., Manning, G., Long, R., & Kamii, C. (1993). Preschoolers' conjunctures about segments of a written sentence. *Journal of Research in Childhood Education, 8*(1), 5–11.

10. Goodman, K. (1965). A linguistic study of cues and miscues in reading. *Elementary English, 42,* 639–643.

    Nicholson, T. (1991). Do children read words better in context or in lists? A classic study revisited. *Journal of Educational Psychology, 83,* 444–450.

11. Ruddell, R. B. (1965). The effect of oral and written patterns of language structure on reading comprehension. *The Reading Teacher, 18,* 270–275.

    Tatham, S. (1970). Reading comprehension of materials written with select oral language patterns: A study at grades two and four. *Reading Research Quarterly, 5,* 402–426.

12. Allington, R., & Woodside-Jiron, H. (1998). Decodable text in beginning reading: Are mandates and policy based on research? *ERS Spectrum, 16,* 3–11.

    Bridge, C., Winograd, P., & Haley, D. (1983). Using predictable materials vs. preprimers to teach beginning sight words. *The Reading Teacher, 36,* 884–891.

    Cunningham, P. (2000). *Phonics they use: Words for reading and writing* (3rd ed.). New York: HarperCollins.

    Kucer, S. (1985). Predictability and readability: The same rose with different names? In M. Douglass (Ed.), *Claremont Reading Conference forty-ninth yearbook* (pp. 229–246). Claremont, CA: Claremont Graduate School.

13. Goswami, U. (1986). Children's use of analogy in learning to read: A developmental study. *Journal of Experimental Child Psychology, 42,* 73–83.

    Goswami, U. (1988). Orthographic analogies and reading development. *The Quarterly Journal of Experimental Psychology, 40,* 239–268.

Moustafa, M. (1995). Children's productive phonological recoding. *Reading Research Quarterly, 30*, 464–476.

14. Anderson, R. C., Wilson, P. T., & Fielding, L. B. (1988). Growth in reading and how children spend their time outside of school. *Reading Research Quarterly, 23*, 285–303.

Elley, W. B., & Mangubhai, F. (1983). The impact of reading on second language learning. *Reading Research Quarterly, 19*, 53–67.

Feitelson, D., Kita, B., & Goldstein, Z. (1986). Effects of listening to series stories on first graders' comprehension and use of language. *Research in the Teaching of English, 20*, 339–356.

Mullis, I. V. S., Campbell, J. R., & Farstrup, A. E. (1993). *NAEP 1992 reading report card for the nation and the states.* Washington, DC: National Center for Education Statistics.

15. DeFord, D. (1981). Literacy: Reading, writing, and other essentials. *Language Arts, 58*, 652–658.

16. Smith, F. (1994). *Writing and the writer* (2nd ed.). Hillsdale, NJ: Erlbaum.

17. Cummins, J. (1981). The role of primary language development in promoting educational success for language minority students. In *Schooling and language minority students: A theoretical framework* (pp. 3–49). Los Angeles: Evaluation, Dissemination and Assessment Center, California State University.

18. Feitelson, D., & Goldstein, Z. (1986). Patterns of book ownership and reading to young children in Israeli school-oriented and nonschool-oriented families. *The Reading Teacher, 39*, 924–930.

Heath, S. B. (1983). *Ways with words.* New York: Cambridge University Press.

Purcell-Gates, V. (1996). Stories, coupons, and the *TV Guide*: Relationships between home literacy experiences and emergent literacy knowledge. *Reading Research Quarterly, 31*, 406–428.

Purcell-Gates, V., L'Allier, S., & Smith, D. (1995). Literacy at the Harts' and the Larsons': Diversity among poor, inner city families. *The Reading Teacher, 48*, 572–578.

Purcell-Gates, V., McIntyre, E., & Freppon, P. (1995). Learning written storybook language in school: A comparison of low-SES children in skills-based and whole language classrooms. *American Educational Research Journal, 32,* 659–685.

Taylor, D. (1998). *Family literacy*. Portsmouth, NH: Heinemann.

Taylor, D., & Dorsey-Gaines, C. (1988). *Growing up literate: Learning from inner-city families*. Portsmouth, NH: Heinemann.

Wells, G. (1986). *The meaning makers*. Portsmouth, NH: Heinemann.

19. Smith, C., Constantino, R., & Krashen, S. (1997). Differences in print environment for children in Beverly Hills, Compton, and Watts. *The Emergency Librarian, 24*(4), 8–9.

Neuman, S. B., & Celano, D. (2001). Access to print in low-income and middle-income communities: An ecological study of four neighborhoods. *Reading Research Quarterly, 36,* 8–26.

20. Anderson, R. C., Wilkinson, I. A. G., & Mason, J. M. (1991). A microanalysis of the small-group guided reading lesson: Effects of an emphasis on global story meaning. *Reading Research Quarterly, 26,* 417–441.

Cantrell, S. C. (1999). Effective teaching and literacy learning: A look inside primary classrooms. *The Reading Teacher, 52,* 370–378.

Freppon, P. (1991). Children's concepts of the nature and purpose of reading in different instructional settings. *Journal of Reading Behavior, 23,* 139–163.

Milligan, J. L., & Berg, H. (1992). The effect of whole language on the comprehending ability of first grade children. *Reading Improvement, 29,* 146–154.

Mullis, I. V. S., Campbell, J. R., & Farstrup, A. E. (1993). *NAEP 1992 reading report card for the nation and the states*. Washington, DC: National Center for Education Statistics.

Sacks, C. H., & Mergendoller, J. R. (1997). The relationship between teachers' theoretical orientation toward reading and student outcomes in kindergarten children with different initial reading abilities. *American Educational Research Journal, 34,* 721–739.

Effective Reading Instruction

21. See the references in the previous endnote.

22. National Commission on Excellence in Elementary Teacher Preparation for Reading Instruction. (2003). *Prepared to make a difference*. Newark, DE: International Reading Association.

23. Cambourne, B. (1995). Toward an educationally relevant theory of literacy learning: Twenty years of inquiry. *The Reading Teacher, 49*, 182–190.

    Taylor, B., Pearson, P. D., Clark, K., & Walpole, S. (1999). *Beating the odds: Teaching all children to read* (CIERA Report No. 2-006). Ann Arbor: University of Michigan.

24. Anderson, R. C., Hiebert, E. H., Scott, J. A., & Wilkinson, I. A. G. (1985). *Becoming a nation of readers: The report of the Commission on Reading*. Washington, DC: National Institute of Education.

25. Bridge, C., Winograd, P., & Haley, D. (1983). Using predictable materials vs. preprimers to teach beginning sight words. *The Reading Teacher, 36*, 884–891.

    Eldredge, J. L., Reutzel, D. R., & Hollingsworth, P. M. (1996). Comparing the effectiveness of two oral reading practices: Round-robin reading and the shared book experience. *Journal of Literacy Research, 28*, 201–225.

26. Anderson, R. C., Wilkinson, I. A. G., & Mason, J. M. (1991). A microanalysis of the small-group guided reading lesson: Effects of an emphasis on global story meaning. *Reading Research Quarterly, 26*, 417–441.

27. Steven, K. C. (1982). Can we improve reading by teaching background information? *Journal of Reading, 25*, 326–329.

28. Duke, N., & Pearson, P. D. (2002). Effective practices for developing reading comprehension. In A. Farstrup & S. J. Samuels (Eds.), *What research has to say about reading instruction* (3rd ed., pp. 205–242). Newark, DE: International Reading Association.

29. Cantrell, S. C. (1999). Effective teaching and literacy learning: A look inside primary classrooms. *The Reading Teacher, 52*, 370–378.

    Elley, W. B. (1989). Vocabulary acquisition from listening to stories. *Reading Research Quarterly, 24*, 174–187.

    Freppon, P. (1991). Children's concepts of the nature and purpose of reading in different instructional settings. *Journal of Reading Behavior 23*, 139–163.

Goodman, Y. M. (2003). *Valuing language study: Inquiry into language for elementary and middle schools.* Urbana, IL: National Council of Teachers of English.

30. Elley, W. B., & Mangubhai, F. (1983). The impact of reading on second language learning. *Reading Research Quarterly, 19,* 53–67.

Neuman, S. B. (1999). Books make a difference: A study of access to literacy. *Reading Research Quarterly, 34,* 286–311.

Taylor, B., Pearson, P. D., Clark, K., & Walpole, S. (1999). *Beating the odds: Teaching all children to read* (CIERA Report No. 2-006). Ann Arbor: University of Michigan.

31. Zaragoza, N., & Vaughn, S. (1995). Children teach us to teach writing. *The Reading Teacher, 49,* 42–47.

32. Gambrell, L. B. (1996). Creating classroom cultures that foster reading motivation. *The Reading Teacher, 50,* 14–25.

33. Guthrie, J. T., Van Meter, P., Hancock, G. R., Alao, S., Anderson, E., & McCann, A. (1998). Does concept-oriented reading instruction increase strategy use and conceptual learning from text? *Journal of Educational Psychology, 90,* 261–271.

34. Cambourne, B. (2002). Holistic, integrated approaches to reading and language arts instruction: The constructivist framework of an instructional theory. In A. Farstrup & S. J. Samuels (Eds.), *What research has to say about reading instruction* (3rd ed., pp. 25–47). Newark, DE: International Reading Association.

35. Pearson, P. D., & Gallagher, M. C. (1983). The instruction of reading comprehension. *Contemporary Educational Psychology, 8,* 317–344.

May 1, 2004

APPENDIX B

A Call to Action: What We Know about Adolescent Literacy and Ways to Support Teachers in Meeting Students' Needs

A Position/Action Statement from NCTE's Commission on Reading
May 2004

Purpose

The purpose of this document is to provide a research-based resource for media, policymakers, and teachers that acknowledges the complexities of reading as a developmental process and addresses the needs of secondary readers and their teachers.

What Is Reading?

The NCTE Commission on Reading has produced a statement, "On Reading, Learning to Read, and Effective Reading Instruction" [see Appendix A], that synthesizes current research on reading. Reading is defined as a complex, purposeful, social, and cognitive process in which readers simultaneously use their knowledge of spoken and written language, their knowledge of the topic of the text, and their knowledge of their culture to construct meaning. Reading is not a technical skill acquired once and for all in the primary grades, but rather a developmental process. A reader's competence continues to grow through engagement with various types of texts and wide reading for various purposes over a lifetime.

Reprinted from http://www.ncte.org/about/over/positions/category/read/118620.htm.

What Is Unique about Adolescent Literacy?

In middle and high school, students encounter academic discourses and disciplinary concepts in such fields as science, mathematics, and the social sciences that require different reading approaches from those used with more familiar forms such as literary and personal narratives (Kucer, 2005). These new forms, purposes, and processing demands require that teachers show, demonstrate, and make visible to students how literacy operates within the academic disciplines (Keene & Zimmermann, 1997; Tovani, 2000).

Adolescents are already reading in multiple ways, using literacy as a social and political endeavor in which they engage to make meaning and act upon their worlds. Their texts range from clothing logos to music to specialty magazines to Web sites to popular and classical literature. In the classroom it is important for teachers to recognize and value the multiple literacy resources students bring to the acquisition of school literacy.

In effective schools, classroom conversations about how, why, and what we read are important parts of the literacy curriculum (Applebee, 1996; Schoenbach, Greenleaf, Cziko, & Hurwitz, 1999). In fact, discussion-based approaches to academic literacy content are strongly linked to student achievement (Applebee, Langer, Nystrand, & Gamoran, 2003). However, high-stakes testing, such as high school exit exams, is not only narrowing the content of the literacy curriculum, but also constraining instructional approaches to reading (Amrein & Berliner, 2002; Madaus, 1998) Limited, "one right answer" or "main idea" models of reading run counter to recent research findings, which call for a richer, more engaged approach to literacy instruction (Campbell, Donahue, Reese, & Phillips, 1996; Taylor, Anderson, Au, & Raphael, 1999).

What Current Research Is Showing Teachers

(1) That literacy is a dynamic interaction of the social and cognitive realms, with textual understandings growing from students' knowledge of their worlds to knowledge of the external world (Langer, 2002). All students need to go beyond the study of discrete skills and strategies to understand how those skills and strategies are integrated with life experiences. Langer found that literacy programs that successfully teach at-risk students emphasize connections between students' lives, prior knowledge, and texts, and emphasize student conversations to make those connections.

(2) That the majority of inexperienced adolescent readers need opportunities and instructional support to read many and diverse types of texts in order to gain experience, build fluency, and develop a range as readers (Greenleaf, Schoenbach, Cziko, & Mueller, 2001; Kuhn & Stahl, 2000). Through extensive reading of a range of texts, supported by strategy lessons and discussions, readers become familiar with written language structures and text features, develop their vocabularies, and read for meaning more efficiently and effectively. Conversations about their reading that focus on the strategies they use and their language knowledge help adolescents build confidence in their reading and become better readers (Goodman & Marek, 1996).

(3) That most adolescents do not need further instruction in phonics or decoding skills (Ivey & Baker, 2004). Research summarized in the National Reading Panel report noted that the benefits of phonics instruction are strongest in first grade, with diminished results for students in subsequent grades. Phonics instruction has not been seen to improve reading comprehension for older students (National Reading Panel, 2000). In cases where older students need help to construct meaning with text, instruction should be targeted and embedded in authentic reading experiences.

(4) That utilizing a model of reading instruction focused on basic skills can lead to the mislabeling of some secondary readers as "struggling readers" and "non-readers" because they lack extensive reading experience, depend on different prior knowledge, and/or comprehend differently or in more complex ways. A large percentage of secondary readers who are so mislabeled are students of color and/or students from lower socioeconomic backgrounds. Abundant research suggests that the isolated skill instruction they receive may perpetuate low literacy achievement rather than improve their competence and engagement in complex reading tasks (Allington, 2001; Alvermann & Moore, 1991; Brown, 1991; Hiebert, 1991; Hull & Rose, 1989; Knapp & Turnbull, 1991; Sizer, 1992). In addition, prescriptive, skills-based reading instruction mislocates the problem as the students' failure to learn, rather than the institution's failure to teach reading as the complex mental and social activity it is (Greenleaf et al., 2001).

(5) That effective literacy programs move students to deeper understandings of texts and increase their ability to generate ideas and knowledge for their own uses (Newmann, King, & Rigdon, 1997).

(6) That assessment should focus on underlying knowledge in the larger curriculum and on strategies for thinking during literacy acts (Darling-Hammond & Falk, 1997; Langer, 2000; Smith, 1991). Likewise, preparation for assessment (from ongoing classroom measures to high-stakes tests) should focus on the critical components above.

What Adolescent Readers Need

♦ Sustained experiences with diverse texts in a variety of genres and offering multiple perspectives on real-life experiences. Although many of these texts will be required by the curriculum, others should be self-selected and of high interest to the reader. Wide independent reading develops fluency, builds vocabulary and knowledge of text structures, and offers readers the experiences they need to read and construct meaning with more challenging texts. Text should be broadly viewed to include print, electronic, and visual media.

♦ Conversations/discussions regarding texts that are authentic, student initiated, and teacher facilitated. Such discussion should lead to diverse interpretations of a text that deepen the conversation.

♦ Experience in thinking critically about how they engage with texts:

• When do I comprehend?

• What do I do to understand a text?

• When do I not understand a text?

• What can I do when meaning breaks down?

♦ Experience in critical examination of texts that helps them to:

• Recognize how texts are organized in various disciplines and genre

• Question and investigate various social, political, and historical content and purposes within texts

• Make connections between texts, and between texts and personal experiences to act on and react to the world

• Understand multiple meanings and richness of texts and layers of complexity

What Teachers of Adolescents Need

♦ Adequate and appropriate reading materials that tap students' diverse interests and represent a range of difficulty

♦ Continued support and professional development that assist them to:

- Bridge between adolescents' rich literate backgrounds and school literacy

- Teach literacy in their disciplines as an essential way of learning in their disciplines

- Recognize when students are not making meaning with text and provide appropriate, strategic assistance to read course content effectively

- Facilitate student-initiated conversations regarding texts that are authentic and relevant to real-life experiences

- Create environments that allow students to engage in critical examinations of texts as they dissect, deconstruct, and reconstruct in an effort to engage in meaning making and comprehension processes

References

Allington, R. L. (2001). *What really matters for struggling readers: Designing research-based programs.* New York: Addison Wesley Longman.

Alvermann, D., & Moore, D. (1991). Secondary school reading. In R. Barr, M. L. Kamil, P. Mosenthal, & P. D. Pearson (Eds.), *Handbook of reading research* (vol. 2, pp. 951–983). New York: Longman.

Amrein, A. L., & Berliner, D. C. (2002). *High-stakes testing, uncertainty, and student learning. Educational Policy Analysis Archives,* 10(18). [Online]. Available at http://epaa.asu.edu/epaa/v10n18

Applebee, A. (1996). *Curriculum as conversation: Transforming traditions of teaching and learning.* Chicago: University of Chicago Press.

Applebee, A., Langer, J., Nystrand, M., & Gamoran, A. (2003). Discussion-based approaches to developing understanding: Classroom instruction and student performance in middle and high school English. *American Educational Research Journal, 40*(3), 685–730.

Brown, R. G. (1991). *Schools of thought: How the politics of literacy shape thinking in the classroom.* San Francisco: Jossey-Bass.

Campbell, J., Donahue, P., Reese, C., & Phillips, G. (1996) *National Assessment of Educational Progress 1994 reading report card for the nation and the states.* Washington, DC: National Center for Education Statistics, U.S. Department of Education.

Darling-Hammond, L., & Falk, B. (1997). Using standards and assessments to support student learning. *Phi Delta Kappan, 79,* 190–199.

Goodman, Y., & Marek, A. (1996). *Retrospective miscue analysis: Revaluing readers and reading.* Katonah, NY: R. C. Owens.

Greenleaf, C., Schoenbach, R., Cziko, C., & Mueller, F. (2001). Apprenticing adolescent readers to academic literacy. *Harvard Educational Review, 71*(1), 79–129.

Hiebert, E. (1991). *Literacy for a diverse society: Perspectives, policies, and practices.* New York: Teachers College Press.

Hull, G. A., & Rose, M. (1989). Rethinking remediation: Toward a social-cognitive understanding of problematic reading and writing. *Written Communication, 8,* 139–154.

Ivey, G., & Baker, M. (2004). Phonics instruction for older students? Just say no. *Educational Leadership, 61*(6), 35–39.

Keene, E. O., & Zimmermann, S. (1997). *Mosaic of thought: Teaching comprehension in a reader's workshop.* Portsmouth, NH: Heinemann.

Knapp, M. S., & Turnbull, B. (1991). *Better schools for the children in poverty: Alternatives to conventional wisdom.* Berkeley, CA: McCutchan.

Kucer, S. (2005). *Dimensions of literacy: A conceptual base for teaching reading and writing in school settings* (2nd ed.). Mahwah, NJ: Lawrence Erlbaum.

Kuhn, M. R., & Stahl, S. A. (2000). *Fluency: A review of developmental and remedial practices* (Report No. 2-008). Ann Arbor, MI: Center for the Improvement of Early Reading Achievement.

Langer, J. (2000). *Teaching middle and high school students to read and write well: Six features of effective instruction.* Albany, NY: National Research Center on English Learning and Achievement.

Langer, J. (2002). *Effective literacy instruction: Building successful reading and writing programs.* Urbana, IL: National Council of Teachers of English.

Madaus, G. (1998). The distortion of teaching and testing: High-stakes testing and instruction. *Peabody Journal of Education, 65,* 29–46.

National Reading Panel. (2000). *Teaching children to read.* Washington, DC: National Institute of Child Health and Human Development.

Newmann, F., King, B., & Rigdon, M. (1997). Accountability and school performance: Implications from restructuring schools. *Harvard Educational Review, 67,* 41–74.

Schoenbach, R., Greenleaf, C., Cziko, C., & Hurwitz, L. (1999). *Reading for understanding: A guide to improving reading in middle and high school classrooms.* San Francisco: Jossey-Bass.

Sizer, T. (1992). *Horace's compromise: The dilemma of the American high school.* Boston: Houghton Mifflin.

Smith, M. I. (1991). Put to the test: The effects of external testing on teachers. *Educational Researcher, 20*(5), 8–11.

Taylor, B. M., Anderson, R. C., Au, K. H., & Raphael, T. E. (1999). *Discretion in the translation of reading research to policy* (Report No. 3-006). Ann Arbor, MI: Center for the Improvement of Early Reading Achievement.

Tovani, C. (2000). *I read it but I don't get it.* York, ME: Stenhouse.

Selected Resources for Teachers

Allen, J. (2000). *Yellow brick roads: Shared and guided paths to independent reading.* York, ME: Stenhouse.

Atwell, N. (1998). *In the middle* (2nd ed.). Portsmouth, NH: Heinemann.

Beers, K. (2003). *When kids can't read: What teachers can do.* Portsmouth, NH: Heinemann.

Fehring, H., & Green, P. (Eds.). (2001). *Critical literacy: A collection of articles from the Australian literacy educator's association.* Melbourne, AU: Intrados Group.

Gee, J. P. (1996). *Social linguistics and literacies: Ideology in discourses.* (2nd ed.). London: Falmer.

Lenski, S., Wham, M. A., & Johns, J. (2003). *Reading and learning strategies: Middle grades through high school.* Dubuque, IA: Kendall/Hunt.

Luke, A. (1995–1996). Text and discourse in education: An introduction to critical discourse analysis. In M. W. Apple (Ed.), *Review of research in education* (Vol. 21, pp. 3–48). Washington, DC: American Educational Research Association.

Moje, E., Young, J., Readence, J., & Moore, D. (2000). Reinventing adolescent literacy for new times: Perennial and millennial issues. *Journal of Adolescent and Adult Literacy, 43*(5), 400–410.

Moore, D., Bean, T., Birdyshaw, D., & Rycik, J. (1999). *Adolescent literacy: A position statement*. Newark, DE: International Reading Association.

Morgan, W. (1997). *Critical literacy in the classroom: The art of the possible*. New York: Routledge.

Robb, L. (2000). *Teaching reading in middle school*. New York: Scholastic.

Smith, M., & Wilhelm, J. (2002). *"Reading don't fix no Chevys": Literacy in the lives of young men*. Portsmouth, NH: Heinemann.

Street, B. (1995). *Social literacies: Critical approaches to literacy in development, ethnography, and education*. London: Longman.

Wilhelm, J., Baker, T., & Dube, J. (2001). *Strategic reading: Guiding students to lifelong literacy*. Portsmouth, NH: Heinemann.

Appendix C

Features of Literacy Programs:
A Decision-Making Matrix

Prepared by the Commission on Reading of the National Council of
Teachers of English

Purpose

The Commission on Reading of the National Council of Teachers of
English regularly undertakes projects to broaden discussion of important literacy issues and to provide support for teachers as they make
informed instructional decisions. Commission members developed the
matrix that follows in response to requests from NCTE members for
sound, standards-aligned criteria to apply as they select program materials or design local programs of instruction in reading. It is intended to
be used as part of professional discussion among colleagues.

Model

The model on which the matrix is based is aligned with the position
statement "On Reading, Learning to Read, and Effective Reading Instruction: An Overview of What We Know and How We Know It"
(http://www.ncte.org/about/over/positions/category/read/118620.htm),
developed by NCTE's Commission on Reading. Reading is a complex,
purposeful, social, and cognitive process in which readers simultaneously
use their knowledge of spoken and written language, their knowledge
of the topic of the text, and their knowledge of their culture to construct
meaning. Effective reading instruction is grounded in a professional
knowledge of how readers make sense of print and how students learn.
All instruction is based on a careful observation of learners' reading to
determine appropriate instruction.

Reprinted from http://www.ncte.org/library/files/About_NCTE/Overview/
ReadingMatrixFinal.pdf?source=gs.

Users

The matrix is intended as a discussion and decision-making tool for teachers and curriculum developers working together to select instructional materials. Educators do this based on their understandings of the nature and uses of literacy and their beliefs about how literacy is developed. The matrix may be found at the NCTE website at http://www. ncte.org/library/files/About_NCTE/Overview/ReadingMatrixFinal. pdf?source=gs.

Matrix Features

The matrix offers categorized features for teachers to consider in making local decisions about appropriate materials and goals for literacy instruction. Blank rows are provided for additional features users find relevant. Instructional emphases will vary depending on students' age and proficiency in reading and writing. For example, the early features listed under word recognition and word study will be most applicable to elementary programs. These features are ranked by the NCTE Commission on Reading as (4) essential, (3) important, (2) less important, or (1) not important for an effective program of literacy instruction. Decisions about the relative importance of various features are based on published research and professional resources. However, each group using the matrix should determine its own rankings by considering local needs, standards, and definitions of reading. Furthermore, *the Commission emphasizes that numeric evaluation of program features is less important than the <u>conversations</u> prompted by the use of the matrix.*

Matrix Use

1. In Column 2 on the matrix, rate each feature in terms of its importance (1–4) for an effective literacy program.
2. For each literacy program under consideration (whether commercially or locally designed), mark each feature to the degree of its presence in the program. Use **H** to indicate high degree/presence in significant amount, **M** to indicate medium degree/presence in some amount, and **L** to indicate low degree/presence in little or no amount. A desirable program will be one in which features seen as essential or important are evident to a high degree. Educators may wish to add other features and compare the ones they rank highly (3–4) with those given high rankings in the matrix designed by the Commission.

* *

You might find it useful to complete the following two statements before using the matrix and starting your conversations.

1. Reading is:

_____

_____

_____

2. Reading instruction should be:

_____

_____

_____

Program Name _____

INTENDED AUDIENCE	
(check all that apply)	
Primary	
Intermediate	
Middle School	
High School	
English Language Learners (ELL)	
Native English Speakers	
Students requiring reading intervention	

NCTE Commission on Reading indicates (4) as essential, (3) as important, (2) as less important, or (1) as not an important feature for an effective literacy program. Decisions about the relative importance of various features are based on published research and professional resources. Rate **H** to indicate high degree/presence, **M** to indicate medium degree/presence, **L** to indicate low degree/presence in each reviewed program. A desirable program will be one in which features seen as essential or important are seen in a high degree.

The "1" column shows NCTE's rating of program features. The "2" column is for your own rating of the features.	1	2	Degree of Presence		
			H	M	L
MEDIA/TOOLS					
Books					
Authentic connected texts, complete & unabridged	4				
Predictable texts	4				
Decodable texts	1				
Abridged texts	2				
Skills-based texts	1				
Leveled texts	2				
Nonfiction texts	4				
Classroom libraries	4				
Controlled vocabulary	1				
Original illustrations	4				
Publisher-substituted illustrations	1				
Videotapes	2				
Internet	2				
Computer software	3				
Audiotapes	3				
School-to-home connections	4				
Suggestions for extended readings	4				
Recall level worksheets	1				

NCTE Commission on Reading indicates (4) as essential, (3) as important, (2) as less important, or (1) as not an important feature for an effective literacy program. Decisions about the relative importance of various features are based on published research and professional resources. Rate H to indicate high degree/presence, M to indicate medium degree/presence, L to indicate low degree/presence in each reviewed program. A desirable program will be one in which features seen as essential or important are seen in a high degree.

The "1" column shows NCTE's rating of program features. The "2" column is for your own rating of the features.	1	2	Degree of Presence		
			H	M	L
MATERIALS REPRESENT					
Authentic multicultural perspectives (text and illustrations)	4				
Accurate, current information	4				
Wide range of purposes	4				
High literary quality	4				
Range of authors	4				
Multiple disciplines	4				
Multiple genres	4				
Content likely to engage and interest readers	4				
Content that is age and developmentally appropriate	4				
Content that is of interest to both genders	4				
Conceptual or thematic structures	4				
PARTICIPANT STRUCTURES/GROUPINGS					
Whole class	3				
Small groups	4				
Individual (instructional and independent)	4				
Flexible groups (interest, ability)	4				
Pull-out instruction	2				
Fixed-ability groups	1				
INSTRUCTIONAL APPROACHES					
Scripted, sequenced, teacher-directed	1				
Student-generated topics and questions	4				
Strategies and skills taught in isolation	1				
Strategies and skills embedded in meaningful text	4				
Scaffolded instruction toward independence	4				
Discussion	4				

NCTE Commission on Reading indicates (4) as essential, (3) as important, (2) as less important, or (1) as not an important feature for an effective literacy program. Decisions about the relative importance of various features are based on published research and professional resources. Rate **H** to indicate high degree/presence, **M** to indicate medium degree/presence, **L** to indicate low degree/presence in each reviewed program. A desirable program will be one in which features seen as essential or important are seen in a high degree.

The "1" column shows NCTE's rating of program features. The "2" column is for your own rating of the features.	1	2	Degree of Presence		
			H	M	L
Role play	3				
Projects	3				
Extensive independent reading (SSR, free choice reading)	4				
Student choice of instructional texts	4				
Literature study	4				
Guided reading	3				
Shared reading	3				
Partner reading	3				
COMPREHENSION					
Development of higher-level thinking and critical literacy	4				
Emphasis on meaning making with connected text, including focus on using fiction and nonfiction text structures and features	4				
Emphasis on application of skills in isolated text excerpts	1				
Multiple perspectives, themes, and interpretations	4				
Independence in learning/self-directed	4				
Development of cognitive strategies (predicting, questioning, confirming, summarizing, inferring)	4				
Development of metacognitive strategies	4				
Support of risk-taking	4				
Development of multiple cueing systems	4				
Opportunities for comprehension work	4				
• before reading					
• during reading					
• after reading					
Intertextuality	4				

NCTE Commission on Reading indicates (4) as essential, (3) as important, (2) as less important, or (1) as not an important feature for an effective literacy program. Decisions about the relative importance of various features are based on published research and professional resources. Rate **H** to indicate high degree/presence, **M** to indicate medium degree/presence, **L** to indicate low degree/presence in each reviewed program. A desirable program will be one in which features seen as essential or important are seen in a high degree.

The "1" column shows NCTE's rating of program features. The "2" column is for your own rating of the features.	1	2	Degree of Presence		
			H	**M**	**L**
Development of schema	4				
• connections to current knowledge					
• development of new knowledge					
WORD RECOGNITION AND WORD STUDY					
Phonemic awareness in isolation	1				
Phonemic awareness in context	3				
Phonological awareness	2				
Phonics in isolation	1				
Phonics in context	3				
Alphabetic principle	4				
Sight words	4				
Reading fluency with comprehension	4				
Reading fluency without comprehension	1				
Miscues as a window into cue and strategy utilization	4				
Decoding of pseudo words	1				
Word families	4				
Experiential base for vocabulary	4				
Etymological focus for vocabulary	3				
Vocabulary lists	2				
Vocabulary from text	4				
Vocabulary building with roots & affixes	3				
Word lists	1				
Concept-driven vocabulary instruction	4				
READING/WRITING CONNECTIONS					
Constructed spelling as approximation	4				
Spelling as a window into phonics knowledge	4				
Response to text in students' own words	4				
Response to text as fill-in-the-blanks	1				

Appendix C

NCTE Commission on Reading indicates (4) as essential, (3) as important, (2) as less important, or (1) as not an important feature for an effective literacy program. Decisions about the relative importance of various features are based on published research and professional resources. Rate **H** to indicate high degree/presence, **M** to indicate medium degree/presence, **L** to indicate low degree/presence in each reviewed program. A desirable program will be one in which features seen as essential or important are seen in a high degree.

The "1" column shows NCTE's rating of program features. The "2" column is for your own rating of the features.	1	2	Degree of Presence		
			H	**M**	**L**
Reading and writing integrated, e.g., text as a source for student writing opportunities	4				
Essay form	2				
Multiple-choice responses to reading	1				
Discussions about individual and social uses of literacy	4				
STUDENT ROLE					
Choice of reading selections	4				
Choice of reading extension activities	4				
Documenting and assessing reading growth via self-reflection, portfolio development, process journals, etc.	4				
Completion of reading logs	2				
Problem-solving & resourcefulness encouraged	4				
Increased independence and responsibility	4				
• social interaction around literacy					
• inquiry into own and others literacy processes and practices					
• risk-taking in reading & writing encouraged					
ASSESSMENT					
Formal, standardized	1				
Unit tests	1				
Classroom-based, ongoing (running record, miscue analysis, retelling, anecdotal observations, student reading histories, records of reading)	4				
Multiple-choice comprehension tests	2				
Student directed	3				
Written reactions and responses to texts	4				

NCTE Commission on Reading indicates (4) as essential, (3) as important, (2) as less important, or (1) as not an important feature for an effective literacy program. Decisions about the relative importance of various features are based on published research and professional resources. Rate **H** to indicate high degree/presence, **M** to indicate medium degree/presence, **L** to indicate low degree/presence in each reviewed program. A desirable program will be one in which features seen as essential or important are seen in a high degree.

The "1" column shows NCTE's rating of program features. The "2" column is for your own rating of the features.	1	2	Degree of Presence		
			H	M	L
Portfolios	4				
Lists of learners' reading experiences	4				
PROFESSIONAL RESOURCES AND DEVELOPMENT					
Scripts for implementation of program	1				
Data on student outcomes	3				
Support for teacher research, e.g., teacher inquiry topics and findings	3				
Support for meeting needs of individual students (resources, instructional approaches)	4				
Resources and professional development experiences to build teacher knowledge about learning and literacy	4				
Research and theory base of the program provided	4				
Support for teacher as instructional decision maker	4				
Provision for parent education, support, and involvement	4				

Having completed the matrix, how close is the match between the program and your definition of reading and what you believe reading instruction should be?

Selected Resources

Allington, R. L. (2005). *What really matters for struggling readers: Designing research-based programs* (2nd ed.). Boston: Allyn and Bacon.

Baker, L., Dreher, M. J., & Guthrie, J. (2000). *Engaging young readers: Promoting achievement and motivation.* New York: Guilford Press.

Braunger, J., & Lewis, J. (2005). *Building a knowledge base in reading* (2nd ed.). Newark, DE: International Reading Association and Urbana, IL: National Council of Teachers of English.

Goodman, K., Olsen, J., Colvin, C., & Vanderline, L. (1966). *Choosing materials to teach reading.* Detroit: Wayne State University Press.

Hammond, W., & Raphael, T. (Eds.). (1999). *Early literacy instruction for the new millennium.* Grand Rapids: Michigan Reading Association and Center for the Improvement of Early Reading Achievement.

Keene, E. O., & Zimmermann, S. (1997). *Mosaic of thought.* Portsmouth, NH: Heinemann.

Kucer, S. (2001). *Dimensions of literacy.* Mahwah, NJ: Lawrence Erlbaum.

Langer, J. (2000). *Guidelines for teaching middle and high school students to read and write well: Six features of effective instruction.* Albany, NY: National Research Center on English Learning and Achievement.

Office of Literacy Programs, Ohio Department of Education. (2001). *Choosing a reading program: A consumer's guide.* Ohio Department of Education.

Peterson, C., Caverly, D., Nicholson, S., O'Neal, S., & Cusenbary, S. (2000). *Building reading proficiency at the secondary level: A guide to resources.* Austin, TX: Southwest Educational Development Laboratory.

Pressley, M. (2002). Effective beginning reading instruction. *Journal of Literacy Research, 34*(2), 165–188.

Robb, L. (2000). *Teaching reading in middle school: A strategic approach to teaching reading that improves comprehension and thinking.* New York: Scholastic Professional Books.

Roller, C. (Ed.). (2001). *Learning to teach reading: Setting the research agenda.* Newark, DE: International Reading Association.

Snow, C., Burns, M. S., & Griffin, P. (Eds.). (1998). *Preventing reading difficulties in young children.* Washington, DC: National Academy Press.

Yatvin, J., Weaver, C., & Garan, E. (2003). Reading First: Cautions and recommendations. *Language Arts, 81*(1), 28–33.

U.S. Department of Health and Human Services. (2000a). *Report of the National Reading Panel. Teaching children to read.* Rockville, MD: NICHD Clearinghouse Publication #00-4769.

U.S. Department of Health and Human Services. (2000b). *Report of the National Reading Panel. Teaching children to read. Reports of the subgroups.* Rockville, MD: NICHD Clearinghouse Publication #00-4754.

INDEX

EDITOR

Stephen B. Kucer is associate professor of language and literacy education at Washington State University–Vancouver. Formerly a fourth-, fifth-, and sixth-grade teacher, he has researched and written on the use of thematic units to promote language, literacy, and concept development in diverse learners in *Curricular Conversations: Themes in Multilingual and Monolingual Classrooms* (1995). He is also the author of *Dimensions of Literacy* (2001) and coauthor of *Teaching the Dimensions of Literacy* (2005). Currently, he is examining the relationship between fluency, miscues, and comprehension in elementary school students.

CONTRIBUTORS

Jane Braunger is a senior research associate with the Strategic Literacy Initiative (SLI) at WestEd, where she conducts research on professional development in literacy among middle and high school teachers; collaborates in the ongoing development of theory and practice in Reading Apprenticeship®; and establishes new networks and contexts for SLI's work, especially in preservice teacher education and community college settings. Her professional experience includes high school and college teaching, K–12 language arts curriculum development, teacher education, research, and writing. She is lead author of a book on preparing middle and high school teachers for content area literacy instruction (*Rethinking Preparation for Content Area Teaching: The Reading Apprenticeship Approach*, 2005). She is coauthor with Jan Lewis of a synthesis of the research on learning to read, *Building a Knowledge Base in Reading* (2006, 2nd ed.). Braunger is the 2005 recipient of WestEd's Paul D. Hood Award for Distinguished Contribution to the Field.

Teaching English to New York City middle-grade students and subsequently receiving the National Council of Teachers of English Promising Researcher Award challenged **Rita S. Brause** to systematically seek to understand the intersections of teaching, learning, and literacy development, most recently using sociocultural and critical literacy lenses. Upon completing her doctoral degree at New York University, she was offered a faculty post at Fordham University, which continues to enable her to pursue answers to professional questions in collaboration with K–12 and university colleagues across the nation and beyond. Representative publications and professional activities include *Enduring Schools: Problems and Possibilities* (1992); *Writing Your Doctoral Dissertation: Invisible Rules for Success* (2003); *Search and ReSearch: What the Inquiring Teacher Needs to Know* (coeditor, 1991); *Succeeding at Your Interview: A Practical Guide for Teachers* (coauthor, 2002); chair of the NCTE Commission on Reading; and member of the Executive Board of the Conference on English Education. She can be reached at Brause@ Fordham.Edu.

Karen Delbridge is currently an instructional facilitator at East High School in Laramie County School District #1 in Cheyenne, Wyoming, and has taught English in grades 7–12 for fourteen years. In addition to serving on the National Council of Teachers of English Commission on Reading, she is president of the Wyoming Association of Teachers of English. Delbridge received her bachelor's degree from Lee University and her master's degree from Tusculum, both in Tennessee. She received her doctorate from the University of Wyoming and conducted research on eighth-grade students reading and responding to multicultural texts. She was awarded the Intellectual Freedom Award from NCTE/ SLATE in 2003, and the Hispanic Organization for Progress & Education awarded her HOPE Teacher of the Year in 2006. Delbridge was also awarded the Richard W. Halle award from NCTE for Outstanding Middle Level Educator in 2006.

Danling Fu is professor of language and culture in the School of Teaching and Learning, College of Education, at the University of Florida. In addition to teaching both undergraduate and graduate literacy courses, she has conducted research in the public schools with a focus on children's writing development and literacy instruction for new immigrant students. Her research has resulted in two books and over sixty journal articles, book chapters, and book reviews. She gives speeches and conducts workshops on various issues pertaining to literacy education for English language learners across the United States.

Yetta M. Goodman is Regents Professor Emerita at the University of Arizona's College of Education in the Department of Language, Reading and Culture. She consults with education departments and speaks at conferences throughout the United States and in many nations of the world regarding issues of language, teaching, and learning with implications for language arts curricula. She has popularized the term *kidwatching*, encouraging teachers to be professional observers of the language and learning development of their students. She is a past president of NCTE and CELT and has served on the executive committee or board of directors of NCTE, CELT, and IRA and been an active member of commissions and committees.

Brenda R. Hawkins has been a reading teacher and literacy educator for more than thirty years. Her professional experience has involved work in schools at all levels, from kindergarten through graduate school, as well as within urban, suburban, and rural communities across the Northeast. Her work has included classroom teaching at the elementary, middle school, high school, and university levels; consultant and tutoring positions at the elementary and middle school levels; and supervision of teacher candidates, paraprofessionals, and Title I reading teachers. In addition to NCTE and the Commission on Reading, Brenda has been involved with IRA, ASCD, WLU, and the Rhode Island Writing Project through committee work and international conference presentations. She currently serves on the boards of directors of the Jamestown Education Foundation and the Friends of the Jamestown Library, and as a Cub Scout den leader. Brenda lives with her husband, their young son, and their dog in the island community of Jamestown, Rhode Island.

Soyong Lee is assistant professor in the TESOL/Bilingual Program at the City University of New York. She has worked with Korean-English bilingual programs in California and with Korean-heritage language schools in the New York metropolitan area. She is interested in how children from linguistically and culturally diverse backgrounds learn to read and write within the classroom context —specifically, the sociocultural and political contexts within which they become readers and writers. Most recently she has been involved in a project that aims to understand the dimensions and dynamics of learning the "basics" among a group of Korean kindergarten English language learners.

Jan Patricia Lewis is professor of education in Pacific Lutheran University's School of Education and Movement Studies/Department of Instructional Development and Leadership. A faculty member for eighteen years, her focus area is literacy education. Coauthored with Jane Braunger, her book, *Building a Knowledge Base in Reading* (2nd ed., 2006), is a synthesis of current research on best practice in K–12 literacy instruction. In addition to presentations of this work at IRA and NCTE conferences, she has worked with colleagues on assessment in teacher education (with Jan Weiss) and integrated teacher education/literacy approaches (with Paula Leitz) at the American Association of Colleges for Teacher Education, the American Educational Research Association, and CEC/TED. Lewis taught grades 1–3 in Boring, Oregon, for ten years. During that time, she was adjunct professor at Lewis and Clark College, teaching in their MA in literacy program. She has a BA in elementary education/English from Oregon State University, MAT from Lewis and Clark College, and PhD from the University of Oregon in reading/curriculum and instruction. Lewis teaches primarily School of Education graduate courses, including both Project LeaD and Project Impact. During fall semesters, she works primarily with Impact students to implement a reading tutoring project in sixteen elementary schools in the Puyallup School District; during the summer, she works with LeaD students on research methods.

Catherine Maderazo is assistant professor at Towson University. Her research interests include early reading, language and literacy learning, and literacy teacher education. Her two children continue to be her greatest and most inspiring teachers.

Prisca Martens received her PhD in language, reading, and culture from the University of Arizona in 1994. She is currently professor in the Department of Elementary Education at Towson University, where she teaches courses on reading, assessment, and children's literature. Her research and writing interests include early literacy, miscue analysis, retrospective miscue analysis, and children's literature.

Marylou M. Matoush is assistant professor of literacy education at Western Carolina University. She has spent the last thirty years working with struggling literacy learners and their teachers in Delaware, Minnesota, Wisconsin, and, most recently, Florida.

Arlene A. Moliterno teaches in the Advanced Literacy Program at Fordham University in New York. She has over thirty years of experience and leadership in public school and college education. Her professional experience includes teaching at early childhood, elementary, secondary, and college levels. At the university level, Moliterno has worked in all areas of teacher training, with an emphasis on literacy and instructional technology. She has extensive experience in developing curriculum for teacher education programs, preparing national accreditation documents, and grant writing. She is coauthor of *Developing Presentation Skills: A Guide for Effective Instruction* (2001) and has written several articles related to literacy, teacher-training, and technology. Her current research focuses on literacy leaders and the role of school principals in developing schoolwide literacy programs.

Margaret Yatsevitch Phinney is professor in the Department of Teacher Education of the College of Education and Professional Studies at the University of Wisconsin–River Falls. She teaches undergraduate and graduate courses in literacy education and is director of the Master of Science Reading Program. She gives workshops on literacy education topics at local, national, and international levels, and is currently on a teaching assignment at Zhejiang Education Institute in Hangzhou, China. Before going into higher education, Phinney served in the Peace Corps and then became an elementary classroom teacher and reading specialist. She is the author of professional articles and the teacher resource book *Reading with the Troubled Reader* (1988). She is a past member of the NCTE Commission on Reading and helped write The Reading Matrix. She is currently working on a developmental continuum in reading with coauthor Gay Ward.

Ruth E. Rigby is a career teacher whose background includes work as a high school English teacher, middle school reading teacher, and school district K–12 reading and language arts coordinator in both Lee County and Charlotte County, Florida. She has also taught a graduate reading course at Barry University. Rigby has served as president of the Florida Council of Teachers of English and president of the Florida Council of Language Arts Supervisors. She is a resident of Cape Coral, Florida, where she works as curriculum specialist/media specialist at Ida S. Baker High School. She is currently serving as director of the NCTE Commission on Reading. Rigby has also been a reviewer of professional development books for NCTE and spearheaded four NCTE Reading Initiative professional study groups. In February 2008, Ruth represented NCTE as a cosponsored speaker at the Write to Learn teachers' conference in Missouri.

A literacy coach and teacher trainer, **Laura Robb** has been a classroom teacher in grades 4–8 for forty-three years. She started her teaching career in Frederick County, Virginia, and spent the rest of her teaching life in Powhatan School and Johnson Williams Middle School, both in Clarke County, Virginia. Robb coaches teachers K–12 and does long-term professional development for the Rockland Boces in New York; in Rockville Center, Long Island; and in Staunton City Schools in Staunton, Virginia. Author of twelve books for teachers, Robb has also coauthored student materials for The Great Source Education Group; she speaks at conferences in the United States and Canada as well. When *Instructor Magazine* conducted a survey in 2005 for teachers to identify the top U.S. educators, Laura Robb was among the twenty named. In addition to serving on the Commission on Reading, Robb is a member of the IRA SIG on Children's Literature and has contributed a chapter to *Young Adult Literature in the Classroom: Reading It, Teaching It, Loving It* edited by Joan B. Elliott and Mary M. Dupuis (2002).

Patrick Shannon is professor of education at Penn State University. He has served NCTE on the Commission on Reading and the Research Committee. His most recent books are *Reading Against Democracy* (2007) and *Pedagogies of the Oppressors* (in press).

Michael L. Shaw is currently professor of literacy education at St. Thomas Aquinas College in suburban New York. He is co-chair of the IRA Professional Standards and Ethics Committee. In addition to serving on the NCTE Commission on Reading, he serves as the liaison between NCTE and IRA. Shaw spent a career of twenty-seven years teaching in Bronx, New York, first as a classroom teacher, then as a reading specialist, and then as a staff developer (aka "literacy coach"). He has published a wide range of articles on professional development, literacy coaching, and developing school-home connections. His current research and professional writing focus on reaching and teaching readers who struggle, including research on characteristics of schools that "beat the odds." He is a literacy consultant to high-needs districts and directs the Literacy Clinic at St. Thomas Aquinas College.

Penny Silvers is assistant professor in the School of Education, Department of Teacher Education, at DePaul University in Chicago, where she teaches undergraduate and graduate reading and literacy courses. She is also a consultant to school districts interested in professional development in language arts, special education, and assessment. Silvers is a former elementary reading specialist, and as a past member of the NCTE Commission on Reading, helped write and field-test The Reading Matrix, which is featured in this book. Her current research is focused on critical literacy, communities of practice, and multiliteracies as an expanded view of literacy practices with young children in primary grades.